VICTORIAN PAIN

Victorian Pain

Rachel Ablow

PRINCETON UNIVERSITY PRESS
PRINCETON & OXFORD

Copyright © 2017 by Princeton University Press

Published by Princeton University Press,
41 William Street, Princeton, New Jersey 08540
In the United Kingdom: Princeton University Press,
6 Oxford Street, Woodstock, Oxfordshire OX20 1TR

press.princeton.edu

Cover image: Plaster cast hands of Princess Beatrice and Princess Louise. From *The Strand Magazine,* No. 26 (February 1893)

All Rights Reserved

First paperback printing, 2020

Paperback ISBN 978-0-691-20288-4

The Library of Congress has cataloged the cloth edition as follows:

Names: Ablow, Rachel, author.
Title: Victorian pain / Rachel Ablow.
Description: Princeton : Princeton University Press, 2017. | Includes bibliographical references and index.
Identifiers: LCCN 2016050649 | ISBN 9780691174464 (hardback)
Subjects: LCSH: English literature—19th century—History and criticism. | Pain in literature. | Pain—Great Britain—History—19th century. | Human body in literature. | Literature and science—Great Britain—History—19th century. | Literature and society—Great Britain—History—19th century. | BISAC: LITERARY CRITICISM / General. | PHILOSOPHY / History & Surveys / General. | PHILOSOPHY / Political. | PHILOSOPHY / Social. | HISTORY / General.
Classification: LCC PR468.P15 A26 2017 | DDC 820.9/353—dc23
LC record available at https://lccn.loc.gov/2016050649

British Library Cataloging-in-Publication Data is available

This book has been composed in Miller

Dedicated to the memory of

Joseph Ablow (1928–2012)

CONTENTS

Acknowledgments · ix

INTRODUCTION	Pain, Subjectivity, and the Social	1
CHAPTER 1	John Stuart Mill and the Poetics of Social Pain	24
CHAPTER 2	Harriet Martineau and the Impersonality of Pain	48
CHAPTER 3	Pain and Privacy in *Villette*	72
CHAPTER 4	Charles Darwin's Affect Theory	93
CHAPTER 5	Wounded Trees, Abandoned Boots	114
AFTERWORD	The Fantasy of the Speaking Body	135

Notes · 141
Works Cited · 173
Index · 187

ACKNOWLEDGMENTS

I AM VERY FORTUNATE in having so many people to thank. At the University at Buffalo, several colleagues provided valuable commentary on portions of this project: James Bono, Tim Dean, Graham Hammill, Ruth Mack, Carla Mazzio, Steven Miller, and Joseph Valente. Cristanne Miller, chair of the English department at UB, provided much-appreciated advice and support. The members of an informal second project group were inspiring fellow travelers and readers: Daniel Hack, Ivan Kreilkamp, Richard Menke, and Rachel Teukolsky. The Upstate New York Victorianists' Group has been a tremendous resource to me over the years. I wish to thank, in particular, Elisha Cohn, Ann Colley, Martin Danahay, Michael Goode, Claudia Klaver, and Supritha Rajan. During a year in Cambridge, Boston Reading, led by the generous Martha Vicinus, provided excellent feedback as well as a model of collegiality: Rosemarie Bodenheimer, Mary Wilson Carpenter, Deb Gettelman, Laura Green, Kelly Hager, Anna Henchman, Sebastian LeCourt, and Maia McAleavy. I also wish to thank Joseph Bristow, William Cohen, Kenneth Dauber, Jason Frank, Elaine Freedgood, Catherine Gallagher, Rae Greiner, Vicki Hseuh, David Kurnick, Jules Law, Andrew Miller, Adela Pinch, John Plotz, Catherine Robson, Cannon Schmitt, Sarah Winter, and Ewa Plonowska Ziarek. Anne Savarese, at Princeton University Press, has been a superlative editor, not least in finding two extraordinarily generous and engaged anonymous readers. Veronica Wong and Rachel McCabe provided assistance with research and proofreading.

I wish, too, to thank audiences at the Eighteenth- and Nineteenth-Century Cultures Workshop at the University of Chicago; the Cornell University English Department; the Harvard Humanities Center; the Victorian Studies Program at Indiana University; the Johns Hopkins University English Department; the Princeton University English Department; the SUNY Binghamton English Department; the University at Buffalo, SUNY, Science Studies Research Workshop; and the Vanderbilt University English Department.

Most of all, I wish to thank Ruth Mack, my partner in this, as in all things. This project owes more to her than I can possibly say. I also wish to thank our children, Simon and Esther, for bringing such extraordinary joy and sweetness into our lives.

I wish to thank my parents, Joseph and Roz Ablow, for their love, support, and encouragement. This book is dedicated to the memory of my father, Joseph Ablow.

A portion of chapter 2 was originally published in *Victorian Studies* 56.4 as "Harriet Martineau and the Subject of Pain." Portions of the introduction and chapter 3 were originally published in *Nineteenth Century Gender Studies* 11.3 as "Hypochondria and the Failure of Relationship." An earlier version of the afterword first appeared in *ELH* 80.4 as "Tortured Sympathies: Victorian Literature and the Ticking Time-Bomb Scenario." I wish to thank all these journals for permission to reprint this material.

This project was completed with the assistance of fellowship support from the American Council of Learned Societies and the Humanities Institute at the University at Buffalo, SUNY.

VICTORIAN PAIN

INTRODUCTION

Pain, Subjectivity, and the Social

"Are you in pain, dear mother?"
"I think there's a pain somewhere in the room," said Mrs. Gradgrind,
"but I couldn't positively say that I have got it."

—CHARLES DICKENS, *HARD TIMES* (1854)

THIS BOOK DESCRIBES Victorian writers' interest in the strange subject position that Mrs. Gradgrind inhabits in this scene: their interest, that is, in what it would mean to experience pain as something that is not self-evidently one's own. As Dickens's satire begins to suggest, pain is often understood as the one thing we cannot help but claim. Mrs. Gradgrind's failure to identify her suffering in this scene seems like evidence that, on her deathbed, she finally inhabits the "view from nowhere" that her husband's utilitarianism seeks to inculcate, and that we are to see the result as being as pathetic as it is ludicrous.[1] As the writers in this project help to demonstrate, however, this is not the only way that the "somewhere" of pain can be understood. As Ludwig Wittgenstein explains, "An innumerable variety of cases can be thought of in which we should say that someone has pains in another person's body; or, say, in a piece of furniture, or in any empty spot."[2] The Victorian writers I examine in this project explore the implications of precisely this thought-experiment—one that suggests Mrs. Gradgrind's confusion may not be entirely unwarranted.

Although pain is a universal phenomenon, historians have long identified the period covered in this project as a watershed in the history of medical, theological, and political-economic accounts of pain. Before the nineteenth century, theological orthodoxy tended to cast pain as the consequence of Original Sin, a trial for the individual sufferer, or a punishment for transgression. Precisely because pain is not subject to human control, it can be understood as divinely ordained. Hence, whether and how an individual endures seems to say something important about her. In the nineteenth century, the development of the first modern anesthetics, along with improvements in analgesics, new understandings of nerve function, and the introduction of vaccination, meant that, for the first time, pain came to seem potentially eradicable.[3] As the anonymous author of "The Function of Physical Pain: Anaesthetics," published in the *Westminster Review* in 1871, explained, the theological, intellectual, and emotional consequences of this new state of affairs were tremendous.

> The fact of a large amount of physical suffering having ... been made optional in all but the first pangs [by anesthetics], necessitates a complete revisal of the theories of the purposes of bodily pain hitherto held by moralists; and our notions of the cosmical plan itself must be fundamentally modified now it is known that it does not permanently include—as has been thought from time immemorial it did—the cultivation of endurance as a virtue.... It is much as though the economy of nature had suddenly been found so all at once altered, as that, when an easterly wind blew, you only had to do a little oiling to the weather vanes, and instantly the breezes became mild.[4]

Other kinds of pain relief had long been available, but the first uses of ether and chloroform made pain seem differently under human control. And while many followed the writer for the *Westminster Review* in welcoming anesthetics with enthusiasm, often seeing them as a guarantee of human perfectibility, others recognized the serious theological questions they raised. Both medical and religious professionals struggled with the problem of how to maintain faith in a benevolent God when one generation is made to suffer what another is able to remediate. As J. Edgar Foster demands, "Has the Author of all things created us merely to gloat over our sufferings?"[5] For Foster, the answer is "no," but he admits the force of the question. Once pain comes to seem eradicable, it also comes to seem superfluous—and hence, too, potentially incompatible with a loving God.

Nineteenth-century understandings of pain were further complicated by the fact that alongside anesthetic optimism existed new forms of pessimism regarding pain's potential eradicability, thanks in large part to the work of Thomas Malthus. Even the most powerful drugs cannot mitigate the consequences of Malthus's basic insight that population increase inevitably outstrips any increase in subsistence, and hence, that suffering and premature death constitute inescapable facts of human existence. "Population, when unchecked, increases in a geometrical ratio," he writes, while "subsistence increases only in an arithmetical ratio."[6] "A slight acquaintance with numbers," he continues drily, "will show the immensity of the first power in comparison of the second."[7] Rather than being vectored toward perfection, in Malthus's account human history is defined by cycles of relative health and procreative success alternating with the "checks," such as famine, disease, war, and vice, that are necessary to cull the resulting surplus population. This is the basic insight that Charles Darwin adapts for his theory of natural selection: "Every being, which during its natural lifetime produces several eggs or seeds, must suffer destruction during some period of its life, and during some season or occasional year, otherwise, on the principal of geometrical increase, its numbers would quickly become so inordinately great that no country could support the product."[8] Profusion here comes to look like a destructive form of profligacy, and death and destruction mere indices of what Catherine Gallagher describes as "procreative vigor."[9]

Nineteenth-century discussions of pain are shaped by the tension between the optimism suggested by the introduction of anesthetics and other medical innovations and the pessimism indicated by Malthus's theory of population. They are also shaped by what both perspectives discover: the fundamental impersonality of pain. Theological doctrines of pain that cast it as a punishment or a trial by no means disappeared in the nineteenth century, and many commentators continued to describe physical suffering as importantly related to or expressive of the person who suffers. Yet both anesthetics and Malthus's theory of population suggest the potential inadequacy of such descriptions: in both contexts, pain comes to seem like the consequence of a historical accident. In the case of anesthetics, this accident involves the state of medical knowledge at one's historical moment. In Malthusian population theory, it relates to one's position in relation to inevitable cycles of plenitude and deprivation. However, in both contexts, the disaggregation of pain from individual merit or demerit raises pressing questions not just about pain but also about the status of, and even the relative importance of, the person who suffers it. Anesthetics and Malthus both suggest that pain might ultimately be, in some sense, beside the point: an unfortunate by-product of historical processes that are in no sense "about" or concerned with human suffering.

All of the writers I examine in this book are engaged with general debates over the desirability, inevitability, and meaning of pain, whether as sufferers or caregivers, religious believers or doubters, novelists, political theorists, or naturalists. They are also interested in the impersonality of pain in the ways indicated by both anesthetics and Malthusian population theory. They are *additionally* concerned with the social status of pain in the sense of its having a collective or interpersonal existence. They are thus interested in what Wittgenstein would call the language game of pain, a formulation that suggests that even the solitude we so often associate with pain is necessarily enmeshed in social life. The writers I discuss are all concerned with the solitariness of pain: its status as one of the aspects of being that we seem least able to share. Yet they are also aware of pain as a fundamental condition of social existence—according to some, the basic justification for the existence of society in the first place. Before there are laws and contracts, Thomas Hobbes writes, "there is no place for Industry... no Arts; no Letters; no Society; and which is worst of all, continuall feare, and danger of violent death; And the life of man, solitary, poore, nasty, brutish, and short."[10] Social life is premised on the fact that we exist as vulnerable, embodied subjects. Thus, even as discussions of pain tend to serve as investigations into the status of persons—as agents, as objects, and as loci of affects—they are also almost invariably questions about the nature and parameters of social life.

The first section of this introduction describes two different recent approaches to the relation between pain and social life. The first position has been advanced most famously by Elaine Scarry in *The Body in Pain* (1985), which casts the pain of the other primarily as an epistemological problem— the thing we cannot, but most need to, know. This approach to pain, I argue, is bound up with a particular account of liberal subjectivity as self-conscious, prior to the social, and private. The second approach to pain that I discuss has been articulated within a tradition that includes such figures as Wittgenstein, Stanley Cavell, and Veena Das, and emphasizes how pain is always already part of a social world. This approach is not exactly opposed to the first, as the Victorian texts I examine in this book indicate, but it does suggest different emphases in approaching the basic problem of the unknowability of the other.

In the second section, I consider some of the terms in which Victorian medical professionals, caregivers, and sufferers understood the social nature of pain. My project here is less to provide a definitive historical context for the readings that follow than to suggest ways in which the philosophical and literary texts that I examine in the rest of the book were engaging with questions being raised in other discourses. In other words, rather than simply contributing to a conversation that was taking place elsewhere, the writers I examine were seeking to use philosophy and literature to address problems that seemed particularly resistant to other modes of explanation. Religion and medicine could not answer questions about the nature or meaning of pain. The writers that I examine in this book make a strong case for philosophy and literature as alternative resources.

In the third section, I describe what I mean by "Victorian Pain." My goal here is to explain why this book seeks to describe not how pain was represented or constructed, but instead how pain was *used* by a range of writers at a particular time. If we are to understand pain as inevitably involving an address to another—in the form of what Wittgenstein calls a pain behavior, or what Stanley Cavell and Veena Das describe as a demand for acknowledgment —that address is never predictable or overdetermined, as the language of constructivism sometimes suggests. Nor is it separable from the pain experience itself, as the idea of representation can imply. My goal in this book is to think with a range of Victorian texts in order to consider the implications of the forms of subjectivity and sociality that the texts themselves explore and seek to produce.

Thinking Pain

Even now, over thirty years after its initial publication, Elaine Scarry's *The Body in Pain* remains the single most influential theorization of aversive physical experience.[11] Regularly cited by literary critics, historians, and political theorists, as well as by journalists, lawyers, and policy makers, *The Body in Pain* makes a forceful argument for what I will be calling an "epistemological" approach to pain—that is, an approach that takes the unknowability of the pain of the other as its central problematic.

Scarry makes four basic claims about the nature of pain. First, she asserts that it is defined by certitude for the one in pain and by doubt for the one who is not: "For the person whose pain it is, it is 'effortlessly' grasped (that is, even with the most heroic effort it cannot *not* be grasped); while for the person outside the sufferer's body, what is 'effortless' is *not* grasping it."[12] Pain thus demonstrates the transparency of the subject to itself, even as it also poses the problem of other minds in its most wrenching form: however intense the pain you endure, I can have no direct knowledge of your experience. Scarry's second claim is that physical pain "shatter[s] ... language" and so is inexpressible and incommunicable. "Unlike any other state of consciousness," she explains, physical pain "has no referential content. It is not *of* or *for* anything." It is "precisely because it takes no object that it, more than any other phenomenon, resists objectification in language."[13] This resistance to language is bound up with its incompatibility with social life, as well. Pain is something we have no choice but to know about ourselves, but that we have no way of communicating to others. Scarry's third claim is related to the second, for while physical pain is unspeakable in her account, "*Psychological* suffering ... *does* have referential content, *is* susceptible to verbal objectification, and is so habitually depicted in art that ... there is virtually no piece of literature that is *not* about suffering."[14] Hence, physical and emotional pain are wholly distinct experiences with different ontologies, phenomenologies, and attendant ethical obligations. While physical pain belongs to the (antisocial) world of the body, psychological pain belongs to the deeply social world of the mind.[15] Finally, Scarry posits that perceiving another's pain necessarily involves wishing it to be relieved: "'Seeing the pain and wishing it gone' ... is a single percipient event in which the reality of pain and the unreality of imagining are already conflated. Neither can occur without the other: if the person does not perceive the distress, neither will he wish it gone; conversely, if he does not wish it gone, he cannot have perceived the pain itself."[16] As a result, language is under an obligation to achieve the impossible: to communicate the incommunicable so as to make it available to amelioration. "The act of verbally expressing pain is a necessary prelude to the collective task of diminishing pain," Scarry writes; in order to encourage ameliorative intervention, "the human voice must aspire to become a precise reflection of material reality."[17] This goal cannot be achieved; it is nevertheless one toward which it is humanity's ethical obligation to strive.

Scarry's claims have been challenged on a variety of grounds. Her equation of pain with certainty, for example, has been called into question by sufferers from chronic pain and phantom limb: for those whose pain resists medical visualization, in particular, self-doubt can be as common a concomitant of pain as certitude.[18] Anthropologists, political theorists, historians, and others have taken issue with her claim that pain shatters language. As Darius Rejali explains, "It would be a mistake to confuse the empirical inability to say or think when one is in pain with a philosophical claim that pain is a preverbal sensation, a sensation that has some quality that, in principle, makes it inexpressible."[19] Medical professionals, among others, have challenged the clarity of the distinction Scarry makes between physical and emotional pain.[20] Finally, at least some commentators on torture have rejected Scarry's claim that the perception of pain involves wishing it gone.[21] For example, according to Peter Singer, torture is not possible unless pain is visible to the torturer: in order to "be an efficient torturer, one would need to be well aware of when one was causing pain and when one was not doing so." Rather than "mak[ing] invisible the agony of the victim," therefore, in Singer's account, torture "puts [its] victims outside the pale of humanity, thus rendering what is done to them morally acceptable."[22]

The "epistemological model" has also been challenged on theoretical grounds, the most sustained critique coming from philosophers and anthropologists engaged with Ludwig Wittgenstein's notion that pain constitutes something akin to a move within a language game, and hence, that pain is something we learn as well as something we feel. These accounts do not deny the skeptical problem that lies at the core of Scarry's philosophy: they, too, admit the impossibility of knowing the pain of the other. However, they reject the notion that the problem of ignorance should or can be met with knowledge. Thus, while Scarry calls attention to the responsibility of language to articulate or "become a precise reflection of material reality," Stanley Cavell insists on the futility of such a proceeding.[23] The "slack of acknowledgment can never be taken up by knowledge," he explains. Knowledge may "fire[] the imagination," but you "cannot always know when the fire will strike."[24] Knowledge here is less the reason for acknowledgment than one possible motivating factor among many—one whose outcome is especially unpredictable. Specifically, once one doubts the other's veracity, or even whether she speaks as a human being, it becomes very difficult to say where that doubt may end. Cavell explores the availability of skepticism through Wittgenstein's famous parable of the picture of the steaming pot. "Of course, if water boils in a pot," Wittgenstein writes, "steam comes out of the pot and also pictured steam comes out of the pictured pot. But what if one insisted on saying that there must also be something boiling in the picture of the pot?"[25] According to Cavell, the question here is not whether we are to assume there is something in the pot (i.e., whether sensations are private). Instead, "The point is to ask us to consider where the suggestion comes from that perhaps (others have it in mind that) nothing is going on inside us. Why is such a suggestion ... so much as worth an answer, even a parable? Why is it alarming?"[26] Cavell thus claims that Wittgenstein asks us to consider the extent to which pain behavior is not about knowledge or reference, but instead constitutes an attempt to elicit acknowledgment that may or may not be forthcoming.[27] Engagement or care cannot be a consequence of knowledge, in Cavell's account; it is instead the corollary of a self-conscious refusal of skepticism.[28]

For the anthropologists who have followed Wittgenstein and Cavell, attending to the "interpersonal grounds of suffering" reveals the extent to which suffering can be understood as a "social experience."[29] As Veena Das explains, Wittgenstein uses "the route of a philosophical grammar" to say that the sentence "I am in pain" is

> not an indicative statement, although it may have the formal appearance of one. It is the beginning of a language game. Pain in this rendering is not that inexpressible something that destroys communication or marks an exit from one's existence in language. Instead, it makes a claim on the other—asking for acknowledgment that may be given or denied. In either case, it is not a referential statement that is pointing to an inner object.[30]

Although she does not mention Scarry by name here, Das seems to have the critic's work in mind in her critique of the notion that pain "destroys communication or marks an exit of language." While in Scarry's work, social life is generated as a way to mitigate suffering that preexists it, in Das's, suffering is coextensive with social life. This move away from epistemology in discussions of pain makes it possible to discuss pain as a problem at the core of the production of social life, rather than as something to which social life belatedly seeks to respond.

Despite the obvious differences between Scarry's epistemological account of pain and Cavell and Das's social models, in the chapters that follow, these models are not simply opposed. Perhaps most importantly, although the epistemological model is clearly compatible with a classical liberal emphasis on liberty and justice, the social model is neither opposed to nor incompatible with an expanded notion of liberalism.[31] Scarry's model of pain assumes a subject that is self-conscious, exists prior to the social, and is private; and it assumes a model of sociality mediated by a language that seeks, yet inevitably fails, to reflect preexisting states of affairs. As I discuss in the afterword, the resulting close connection between liberalism and an epistemological model of pain may help account for the latter's longevity. Social models of pain are not simply opposed to liberalism, however, although their relation to any political formation may be complicated. The nature of this complexity becomes particularly apparent in the first chapter of this project. John Stuart Mill is often identified as the most important liberal philosopher of the nineteenth century. Yet in chapter 1, I argue that the model of pain that emerges from his *Autobiography* (1873) has as much in common with Das's account as with Scarry's. His account of pain as something that can only ever be experienced alone, but that is only ever understood through others, maintains a delicate balance between ways of thinking about pain, refusing to relinquish the guarantee of privacy and uniqueness promised by the epistemological model, even as it gives priority to social life.

This description of Mill suggests a tension around questions of privacy, which runs throughout this book. According to Cavell, Wittgenstein's rejection of the possibility of a private language suggests that "the fact, and the state, of your (inner) life cannot take its importance from anything special in it. However far you have gone with it, you will find that what is common is there before you are."[32] For Cavell, this recognition is primarily a source of what he calls "interest." Yet for Mill—and then in chapter 3, for Charlotte Brontë, as well—it is also a source of great anxiety or even anguish. In Mill's nightmares of overdetermination, and Brontë's of drowning, one can see two different versions of the lament for privacy as secrecy that a social model of pain disallows. Harriet Martineau, Charles Darwin, and Thomas Hardy maintain less problematic relations to social models of pain. All three, however, still grapple with the problem of how to maintain some hold on the subject. In a view from nowhere, these writers ask, does the individual still matter? What do we give up if the answer is no?

All the writers that I address in this project thus draw on both models I have discussed thus far, moving between imagining pain as something incommunicable, private, and prior to the social, and understanding it as produced through and in the context of social life. But, as I have already begun to suggest, they are by no means limited to these two ways of thinking about pain. The alternatives they imagine take a variety of different forms. Yet consistently, what emerges at the moments of crisis that I examine is a reconfiguration of the boundaries between persons, as well as between persons and things—a reconfiguration that is often signaled by the eruption of insistently "literary" or noninstrumental language. This is not to say that pain "destroys" language; only that it rearranges common protocols, often becoming lyrical, poetic, or rhapsodic in ways that clearly call attention to themselves as literary.[33] My selection of primary texts highlights the consistency and consequences of such linguistic shifts in both fictional and nonfictional writing—and specifically, the way that discussions of pain tend to strain against the most commonly recognized protocols of language.

I will be using two terms, in particular, to describe this reconfiguration: *impersonality* and *affect*. Briefly, I take the term impersonality from Sharon Cameron's claim that representations of impersonality take as their goal "to have no preference, to see from no point of view"—a perspective akin to that which Mrs. Gradgrind inhabits when she fails to identify her pain as her own.[34] As a result of this perspective, Cameron writes, "representations of impersonality suspend, eclipse, and even destroy the idea of the person as such, who is not treated as a social, political, or individual entity."[35] The person rarely disappears entirely from the texts I discuss, although in the work of Hardy and Darwin it comes close to doing so. Yet all the writers I examine are interested in what it would mean to "see from no point of view" in the way that Cameron describes. For Mill, that possibility is both compelling and terrifying. For Martineau, it is empowering. For Darwin and Hardy, it raises fascinating questions regarding the stability of both mental and object worlds. For Brontë, as I have already suggested, it looks like drowning.

Affect and impersonality constitute closely related terms in my account, both defined by the pressure they place on the notion of the individual.[36] Hovering ambiguously between body and mind, irreducible to either emotion or sensation, Benedict de Spinoza's notion of affect as "affections of the body by which the body's power of acting is increased or diminished, aided or restrained" offers a way to consider feeling (with all the attendant ambiguity of that term) in the absence of personhood.[37] "By singular things I understand things that are finite and have a determinate existence," he writes. "And if a number of individuals so concur in one action that together they are all the cause of one effect, I consider them all, to that extent, as one singular thing."[38] This account of affect as tending toward the redefinition of the "thing" has not often been used to think about pain. This book suggests that this is a serious oversight, and one whose remediation requires a shift in how both "affect" and "pain" have most commonly been defined.[39] Pain, too, I suggest, has the potential to pull against the idea of the individual as a self-evident unit of measure or object of observation. At the very least, in the work of the writers I examine, it raises serious questions regarding where one person ends and another begins.

The End of Pain

Thus far I have relied exclusively on recent accounts to explain the distinction I make between epistemological and social accounts of pain. In this section, I shift focus and attend instead to nineteenth-century accounts of aversive physical experience. My goal is to suggest the extent to which the philosophical and literary engagements that I examine in the rest of this book constitute attempts to intervene in an ongoing conversation regarding the nature, uses, and consequences of physical suffering that was also taking place among scientists, medical professionals, religious writers, and sufferers. This conversation suggests just how widespread were the questions raised by nineteenth-century writers.

The first question often raised in nineteenth-century discussions of pain is that of how to define it. This is not a question to which medicine, political economy, or theology provided clear answers. As I discuss at length in chapter 1, even utilitarianism, the philosophy of pleasure and pain, provides no definitive account of what pain is, but instead consistently falls back on the notion that pain is defined by the experience of it. Physiology and medicine went little further. Although the nineteenth century was "a time of rapidly increasing physiological knowledge as well as one of great therapeutic advances," Lucy Bending explains, "the ability to alleviate pain far outstripped medical understandings of its functioning."[40] One can see this divergence consistently in both scientific research and medical practice: knowing what alleviates pain does not necessary mean that one has any idea of why it does so. Victorian writers may have meant very different things when they posed the question, "What is pain?" but they nevertheless tended to agree that it is fundamentally unanswerable. As the anonymous author of "What Is Pain," published in *The Lancet* in 1887, explained, "We think we know what it is to live and feel pleasure or pain, but when we attempt to express our thoughts by words we discover that the feat is impracticable. The answer to the question, 'What is pain?' must therefore be, 'No one knows.'"[41] Similar claims are repeated again and again in scientific, medical, and popular writings on pain.

Medicine clearly had an especially great stake in defining pain, particularly in the context of its breakthroughs in pain remediation. Such certainty was difficult to achieve, however, when the precise relation between the mind, brain, and nerves remained a mystery. Despite Scarry's insistence on the unmistakable difference between physical and mental pain, nineteenth-century physiologists often move seamlessly between these categories. I discuss this refusal to differentiate between forms of suffering at length in chapter 4 on Charles Darwin. In *The Expression of the Emotions in Man and Animals* (1872), in particular, the naturalist repeatedly juxtaposes occasions of mental and physical anguish as if they were interchangeable. Such apparent confusion often looks like a deliberate refusal of the premature disaggregation of phenomena whose relations had yet to be defined clearly. One can see a similar refusal in the work of one the most important physiologists of the time, Alexander Bain. Depending on the passage one reads, suffering—along with other mental phenomena—seems wholly attributable either to mind, or brain, or to some combination of the two. Rather than simple inconsistency, however, such shifting explanations seem like attempts to keep many different kinds of explanation in play concurrently. Lorraine Daston claims that for Bain, pain and pleasure ultimately remain "feelings, not neural tremors": he "couched his explanations in psychological terms," she argues, rather than physiological ones.⁴² Yet, it is oftentimes difficult to say where the line between the psychological and the physiological might be drawn. "The organ of mind is not the brain by itself," Bain writes, for example,

> it is the brain, nerves, muscles, organs of sense and viscera.... When the mind is in the exercise of its functions, the physical accompaniment is the passing and re-passing of innumerable streams of nervous influence. Whether under a sensation of something actual, or under an emotion or an idea, or a train of ideas, the general operation is still the same. It seems as if we might say, no currents, no mind.⁴³

Aside from anything else, this is a far cry from seventeenth- and eighteenth-century associationism. One consequence in terms of Bain's discussions of pain is that he often slides between accounts of physical and psychological suffering, and between describing suffering itself as a psychological, a neurological, or a physiological phenomenon.

Medical uncertainty regarding the nature of pain corresponded to an equal uncertainty regarding what pain does—and hence, the desirability of relieving it. So, for example, despite repeated demonstrations of the safety of anesthetics, many surgeons remained reluctant to employ them: Thomas Dormandy claims that approximately one third of limb amputations performed "for compound fractures at the Pennsylvania Hospital [1853–62] were still carried out on conscious patients."⁴⁴ This statistic was due in part to medical professionals' concerns regarding potential side effects of the drugs themselves: ether was plagued by "occasional ineffectiveness," "accompanying sickness," and "chest complications."⁴⁵ Chloroform had fewer side effects, but it was still attended by the risks of addiction and the occasional unexplained death.⁴⁶ Medical professionals were additionally concerned about suppressing the potential benefits of pain. "Were it not for the stimulation induced by pain," John P. Harrison, vice president of the American Medical Association, complained in 1849, "surgical operations would more frequently be followed by dissolution."⁴⁷ Meanwhile, as Martin Pernick explains, "natural healers preferred to passively 'do no harm' rather than risk causing harm directly," and the "heroic" professional tradition "opposed the use of anesthetics to avoid suffering" that did not endanger the life of the patient.⁴⁸ Only so-called "conservative professionalism permitted the cautious use of anesthetics, both to relieve emotional suffering and to prevent physical damage."⁴⁹ Yet even these doctors' use of anesthetics could be inconsistent and, from a contemporary perspective, parsimonious.⁵⁰ Pain was not simply an evil to be eliminated at any cost: it was assumed to have uses, even if those uses were not always fully understood.

Religious commentators brought their own concerns to the "anesthetic revolution." As I have already mentioned, the potential elimination of pain led some to question the existence of a benevolent God. Meanwhile, it led others to question the religious acceptability of pain relief. Joanna Bourke describes the concerns that arose over dying under the influence of painkillers. While some Christian physicians claimed that "sufferers were incapable of piety" and so should receive pain relief in their final illness, others were concerned that opiates "could befuddle the mind, making dying believers less capable of focusing on their otherworldly fate."[51] According to Bourke, this last concern was most relevant for Catholics.[52] However, even non-Catholics debated whether pain relief was more likely to enable or inhibit religious devotion. The writings of Priscilla Maurice show the resulting strain especially clearly. In *Sickness, Its Trials and Blessings* (1850), Maurice acknowledges sufferers' fear of addiction, and their "questionings whether it can be right in them to subdue the sense of pain, when God Himself has sent the pain; when Christ Himself endured such extreme suffering, and refused to drink, even in the midst of His agonizing thirst."[53] Although she ultimately argues for the understanding of pain relief, too, as a gift from God, she raises a real problem: that of how to reconcile religious conceptions of suffering with contemporary medical technologies.

These questions ultimately point to a concern over how to account for the existence of pain in the first place—a problem that at least some Christian apologists sought to resolve by insisting on what G. A. Rowell called the "beneficent distribution of the sense of pain," or the notion that pain serves certain necessary functions in relation to the individual or the community. Pain was still sometimes cast as a consequence of Original Sin, or a punishment for personal transgressions, but it was also often described as part of God's benevolent design. As Rowell explains, "There may be pain and suffering, the use of which it may be difficult to see; but I would rather attribute this to a want of knowledge, than believe that the rule which holds good in so many cases does not hold good in all."[54] James Hinton agreed, arguing in *The Mystery of Pain: A Book for the Sorrowful* (1866), that pain "prompts us to many actions which are necessary for the maintenance or security of life, and warns us against things that are hurtful."[55] The notion that pain serves a protective function appealed to medical as well as to religious professionals. Particularly in the early part of the century, before the picture was complicated by theories of evolution, one can see it reiterated often in *The Lancet* and the *British Medical Journal*.

On the one hand, then, pain was often described as beneficent because of its medical function in relation to the individual. On the other—and more interestingly for my purposes—pain was also often ascribed an important function in the reconfiguration of the relation between the individual and the community. Pain, many writers insisted, is never experienced in isolation, however much it may seem as if it is. Instead, it exists in the context of social and religious relations that stand to be shaped by that suffering. Thus, some writers emphasize how pain can encourage sufferers to turn away from the inevitable limitations of human consolations and, instead, to turn toward God. "No one can fully see the extent and details of the trial which another is called to bear," Priscilla Maurice explains. "One comes near and says words of sympathy for one part of the trial; another for some other part; a third sees no trial in it at all; a fourth thinks it must be much less trying than some other form of suffering, or than his own. No one but the sufferer sees it in all its bearings and forms of inward suffering; no one else feels the acute pain of heart and all its throbbings."[56] In the absence of human sympathy, Maurice urges the sufferer to turn to God, whose omniscience suggests infinite compassion. In *A Companion for the Sick Chamber* (1837), John Thornton makes a related claim, describing pain's power to "excite a serious and most earnest concern about the salvation of the soul in those who have been totally negligent" and to show us the "utter emptiness, vanity, and barrenness of the present world, and the folly and misery of seeking our portion in it."[57] In his account, to experience pain could also "lead us to Christ" and to a contemplation of His sufferings.[58]

While some commentators emphasize the role of pain in binding sufferers to God, others stress the extent to which pain serves to consolidate human communities. Thus, even Thornton describes how the sufferer, "when raised and restored, if such be the will of God, [may] enter with feeling and tenderness into the sufferings of our brethren and fellow-men, and prepare us to make sacrifices to serve them."[59] Meanwhile, the Reverend George Martin asks his congregation to remember the impact suffering has on witnesses, encouraging his congregation to "learn those lessons of wisdom and of truth which [pain] is calculated to teach" by allowing the spectacle of the Prince of Wales's affliction to bring them to God.[60] Maurice, too, emphasizes the extent to which suffering inevitably takes place in relation to others. "At this very moment, many other persons are suffering, in mind, body, and estate, just as you are suffering," she explains. "They have the same trials, the same temptations, though you know them not, and they know nothing of you." Nevertheless,

> *how* you suffer is very important to them, for you insensibly affect them, though you do not indeed exactly know *how*; but this you know, that every member of the Body is necessary to, and affects, the whole Body.... 'I believe in the communion of Saints,' and so I am not alone, I cannot be; my trials are not mine alone; my conflicts and my temptations are those of some other member of Christ's Church. In fighting, I fight for them as well as for myself; in overcoming, weaken Satan's power over them, as well as over myself.[61]

Here, the sufferer does not simply perform her suffering for an audience. Instead, she is encouraged to experience her own sufferings as bound up with the needs of others. How she suffers affects all other members of the community, although it may not be possible to say exactly how.

In their interest in the relation between individual suffering and that of the larger community, religious commentators are unexpectedly similar to the medical writers who were influenced by evolutionary theory. Despite the obvious differences between them, both groups assume the fundamental inevitability of suffering, both manifest great compassion toward individual sufferers, and both consistently assume that how the sufferer understands the relation between her distress and that of her community will have considerable consequences for how she experiences it. Thus, both consider the individual's experience of pain to be bound up with social life. This commitment becomes particularly clear in the context of a debate sparked by H. Cameron Gillies's article, "The Life-Saving Value of Pain and Disease," published in *The Lancet* in August 1887. As the title of his piece suggests, Gillies was a profound optimist in relation to pain, claiming that "pain never comes where it can serve no good purpose," for "pain is in direct proportion to the powers of repair—that is to the probability of recovery."[62] Pain, in other words, always signals a problem that is available to amelioration. Therefore, when pain can "serve no good purpose, … there is no pain."[63] Gillies does admit a few exceptions to this rule, but ultimately resolves them by claiming they indicate that something is wrong with common methods of treatment. The fact that many people suffered horrendously as a result of compound fractures, for example, he sees as necessary to make clear that *"there was something wrong* in our treatment of compound fractures"—a wrong eventually corrected by Joseph Lister.[64]

Nearly all of the medical professionals who responded in *The Lancet* disagreed with Gillies's assessment. Pain is *not* reliably meaningful in relation to the individual, they insisted. Nor does it always indicate a problem that can be solved. Pain, they claimed, is instead best understood as a byproduct of processes that, at this late point in the century, they often identified with evolution.[65] Thus, pain is no simple utilitarian signaling system, designed to indicate problems subject to remedy. Instead, it is often in great excess of any conceivable function. As A. St. Claire Buxton insisted, "We see in pain the expression of a high degree of sensibility in the nervous system; and we believe the nervous system has attained its present high degree of sensibility by reason of long and steady development—evolution, in fact."[66] As a result, for the student of evolution, it may be possible to see "a reason for the existence of pain, but no motive or purpose."[67] We can understand the cause of pain in evolutionary terms, but that does not mean that the pain of an individual indicates anything distinctive or remediable about her case.

Lucy Bending points out the extent to which this debate suggests that "evolutionary theory had won the battle, and Christian rhetoric was forced to shape its own arguments in the light of its claims."[68] Another less obvious implication is the continuity between religious and evolutionary understandings of the role played by a sense of the community in the sufferer's experience. Thus, Gillies was condemned for the cruelty of his claims for the benevolence of pain, and evolutionary theory was offered as a potentially comforting alternative. "To a reverent believer in evolution," W. J. Collins explained,

> pain is more nearly comprehended in its true light and meaning, and much of its sting removed in proportion to that comprehension.... Here there is to be found the comfort which science affords—comfort in the knowledge that pain is in obedience to law, is bound up with the progress of the race. With this knowledge and with this hope, far more than with blind assertions as to the invariable beneficence of pain, one can "kiss the rod," and be "patient of pain, though as quick as a sensitive plant to the touch."[69]

Evolutionary theory here becomes a substitute for Christian orthodoxy, both as a way to explain the existence of pain and as a way to use that explanation to conceive of the sufferer as part of a larger whole. Evolutionary theory does not make pain less painful, but it is imagined as consoling sufferers with the "knowledge" that there is some relation between their suffering and the "progress of the race." However isolated sufferers may feel, both Christianity and science insist that their suffering is not simply theirs alone. In both contexts, the sufferer is imagined as, in some sense, a member of a larger community, and hence, as one whose sufferings have positive implications for others.

One consequence of this reconfiguration is to cast medical professionals as something akin to spiritual advisers, both in the sense that they are truth-tellers and in the sense that they have the power to help patients shape their experiences in tangible ways. Thus, Gillies was not simply wrong, the physicians and surgeons who wrote to *The Lancet* insisted, he was cruel in a way wholly at odds with his responsibilities as a medical professional. "Is this the grim comfort [Gillies] would bring to a suffering woman tortured slowly to death by a sloughing scirrus of the breast," Collins demands, "or to a man, made almost unhuman and killed by inches by the slow yet sure ravages of a rodent ulcer?"[70] E. R. Williams is even more vitriolic, citing the case of a woman whose breast cancer begins as a small tumor of which she is unconscious:

> For months, may be, she is quite ignorant of the fact that she has within her the beginning of what will ultimately be her end. The tumour grows, neighbouring structures become contaminated, and pain comes on and persists, which by the exhaustion it induces hastens on the inevitable. In this stage, of what service is her pain? The diagnosis is made, the disease is to [*sic*] far advanced for operation, the patient knows that she is beyond the reach of surgery, and so, tortured with pain night and day, she waits, and prays for a speedy release. And yet the writer stoically says, "Pain is merciful."[71]

The tone of righteous indignation toward Gillies is unmistakable, as is the compassion for the individual sufferer. Williams does not simply seek to prove

Gillies wrong; he seeks to evoke real pity for the woman he casts as his opponent's victim. Pain, these writers assume, is produced at least in part between doctor and patient. It is thus incumbent on those who minister to be mindful of the full extent of their responsibilities. As J. Russell Reynolds insisted in the president's address, delivered at the Annual Meeting of the Metropolitan Counties Branch of the British Medical Association in 1871, "We must ever remember that in the practice of our noble profession we have to deal with man as a whole, to examine him and to treat him as such."[72] Reynolds's concern with the patient as a whole, and his recognition of the way in which the doctor plays a role in that patient's overall well-being, suggest a sensitivity to the patient's perspective that was certainly not universal, but was also not entirely isolated.

Particularly in the wake of Michel Foucault's influential *The Birth of the Clinic*, statements like Reynolds's might be surprising. The story Foucault tells of the replacement of patients by disease involves an effective erasure of the sick person as an object of concern. According to Foucault, in place of people with illnesses, the clinic was concerned with diseases that manifested, more or less perfectly, in cases that happened to be located in human bodies. As a result, he explains, the patient becomes the "rediscovered portrait of the disease; he is the disease itself, with shadow and relief, modulations, nuances, depth."[73] According to Mary Fissell, one consequence of this shift was that the "patient's narrative of illness was made utterly redundant. Hospital medicine came to focus on signs and symptoms, which provided doctors with a disease-oriented diagnosis conducive to the demands of hospital practice and reflective of its social structure."[74] Meanwhile, laboratory medicine imposed an "object oriented role system" in place of the "person oriented role system" associated with older forms of bedside medicine.[75] Foucault summarizes this system of changes in the conception and practice of medicine in terms of the difference between the question, "'What is the matter with you?' with which the eighteenth-century dialogue between doctor and patient began" and "that other question: 'Where does it hurt?,' in which we recognize the operation of the clinic and the principle of its entire discourse."[76] The patient effectively disappeared behind her own symptoms and the disease they were understood to signify.

As both historians and literary critics have pointed out, Foucault's focus on France means his history cannot simply be transferred to the British context.[77] So, for example, despite the centrality of the hospital in the training of medical students and the care of the lower classes, the patient-doctor relationship remained extremely personal and personality-driven for the middle and upper classes.[78] "Sound clinical judgment needed to be backed up by other, more personal, attributes if a practitioner was to obtain the confidence of a patient," Anne Digby explains. Particularly "since their therapeutic impotence in the face of many diseases remained, practitioners continued to need good personal qualities to retain the faith of patients."79 Patients may very well have been accorded decreasing authority over their care throughout the century, but the authority of doctors was nevertheless constantly challenged, particularly by patients with economic resources.80 This balance of power is especially evident in some of the figures examined in this book: while Harriet Martineau dispensed with her medical advisers almost entirely once she thought her (unauthorized) mesmeric treatment began to take effect, Charles Darwin employed a wide range of medical professionals in order to compare and evaluate their recommendations.81

What interests me is not simply the extent to which patients retained the power to define their illness, but instead the way in which, against Foucault's disciplinary account, suffering was regarded as *both* social *and* as inherent in individual, identifiable persons. Nowhere is this conviction more evident than in the context of hypochondria, an illness largely defined by the dangerous isolation of the person who suffers it. Hypochondria holds particular interest for this project insofar as it was commonly understood as a pathology of social life: a product of its breakdown, whether in the life of an individual or the community as a whole. It also constitutes one of the few contexts in which one person can say, "I am in pain," and her interlocutor can legitimately respond with an alternative interpretation. According to Veena Das, such a refusal of belief is never acceptable: "My expression of pain compels you in unique ways—you are not free to believe or disbelieve me—our future is at stake."82 In her account, the social fabric depends on a setting aside of skepticism: it requires of us the assumption that the other speaks truthfully as a vulnerable human being like ourselves. In the context of hypochondria, Victorians implicitly assume that such doubt registers the fact that the future has *already* been imperiled: the existence of the illness in the first place suggests that the stability of the ordinary has already come under threat.

Hypochondria in the nineteenth century has no single, simple definition. As Esther Fischer-Homberger has shown, in the eighteenth century, hypochondria was a "real and serious illness with its seat in the upper abdomen ... [that] involved spiritual as well as physical pain to those who suffered from it, and ... could be induced either mentally or somatically."83 Only in the later eighteenth and nineteenth centuries did it become usual to associate hypochondria with what Fischer-Homberger calls "pathophobia," or the fear of illness, and even then the connection was by no means universal.84 Hence, some nineteenth-century commentators define hypochondria in terms of the fear of illness, while others saw such an anxiety as incidental to, rather than constitutive of, the disease—as evidenced, for example, in recurring interest in "religious hypochondria," or the belief in one's damnation in the absence of any particular crime.85 In his "Lecture on Hypochondriasis" (1873), for example, published in the *British Medical Journal*, Thomas King Chambers moves seamlessly between medical and religious forms of hypochondria, repeatedly quoting John Bunyan's *Grace Abounding unto the Chief of Sinners* (1666) as "the most vivid picture extant of an [*sic*] hypochondriac."[86] Meanwhile, other writers associated the term "hypochondria" with what we might call anorexia or obsessive compulsive disorder—as in the case of Stonewall Jackson, whose "hypochondria," as reported in *The Lancet*, consisted of believing "that everything he ate went down and lodged in his left leg" and of going for long periods in which he would not eat "except by the watch, at a precise moment."[87] Jackson did not exactly think he was ill, although he clearly had unconventional ideas about the workings of his own body; nevertheless, the anxiety he attached to those workings led him to be categorized as a hypochondriac.

Despite the lack of consensus regarding its symptomatology in the nineteenth century, both medical professionals and lay commentators generally agreed upon two aspects of the illness. First, hypochondria was regarded as a disorder of the senses as much as an error of belief: the problem is not simply that the hypochondriac thinks she is ill when she is not, but instead that she *feels* ill (or damned) in the absence of any verifiable cause. So, for example, John Conolly claimed in 1849 that hypochondria originates not in the mind, but in the "peripheral extremities of the nerves; from which ... uneasy impressions are transmitted to the brain."[88] The consequence is an "intense acuteness of smell, and extreme sensibility to the impression of the external air on the surface ... conveying to the mind of the patient ideas of functional or even organic disease of a serious nature, when there is, at least, no structural change."[89] By this account, hypochondriacs are not exactly wrong to think they are ill; instead, they are victims of a faulty nervous system that makes them feel as if they are ill when they are not. Thomas King Chambers largely agreed, claiming in 1873 that "the patient feels all wrong but understands all right": it is their nervous systems that are disordered rather than their mental faculties.[90] "Feeling general misery," he continues, "often accompanied by local pain, [hypochondriacs] construct a theory to account for the same; and, as they are for the most part intelligent and ingenious persons, the theory runs a chance of being a very plausible one."[91] The result is that they often convince not just "themselves and their friends, [but] often their medical advisers."[92] Not all medical professionals thought hypochondria originated in the senses; many attributed it to pathological forms of self-regard. Regardless of its understood cause, however, the consensus was that hypochondriacs do experience real suffering, even if it is unaccompanied by lesion.

The second aspect of hypochondria upon which commentators almost invariably agreed has to do with the illness's relation to isolation: whether as cause or as effect, hypochondriacs were often assumed to be cut off from others. As Michael J. Clark writes of the closely related and often overlapping diagnosis of "morbid introspection," according to many experts on psychological medicine, "introspection and self-absorption, persistent abstention from ordinary social intercourse, and neglect of active pursuits all tended to weaken the will, undermine the 'natural' social affections, and encourage idleness, eccentricity, and the growth of perverse or immoral tendencies. Absorption in purely 'subjective' states of consciousness, they argued, upset the 'natural' mental balance by impairing the capacity to receive and react to external impressions."[93] As in hypochondria, in morbid introspection, isolation could all too easily result in emotional or sensory extravagance. As the anonymous commentator in *The Quarterly Review* explained in 1810, "Of all morbid habits, that of watching our own sensations is one of the most unfortunate; it is by this habit that the miserable hypochondriac induces upon himself the symptoms of any disease that his fancy apprehends, and endures thereby actual suffering from an imaginary cause."[94] Self-absorption leads to an excessive sensitivity to one's own sensations—a sensitivity that could be experienced as pain, suffering, or sensations resembling illness.[95]

Such self-absorption could take many different forms. At one end of the spectrum is the literal-mindedness of W. H. Ranking, who, in 1843 identified the illness with celibacy, or of John Elliotson's insistence in 1832 that almost all sufferers are sexually deficient: "They have nightly emissions, or excessive emissions, or no desire, or if they go to a female they 'do no good.'"[96] At the other end of the spectrum is the frequently reproduced excerpt from Dr. Bruck's "Hypochondria Politica in Germany," which first appeared in 1848 in Casper's *Wochenschrift* and was then translated for English audiences in *The Lancet*. Identifying hypochondria with "the recent violent political commotions in Prussia," the author attributes his countrymen's ill-health to their reluctance to become politically engaged.

> Twenty-one years ago I mentioned, in a memoir on psychical medicine, that the numerous cases of hypochondria in our country among the higher and middle classes, were mainly owing to the want of interest in public affairs, and the total absence of co-operation between the citizens and the state. It is now evident that I was right, for the peculiar effects which the late political changes have produced, and from the nervousness with which we watch the events, prove that we have become more or less hypochondriacal. We are afraid of public life; all news of a political nature, which, amongst more advanced nations, are quietly discussed, has with us an immediate effect on the ganglionic system, frightens and unnerves us; the appetite disappears, sleep is disturbed, and the train of symptoms above mentioned make their appearance.[97]

The failure of civil society here constitutes a problem not just for the body politic, but for the individual body, as well: an entire population becomes sick because of individual refusals to engage in public life.

Regardless of whether they located hypochondria's origin in the nerves or in the mind, most medical practitioners prescribed social engagement as the cure. For example, in 1825 Dr. Armstrong advised his pupils "to appeal to [hypochondriacs'] common sense, so that they may, at the commencement, withdraw the mind from the contemplation of themselves, and fix it upon some external object with interest sufficiently intense, as a diversion from the distemper."[98] Meanwhile, William Withey Gull and Francis Edmund Anstie insisted in 1876 that "it is a fallacy to suppose that the sufferings of the patient are unreal; on the contrary, they are most vividly real, and it is impossible that he should forget them till they cease."[99] Yet they also go on to claim that mental therapies can be salutary because "the mind has a reflex influence upon the bodily disorder, which may be as effective for good as for evil.... The key to the moral treatment is the breaking down of the patient's morbid self-concentration, and this object may be achieved to some extent in many cases by a change in the course of his daily life."[100] Hypochondriacs suffer from an excess of self; it is thus only reasonable to associate their cure with distraction, social engagement, and an increased sense of civic responsibility.

Rather than a purely subjective experience, or simply the product of a social exchange, suffering here appears to exist between these two possibilities. It is simply not always possible to know what we feel in isolation, doctors writing on hypochondria assume—or, rather, what we do feel can become exaggerated without the normalizing presence of others. Clearly such a recognition of the social nature of pain could be deployed so as to undermine the patient's authority over the one arena from which medical professionals might seem to be excluded: her own experience. It could also, ironically, be used to hold patients responsible for their own physical illness—as in M. Andral's 1833 account of how excessive attention to the nerves leads to physical lesion: "Consecutive to this delusion [of hypochondria]," he explained in *The Lancet*, "various nervous derangements may supervene, and terminate in functional disorders or organic changes in different parts of the system."[101] As a result, "in the hypochondriac, it is not rare to find that the attention, fixed on the lungs, has actually induced the disease which was the subject of the delusion."[102] Yet, it also suggests a far more nuanced understanding of the social experience of pain than has tended to be recognized. Such understandings could have very practical consequences for how the patient-doctor relationship was conceived. For many practitioners tasked with caring for hypochondriacs, skepticism was simply not an option, but nor was the meaning of any given statement necessarily self-evident. In this context, the claim, "I am in pain," was deeply meaningful and expressive of a felt need. The problem for the caregiver was to diagnose the nature of that need rather than—or in addition to—search for any physical lesion.

Victorian Pain

The past few years have seen a proliferation of historical studies on sensation and emotion—one consequence of which has been a lively debate over the best ways to describe the historical status of experiences that can so easily seem to have no history. According to Joanna Bourke, pain can best be understood as an "event" in the sense that "people are active in its construction in sensual, cognitive, and motivational terms."[103] This definition has the benefit of resisting what David B. Morris calls the "Myth of Two Pains," or the notion that "physical pain" can be clearly distinguished from "mental pain."[104] Further, the "event-ness of pain ... points to the fact that the individual's perception of what she signifies as a pain-event can also be profoundly affected by environmental interactions."[105] Describing pain in these terms, however, threatens to make pain seem like something that involves only sufferers rather than something in which their interlocutors also participate. This is a problem Javier Moscoso seeks to resolve in his description of his object of study as a "social drama": "Pain mobilizes all the elements of theatrical representation. The experience of harm has its actors, plot, stage, costumes, props, scenography, and, of course, its audience."[106] Moscoso's theatrical model makes clear that pain requires an audience. Yet the notion of pain as a kind of performance places sufferers behind an imaginary scrim, rather than casting them as engaging with their interlocutors in what Veena Das helpfully describes as "transactions."[107] In writing this book, I have often relied on Das's model of pain, but I have also sought to heed her warning: "The absence of any standing languages of pain is perhaps symptomatic of the fact that I cannot separate my pain from my expression for it—another way of saying this is that my expression of pain compels you in unique ways."[108] Part of what I take this to suggest is the multiplicity of ways in which a "transaction" can be conceived or inhabited. Part of my project, therefore, has been to tease out writers' own understandings of pain's social status, rather than attempt to impose a model from without.

The first two chapters of this project address the problem of social suffering in the context of liberalism. Specifically, they seek to demonstrate the deep commitment on the part of two of the period's most important liberal thinkers to the non-self-evidence of precisely that sensation ordinarily understood as most private. The consequence is a revised notion of liberal subjectivity, not as prior to the social, but instead as inevitably enmeshed within it. Chapter 1, "John Stuart Mill and the Poetics of Social Pain," describes Mill's attempt to redefine sensory experience as a way to reimagine the social order posited by the utilitarianism of both his father, James Mill, and Jeremy Bentham. While James Mill describes pain as profoundly personal, interiorized, and private—and so imagines society as a more or less simple aggregate of essentially isolated individuals—in his *Autobiography*, John Stuart stages his famous mental crisis as a way to introduce a different model of pain that casts it as something we learn as well as something we feel. Pain is something each of us may experience alone, Mill concludes, but we only ever understand it through our encounters with others—encounters ideally mediated by poetry. Ultimately this notion of pain suggests a model of liberal sociality organized like a Wittgensteinian language game in which the terms of the discussion may be endlessly renegotiated among individuals who share the same fundamental pain of self-alienation.

Chapter 2, "Harriet Martineau and the Impersonality of Pain," argues that one of the most famous invalids of the age—and one of the most important political theorists—used her many writings on illness to imagine a model of impersonality uniquely well suited to the responsibilities of legislation. The relation of the legislator to the community represents a recurring problem for utilitarianism: if self-interest is the only reliable motivation, it becomes difficult to account for the legislator's—and hence, the ideal citizen's—supposed commitment to the common good. In Martineau's account, only the enlightened sufferer is able to regard all persons as equally valuable, and hence, her or his own pain as of no greater or lesser consequence than that experienced by anyone else. Working with a radical version of Hartleyan psychology, Martineau insists on the extent to which all sensation—including all painful sensation—has the potential to be attached to new associations, experiences, or beliefs. What makes pain unique, however, is the license it grants the sufferer to retreat from the world of face-to-face encounters. As a result, the sufferer comes to constitute the ideal legislator, albeit one who is prohibited by her condition from acting in the world.

Chapter 3, "Pain and Privacy in *Villette* (1853)," shifts away from politics to the novel, yet remains focused on pain's ability to configure the relation of the subject to the social. Specifically, this chapter argues that Charlotte Bronte's novel uses the phenomenology of pain as a way to imagine the compatibility of privacy—offered as the locus of the individual's value—with community. Here, I am particularly interested in Lucy Snowe's practice of using the language of physical sensation as a substitute for any account of the precise nature of her emotional trauma. In this chapter, I argue that these carefully staged refusals of readers' sympathy constitute an attempt to offer recognition and acknowledgement—here, counterintuitively couched in terms of the painful sensations of the body—in place of an implicitly normalizing fellow-feeling. We may not be able to enter into one another's feelings, Brontë insists, but we can nevertheless recognize that we all possess them. Such a model may preclude intimacy, but it enables a form of compassionate coexistence that has a family resemblance to that which Martineau and Mill imagine as the grounds of liberal sociality.

Although still connected to the issues of social life that inform the first three chapters, chapters 4 and 5 home in on the particular questions raised by

Darwin's engagement with Malthus. Chapter 4, "Charles Darwin's Affect Theory," considers how Darwin's meditations on pain complicate the optimism not just of his own historical moment but of some of the recent affect theory that claims to depend on his work. Specifically, Darwin's use of the idea of pain to ambiguate the relationship between the biological and the cultural, and to interrogate the basic unit of analysis, leads to a strange phenomenology in which it is often difficult to say who or what suffers: a person, a population, a species, or a limb. As such, it offers a model for a version of affect theory that refuses to take the individual for granted as its object. This chapter suggests the radical revision Darwin offers to any account of the social that naturalizes an autonomous subject as its starting point. It additionally indicates how Darwin's work on the expression of pain might prove useful for a renovated version of affect theory, albeit one devoid of the political optimism sometimes taken for granted by recent theorists.

Chapter 5, "Wounded Trees, Abandoned Boots," explores Thomas Hardy's post-Darwinian accounts of pain that hover ambiguously between and beyond subjects, that are attributed to no malign agent, and that hold no hope of prevention or remediation. Such accounts tend to be troubling in their vividness as well as in the profundity of the sorrow they describe and convey. They can certainly be called "pessimistic" in the sense that they offer no clear path for either action or catharsis; however, this chapter argues that for that very reason they invite us to consider the disposition that might be at issue in the reading practices they encourage: affectively engaged practices that ask us to experience ourselves less as potentially responsible observers of pain than as fellow sufferers. However much Hardy's work may seem like a retreat from the political, therefore, it nevertheless suggests an account of the social, grounded in the recognition of universal and yet differential relations to suffering.

Throughout *Victorian Pain*, I argue that "modern pain" is characterized by its imbrication with the social. In the afterword, I offer a very brief account of what epistemological accounts of pain can look like when conceived in isolation from social life. This way of thinking about pain does not originate in the nineteenth century, but it is importantly reformulated during this period. In the afterword, I describe the nature of this reformulation and begin to point to the consequences of its lingering pervasiveness. As I have already begun to suggest, *Victorian Pain* asserts a basic compatibility between a model of atomistic individualism often identified with liberalism and an exclusively epistemological model of pain. The afterword "The Fantasy of the Speaking Body" attends to a few symptoms of this compatibility.

CHAPTER ONE

John Stuart Mill and the Poetics of Social Pain

Human nature is not a machine to be built after a model, and set to do exactly the work prescribed for it, but a tree, which requires to grow and develop itself on all sides, according to the tendency of the inward forces which make it a living thing.

—JOHN STUART MILL, *ON LIBERTY* (1859)

JOHN STUART MILL'S *Autobiography* (1873) tells the story of a machine that turns into a tree. Before the "mental crisis" described in chapter 5, Mill claims that he had been "built after a model" by his father, James Mill, along with Jeremy Bentham, and "set to do exactly the work prescribed for it," devoid of any personal investment in the object of that work. He was "a mere reasoning machine," committed to "the good of mankind" out of a "zeal for speculative opinions," rather than "genuine benevolence, or sympathy with mankind."[1] After the crisis, by contrast, he was able to question certain of his makers' assumptions and take pleasure in activities with no immediate, practical end. He achieved this new state as a result of identifying the precise therapy he required. "What made Wordsworth's poems a medicine for my state of mind," and "the very culture of the feelings, which I was in quest of," he explains, is that "in them I seemed to draw from a source of inward joy, of sympathetic and imaginative pleasure, which could be shared in by all human beings; which had no connexion with struggle or imperfection, but would be made richer by every improvement in the physical or social condition of mankind" (*A* 151). By reading about trees—and tree-like poets—Mill effectively becomes one: an organism able to "grow and develop itself on all sides, according to the tendency of the inward forces which make it a living thing."[2]

But how can a machine become a tree? How, in other words, can a manufactured tool, designed and constructed to perform a particular function, turn into an organism characterized by "inward forces" that require expression? In this chapter, I argue that Mill stages this miraculous transformation as a way to demonstrate the limitations of classical utilitarian conceptions of pain. Utilitarianism purports to attend to pain and pleasure above all else. "Nature has placed mankind under the governance of two sovereign masters, *pain* and *pleasure*," Bentham asserts at the beginning of *The Principles of Morals and Legislation* (1789). "In words a man may pretend to abjure their empire: but in reality he will remain subject to it all the while."[3] Bentham's "principle of utility ... recognizes this subjection, and assumes it for the foundation of that system, the object of which is to rear the fabric of felicity by the hands of reason and of law."[4] In Mill's account, however, it is simply not sufficient to take pain seriously: according to him, utilitarianism is fundamentally limited by its misunderstanding of what pain is. The "mental crisis" described in the *Autobiography* thus narrativizes his own passage from a utilitarian model that casts pain as prior to the social, to a model that regards both pain and the subject as inescapably social. Pain is something each of us may experience alone, Mill concludes, but only insofar as we also experience it in relation to others. In this way, his mental crisis ultimately serves not just as a way to imagine a different model of pain, but also as a way to offer different ways of thinking about the subject, the relations between subjects, and the relations between the subject and the social. Put most simply, while before the crisis, Mill inhabits the social order as a more or less simple aggregate of fundamentally isolated individuals—as Bentham explains, "The interest of the community is ... the sum of the interests of the several members who compose it"[5]—afterward, he embraces a model of liberal sociality organized like a Wittgensteinian language game in which the terms of the discussion are endlessly renegotiated among individuals who share the same fundamental pain of self-alienation.[6] That "game" serves as a common ground, but it also constitutes a kind of bond, able to generate felt investments in others who participate in it. As a result, it begins to resolve one of the key problems of utilitarianism: that of how to connect individual pains and pleasures to collective well-being.

In the first section of this chapter, I examine the understanding of the human mind that subtends the education Mill describes receiving in the *Autobiography*. Even as James Mill and Jeremy Bentham were committed to the self-evidence of pain and pleasure, they also believed in the radical educability of the associations between the ideas to which those sensations give rise. In the *Autobiography* and elsewhere, by contrast, Mill argues for the limits of human educability in terms that reinstall something like an intuitive and foundational attachment to self. In other words, against his tutors' commitment to the eradicability of such an attachment—and hence, the viability of aspiring to a naturalized form of impersonality—Mill insists on the inevitability of experiencing one's own happiness differently from the way one experiences the happiness of others. In the second section of this chapter, I consider the alternative model of the relation between the self and the social that Mill proposes through his encounter with Jean François Marmontel's *Memoires* (1804). In place of a utilitarian subject isolated in her own sensorium, Mill uses his experience of reading about another's tragedy to imagine a social subject who enters into self-consciousness through its relationships to and within a social field. This model of subjectivity may not eliminate skepticism, or the recognition of the tragic inaccessibility of others, but it insists on the extent to which all subjects are implicated in it: the self as well as others. In the third section, I consider what that subject looks like when activated within the social field through which it has emerged. Through Wordsworth, I argue, Mill imagines a distance between self and experience that suggests one learns what Wittgenstein calls "pain behavior" in the process of becoming a recognizable member of a community.[7] The result is a reimagination of the bonds between the individual and the collective through a shared "form of life" involving pain.[8] Thus, while Wendy Donner claims that "Mill's individualism assumes social beings," and Nancy Yousef argues that "solitariness and privacy remain existentially fundamental to Mill's conception of the individual," this chapter argues that these are not opposing alternatives: in the terms that Wittgenstein provides, privacy is neither more nor less than the condition of the language game of pain.[9]

Utilitarian Pain

Critics have offered a variety of accounts of the "real" cause of the mental crisis at the center of Mill's *Autobiography*. Alexander Bain summarily rejects Mill's own claims of ennui on the grounds that "it was too early to have exhausted his whole interest in life" and turns instead to his friend's notorious industriousness: "I am unable to produce an instance of a man going through as much as Mill did before twenty."[10] A. W. Levi, by contrast, rejects Bain's account on the grounds that "no one ... has ever suffered a nervous breakdown from mere overwork" and instead attributes Mill's breakdown to his repressed hatred for his father.[11] This is the "unacknowledged trauma, that unassigned conflict, which, lying latent and malignant, needed but the strain of the year 1825 to transform itself into the mental crisis of the year 1826."[12] Janice Carlisle takes a different tack entirely, pointing to Mill's unhappiness with his position in the India House and his father's refusal to give him the "opportunity to prepare himself for a public career through the conventional route of university attendance."[13] And John M. Robson emphasizes Mill's sense of alienation from his fellows and his recognition that his father's "science of morality ... had no power to motivate his actions."[14] Despite the diversity of offered explanations, however, most commentators agree that Mill himself sought to place much of the blame on what Carlisle calls the "emotional poverty of his education."[15] As John Durham writes, fairly typically, "the period of melancholy seems to have been caused by emotional exhaustion, an exhaustion resulting from the peculiar nature of his education which had not allowed natural emotions to develop."[16] In other words, Mill had an unnatural childhood, during which his training in utilitarianism forced him to repress his emotions. The breakdown was a simple consequence of this repression and a necessary step toward establishing a more "natural" emotional balance.

To some extent, claims like these seem to be legitimated by Mill's repeated references to his father's suspicion of the way emotions tend to be invoked and described. "Offended by the frequency with which, in ethical and philosophical controversy, feeling is made the ultimate reason and justification of conduct," John Stuart explains, James Mill "had a real impatience of attributing praise to feeling, or of any but the most sparing reference to it either in the estimation of persons or in the discussion of things" (*A* 113). Furthermore, "for passionate emotions of all sorts, and for everything which has been said or written in exaltation of them, he professed the greatest contempt" (*A* 51). The impression that James Mill and Bentham sought to repress emotion is additionally reinforced by the consistency with which both men voiced concern about the injustices committed in its name. In *The Principles of Morals and Legislation*, for example, Bentham describes "the *principle of sympathy and antipathy*" as effectively a "*principle of caprice*."[17] Whether one calls it a "*moral*" or a "*common*" sense, a "Law of Nature, Law of Reason, Right Reason, Natural Justice, Natural Equity, [or] Good Order," the appeal to supposedly universal or natural feelings is merely a way of expressing that one likes or dislikes a thing and cannot give any good account of why.[18] "The various systems that have been formed concerning the standard of right and wrong ... consist all of them in so many contrivances for avoiding the obligation of appealing to any external standard, and for prevailing upon the reader to accept of the author's sentiment as a reason for itself."[19]

As Frances Ferguson explains, Bentham and James Mill's rejection of the explanatory value of feeling constituted an attempt to make "judgments look plausible to those who were not themselves parties in a dispute" and so to ground decision-making in something more consistently predictable than individual preferences or attachments.[20] This commitment has been extremely important in the twentieth and twenty-first centuries. One can see its influences, for example, in John Rawls's "veil of ignorance," which constitutes a way to "nullify the effects of specific contingencies which put men at odds and tempt them to exploit social and natural circumstances to their own advantage."[21] While comprehensible and even laudable in the context of public policy, however, this suspicion of "strong feeling" can seem bizarre, and possibly even cruel, when brought to bear on personal relations—as it seems to have been in relation to John Stuart. The schoolmaster M'Choakumchild insists in Charles Dickens's *Hard Times* (1854), "Facts alone are wanted in life.... You can only form the minds of reasoning animals upon Facts; nothing else will ever be of any service to them."[22] The mouthpiece may be grotesque, but this nevertheless seems like an opinion with which Bentham and James Mill might have agreed.

To claim that James Mill and Bentham rejected emotion as a reliable guide to legislation is not at all the same as to claim that they sought to suppress feeling, however. In fact, their commitment to pain and pleasure—along with the emotions to which they give rise—as the springs of all action, effectively place the emotions at the center of their understanding of human psychology, and hence, too, of the legislation they sought to develop. The notion that "Nature has placed mankind under the governance of two sovereign masters, *pain* and *pleasure*," itself assumes that these masters lie at the core of even the most complex emotions: our commitments and beliefs, our relationships to others, and our ambitions and aspirations. As John Stuart explains in his essay, "Sedgwick's Discourse" (1835), for example, "In all circumstances ... the determination of the will is wholly by feeling. Reason ... teaches us to know the right ends, and the way to them; but if we desire those ends, this desire is not Reason, but a feeling."[23] This is a claim his father makes at much greater length in his treatise on utilitarian psychology, *Analysis of the Phenomena of the Human Mind* (first published in 1829, published with notes by John Stuart Mill, Alexander Bain, Andrew Finklater, and George Grote in 1869). In addition to a chapter on "Pleasurable and Painful Sensations," James Mill includes one chapter on the "Causes of the Sensations of Pleasure and Pain," another on "Ideas of Pleasure and Pain and of the Causes of them," another on "The Pleasurable and Painful Sensations, contemplated as passed, or future," and still another on "The Causes of Pleasurable and Painful Sensations, contemplated as passed, or future."[24] The list can seem almost comical, but under this last heading alone, James Mill accounts for our attachments to wealth, power, and dignity; our capacity for friendship and kindness; our attachment to family, country, party, and mankind; and even our senses of the sublime and the beautiful.[25] In his view, all emotions—no matter how apparently complex—can be broken down into their basic components of pain and pleasure. Far from being dispensable, therefore, emotions are bound up with the basic claims of utilitarian theory, and the problem Mill and Bentham diagnose is not that feelings themselves are too powerful but instead that the fact of their power is so rarely acknowledged.

Considering the centrality of the emotions to utilitarian theory, then, it would be strange for John Stuart to claim his educators sought simply to suppress them. Nor does he ever make exactly this claim. Instead, he objects much more specifically to what he describes as the artificial ends to which his teachers sought to put his emotions. According to James Mill, rewards and punishments can effectively establish almost any association: "When Education is good, no point of morality will be reckoned of more importance than the distribution of Praise and Blame.... They are the great instruments we possess for ensuring moral acts on the part of our Fellow-creatures."²⁶ According to John Stuart, however, his father vastly overestimated the power of those "instruments." He writes:

> I had always heard it maintained by my father, and was myself convinced, that the object of education should be to form the strongest possible ... associations of pleasure with all things beneficial to the great whole, and of pain with all things hurtful to it. This doctrine appeared inexpugnable; but it now seemed to me on retrospect, that my teachers ... seemed to have trusted altogether to the old familiar instruments, praise and blame, reward and punishment. Now I did not doubt that by these means ... intense associations of pain and pleasure, especially of pain, might be created.... But there must always be something artificial and casual in associations thus produced. (*A* 141)

Despite the nobility of their goal, Mill argues, because there is no "natural tie" between the pains and pleasures used to educate him and their desired associations, those associations will be unable to withstand analysis. As a result of his mental crisis, therefore, "I now saw, or thought I saw, what I had always before received with incredulity—that the habit of analysis has a tendency to wear away the feelings" (*A* 141). It would have required a much more strenuous emotional education to make "indissoluble" the associations his educators wished to establish, Mill insists, if they could in fact be established at all.

Part of what Mill points to in the passage cited above is what he sees as a tension between the supposed self-evidence and privacy of pain and pleasure, on the one hand, and the radical availability of associations to education, on the other. For while the one suggests their irreducible attachment to self, the other makes that self seem available to extremes of self-denial in the interest of the collective. The notion that sensations are intuitively available is central to James Mill's psychology. He explains in his *Analysis*, "A man knows [the difference between different sensations], by feeling it; and this is the whole account of the phenomenon."

> I have one sensation, and then another, and then another. The first is of such a kind, that I care not whether it is long or short; the second is of such a kind that I would put an end to it instantly if I could; the third is of such a kind, that I like it prolonged. To distinguish those feelings, I give them names. I call the first Indifferent; the second, Painful; the third, Pleasurable.... It is obvious ... that having three sensations, an Indifferent, a Pleasurable, and a Painful, and knowing them for what they are, are not different things, but one and the same thing.²⁷

Pain is simply what the sufferer feels to be painful. It is private, intuitively available, and can never be experienced by anyone other than the sufferer herself. James Mill thus effectively predicts Elaine Scarry's account of pain as "so incontestably and unnegotiably present ... that 'having pain' may come to be so thought of as the most vibrant example of what it is to 'have certainty.'"[28] This is not to say that sympathy and compassion are inconceivable to James Mill any more than they are to Scarry: contrary to Dickens's assumption of the inevitable selfishness of utilitarianism, Bentham and James Mill are very explicit that the other-regarding pleasures of "benevolence" (and "malevolence") take their places alongside the self-regarding pleasures of "sense," "wealth," "skill," "a good name," "power," and so on.[29] But it is to say that whatever knowledge we might think we have of others' feelings are simply extrapolations from the feelings we have *ourselves*. Despite the fact that we "never feel any pains and pleasures but our own," therefore, we may still imagine another's feelings, but in doing so, we necessarily assume they resemble our own: "The fact, indeed, is, that our very idea of the pains or pleasures of another man is only the idea of our own pains, or our own pleasures, associated with the idea of another man."[30] Each of us may be locked inside our own experiences, but by associating those experiences with those of someone else, we come to feel some investment in that person's well-being.

The key term in this discussion is *association*: according to James Mill's account of the human mind, while sensations are immediate and intuitive, ideas, or what he calls the "remainder" of the sensation, exist at one remove from those sensations—as do the associations between ideas that make up the better part of our mental landscape.[31] "It is a known part of our constitution," James Mill explains, "that when our sensations cease, by the absence of their objects, something remains ... which, though I can distinguish it from the sensation ... is yet more like the sensation, than anything else can be."[32] We thus have "two classes of feelings; one, that which exists when the object of sense is present; another, that which exists after the object of sense has ceased to be present. The one class of feelings I call SENSATIONS; the other class of feelings I call IDEAS."[33] James Mill's account up to this point closely resembles John Locke's description in his *Essay Concerning Human Understanding* (1689) of how "the Senses at first let in particular *Ideas*, and furnish the yet empty Cabinet."[34] But while Locke emphasizes the importance of ideas, per se, James Mill is far more interested in the associations we make between them:

> Thought succeeds thought; idea follows idea, incessantly. If our senses are awake, we are continually receiving sensations, of the eye, the ear, the touch, and so forth; but not sensations alone. After sensations, ideas are perpetually excited of sensations formerly received; after those ideas, other ideas: and during the whole of our lives, a series of

those two states of consciousness, called sensations, and ideas, is constantly going on.[35]

James Mill goes on to describe a number of different bases for association, but ultimately, he concludes, "The causes of strength in association seem all to be resolvable into two; the vividness of the associated feelings; and the frequency of the association."[36]

These few simple principles constitute the basis of an entire system of education. "As the sequences among the letters or simple elements of speech, may be made to assume all the differences between nonsense and the most sublime philosophy," James Mill explains in his article, "Education," first published in the *Encyclopedia Britannica* (1825), "the sequences, in the feelings which constitute human thought, may assume all the differences between the extreme of madness and of wickedness, and the greatest attainable heights of wisdom and virtue: And almost the whole of this is the effect of education."[37] As a result, he continues, it is in the interest of every legislator or reformer to take seriously the role of education in forming people's attachments to the common good, and in teaching them that "the happiness of the individual is bound up with that of his species, [and that] that which affects the happiness of the one, must also, in general, affect that of the other."[38] James Mill recognizes the difficulty of promoting this attachment and so provides concrete instructions regarding how educators should reinforce the natural sequence whereby "the pleasures of those who are about [the child] are most commonly the cause of pleasure to himself; their pains his pain."[39] But the goal is worth the trouble: that of guaranteeing that the child will associate ideas in ways most conducive to benevolence: "A train of ideas, in the highest degree pleasurable, may thus habitually pass through his mind at the thought of happiness to others produced by himself; a train of ideas, in the highest degree painful, at the thought of misery to others produced by himself."[40] What education should seek to inculcate, therefore, is nothing more nor less than the absolute identification of the interests of the individual with those of the collective, a process that so expands the definition of self-interest as to make it nearly indistinguishable from selflessness.

As described by James Mill, it seems as if education needs only to underscore associations that arise naturally from a social order characterized by interdependency: in the long run, the pupil's interests are truly bound up with those of everyone around her; the goal of education is only to bring that fact home and so counter the common misunderstanding that her interests are in competition with those of others. This identity of interests is not, however, as self-evident as James Mill suggests—a fact that utilitarian theory elsewhere recognizes. Bentham writes: " 'Tis in vain to talk of adding quantities which after the addition will continue distinct as they were before, one man's happiness will never be another man's happiness: a gain to one man is no gain to another: you might as well pretend to add 20 apples to 20 pears."[41] Malthusian principles of population only underscore the potential incompatibility of interests, since they suggest the extent to which all persons are locked in a struggle for life in which the success of some will necessarily come at a cost to others.[42] As a result, as Elie Halévy explains, "[Benthamism] is incessantly appealing to two distinct principles, which are in a sense in competition within the system: the one in virtue of which the science of the legislator must intervene to identify interests which are naturally divergent; the other in virtue of which the social order is realised spontaneously, by the harmony of egoisms."[43] Even were one simply to rely on the legislator's ability to "intervene to identify interests which are naturally divergent," as Harold Perkin points out, this still leaves the problem of the legislator whose own interests may interfere with her or his ability to legislate fairly.[44] In a democracy, such a "legislator" is in some sense identical to the citizen insofar as each of us is responsible for decision-making in relation to others. One way of understanding the purpose of the education Mill received is as an attempt to remedy this last problem by creating a legislator (or citizen) who *does* experience her or his interests as identical with those of the collective. Yet in a context in which there is no natural identity of interests, any education that seeks to attach the child's feelings in this way can seem less to encourage enlightened self-interest than a sentimental or even a masochistic psychology whereby one consistently privileges others' interests above one's own.

In his extended discussion of sympathy in the *Analysis*, James Mill implicitly acknowledges the difficulty of identifying one's own interests with those of others—or at least with those of persons in whom one does not have an obvious investment. In a section on "Our Fellow-Creatures contemplated as Causes of our Pleasures and Pains," he emphasizes not disinterested sympathy but instead the proximate or causal relationships that make others seem connected with oneself. His paradigmatic example is that of a parent whose sympathy with a child is due at least in part to the fact that their interests may actually be bound together. "A parent is commonly either led or impelled to bestow an unusual degree of attention upon the pains and pleasures of his child," he explains, "and hence a habit is contracted of sympathizing with him."[45] Meanwhile, "the perfect dependence of the child upon the parent is a source of deep interest."[46] A man may thus look "upon his child as a cause to him of future pains or pleasures" and so regard the child's happiness as causally bound up with his own.[47] "Domestic affections" seem relatively easy to come by. It is not entirely clear, however, how to move sympathy beyond the family unit. Hence, while James Mill spends several pages describing the sources of the Domestic Affections, the other three objects to which he turns in this section—"Country," "Party or Class," and "Mankind"—are discussed extremely briefly and, to a large extent, are modeled on familial relations. James Mill claims we feel an "interest" in a country both because we have pleasurable associations with the objects it contains (mountains, plains, valleys, etc.) and because it includes "all that portion of our fellow-creatures with whom we have been accustomed to associate our Pains and Pleasures. Here are our Parents, our Brothers and Sisters, our Sons and Daughters. Here are the men, and here the women, who have engaged our affections."[48] He then goes on to include, as additional sources of pleasurable association, "our Benefactors ... our Instructors, [and] the Institutions from which we have derived Protection."[49] The implication is that our attachments to abstractions such as "country," and later, "mankind," are deeply bound up with the selfish, or at least self-regarding pleasures we have taken in other individuals. The collective abstractions of "Party or Class" and "Mankind" are similarly bound up with the selfishness of family life. As a result, it is difficult to imagine the circumstances under which one's commitment to a more abstract category could outweigh more proximate ties. As James Mill admits, "A very general idea, such as that of *Mankind*, is an indistinct idea; and no distinct association is formed with it, except by the means of Education."[50] Even education, it seems, may have a difficult time countering such foundational selfishness.

In his notes to this section of the *Analysis*, John Stuart makes at least two objections to his father's account of sympathy.[51] The first is that James Mill offers no clear account of how imagining our feelings in another's body will attach us to that person. John Stuart writes: "That the pleasures and pains of another person can only be pleasurable or painful to us through the association of our own pleasures and pains with them, is true in [the] sense ... that the only pleasures and pains of which we have direct experience being those felt by ourselves."[52] This, however, in no way accounts for the totality of the experience, for by "the acts or other signs exhibited by another person, the idea of a pleasure (which is a pleasurable idea) are recalled, sometimes with considerable intensity, but in association with the other person as feeling them, not with one's self as feeling them."[53] When I sympathize with another, in other words, my sympathy is with their feelings as theirs, Mill insists, not just with my feelings as theirs. This distinction is especially significant insofar as it insists on the role of self-consciousness in all feelings—a point to which I return in the next section.

The second objection Mill makes to his father's account of sympathy is to be found not in the notes to the *Analysis*, but in the *Autobiography*, where he stages a critique of the limits of utilitarian understandings of the felt tie between the individual and the collective. However much one might wish to imagine that one's own happiness will come to be identified with the well-being of the collective, Mill argues, the commitment of utilitarians to the essential privacy of sensations suggests just the opposite: that one's pains and pleasures are only ever one's own. Education may be able to generate certain associations through praise and blame, reward and punishment, but those associations will always be "artificial and casual." We have no choice but to experience others' sensations as different from our own. Finally, by instilling habits of analysis, one effectively guarantees that the object of education will eventually discover the fraud.

Social Pain

Thus far I have suggested that Mill's disagreement with his educators revolves around their attempt to attach the feelings of the individual to the well-being of the collective. To be more precise, I have begun to suggest that Mill takes issue with the way their model of mind makes such an attachment both inconceivable and mandatory. So long as pain and pleasure are understood as self-evident, private, and foundational, it will be impossible to regard the pains and pleasures of other people—particularly other people to whom one has no self-regarding tie—as critical to one's happiness. Education can seek to generate *associations* of pleasure and pain with the welfare of the community, but because those associations have no grounding, they are vulnerable to dissolution by analysis. As a result, even though Mill wishes he could feel sympathy with or an investment in human beings in general, he cannot. "All those to whom I looked up," he writes, "were of opinion that the pleasure of sympathy with human beings, and the feelings which made the good of others, and especially of mankind on a large scale, the object of existence, were the greatest and surest sources of happiness. Of the truth of this I was convinced, but to know that a feeling would make me happy if I had it, did not give me the feeling" (*A* 115). One cannot feel a thing simply because one knows it would be convenient to do so. That feeling needs some more substantial foundation.

In this section, I turn to Mill's description of his "mental crisis" in the *Autobiography* as a narrativization of his passage from a utilitarian model of mind—characterized by both the privacy of his sensations and his subjection to the artificial associations produced by his education—to what I call a social model, whereby one's self-conscious difference from the collective constitutes the condition of one's attachment to it. This latter model of mind does not require one to generalize from one's own feelings to others, or from one's local attachments to those felt toward the collective. Instead, it presumes that it is only through social engagement that one's feelings become recognizable in the first place. Rather than simply characterizing the universal ontology of pain, in Mill's account, the self-evidence and privacy his father associates with pain come to seem like the conditions of a language game in which we are all always already participating. As I discuss in the third section of this chapter, that game is not all-determining: the gaps between sensation and understanding enable a fair amount of free play, creativity, and disagreement. It does, however, serve as the basis of a felt bond with other people.

The trajectory of Mill's mental crisis is well known: in the fall of 1826, when he was twenty years old, Mill claims he experienced a "dull state of nerves, such as everybody is occasionally liable to; unsusceptible to enjoyment or pleasurable excitement":

> In this frame of mind it occurred to me to put the question directly to myself, "Suppose that all your objects in life were realized; that all the changes in institutions and opinions which you are looking forward to, could be completely effected at this very instant: would this be a great joy and happiness to you?" And an irrepressible self-consciousness distinctly answered, "No!" At this my heart sank within me: the whole foundation on which my life was constructed fell down. All my happiness was to have been found in the continual pursuit of this end. The end had ceased to charm, and how could there ever again be any interest in the means? I seemed to have nothing left to live for. (*A* 112)

Jerome H. Buckley has pointed out the parallels between this passage and the "Everlasting No" passage in Thomas Carlyle's *Sartor Resartus* (1833–34): "All at once, there rose a Thought in me, and I asked myself: 'What *art* thou afraid of? ... Hast thou not a heart; and, as a Child of Freedom, trample Tophet itself under thy feet ... ?' And as I thought, there rushed like a stream of fire over my whole soul; and I shook base Fear away from me for ever."[54] But while the origins of Teufelströckh's crisis are vaguely romantic—the character appears to have been disappointed in his love for the woman he calls "Blumine"—Mill's breakdown is couched as the product of a nearly automatic process whereby, in the absence of other objects of analysis, the machine turns its attention on itself. The consequence is a crisis that also constitutes the birth of self-consciousness: as a child, Mill claims, "I never thought of saying to myself, I am, or I can do, so and so. I neither estimated myself highly nor lowly: I did not estimate myself at all" (*A* 37). After the crisis, by contrast, he becomes all too aware of himself as both a self and a problem, the solution to which eludes him. As a result, for the next few months, "the cloud seemed to grow thicker and thicker" as he "became persuaded, that my love of mankind, and of excellence for its own sake, had worn itself out" (A 139).

According to Jonathan Loesberg, the passage cited above serves most importantly to provide "both support and justification for Mill's theories of free will and self-consciousness."[55] As Mill himself admits, during the period of his crisis, he was tortured by "the doctrine of what is called Philosophical Necessity," or the notion that the associationist rejection of innate ideas necessarily suggests that the subject is wholly defined by circumstances. Mill himself claims he arrived at the solution to the quandary during this period:

> I pondered painfully on the subject, till gradually I saw the light through it. I perceived, that the word Necessity, as a name for the doctrine of Cause and Effect applied to human action, carried with it a misleading association.... I saw that though our character is formed

by circumstances, our own desires can do much to shape those circumstances; and that what is really inspiriting and ennobling in the doctrine of freewill, is the conviction that we have real power over the formation of our own character; that our will, by influencing some of our circumstances, can modify our future habits or capabilities of willing. (*A* 177)

We may be made by circumstances, in other words, but our own will constitutes one of those circumstances.[56] Mill was clearly committed to this account: he articulates it first in *A System of Logic* (1843) and reiterates it several times in his work. As Alan Ryan explains, "Mill was, in fact, more pleased with his discussion of [the problem of determinism] than with any other part of the *System of Logic*. He never lost his belief that his argument did reconcile freedom and necessity, by showing that our actions are both freely chosen and causally determined."[57] Yet, however satisfied Mill may have been with this solution, it has struck many commentators as inadequate, and Loesberg is one of the doubters. Mill "has perhaps explained our *impression* that we are free agents," he argues, "but he has not proved that we can be causally determined and still remain truly free agents. In effect, the argument opens up a space between cause and effect and slips the agent's will into that space."[58] This logical weakness, Loesberg continues, is shored up in the *Autobiography* only through the narrative of the crisis itself—not through any logical means. In order to reconcile associationism with free will, Loesberg explains, Mill needs to describe his crisis in "such a way that it is externally caused but possible only because of internal responses."[59] He does this by making everything about the crisis the product of association, with the sole exception of the moment in which "an irrepressible self-consciousness distinctly answered, 'No!'" to the question he puts to himself. "Only the moment itself," Loesberg argues, "in its psychological inexplicability, is entirely free. And yet, that one slight moment is enough. To create that moment, he opened a space in his father's psychological theory, a space to be filled by an ultimate principle that he supports by the supposedly empirical evidence of the event he describes here."[60]

Loesberg's description of Mill's entrance into self-consciousness as a way to resolve the problems posed by determinism seems accurate, and yet, it is worth noting how little is ultimately altered by a transformation one might expect to be earth-shattering. Teufelströckh's self-interrogation, for example, enables him to embrace a new will to live and to conceive of himself as a possessor of free will: "The Everlasting No had said: 'Behold, thou art fatherless, outcast, and the Universe is mine (the Devil's);' to which my whole Me now made answer: '*I* am not thine, but Free, and forever hate thee!'"[61] If Mill's moment of self-interrogation solves his philosophical issues relating to free will and determinism as neatly as Loesberg suggests, one would expect the passages that follow it to be similarly triumphant. Instead, the change is nearly undetectable: before his entrance into self-consciousness, Mill claims he felt "dull" and "unsusceptible to pleasure or pleasurable excitement"; afterward, he describes himself as feeling he "has nothing left to live for" (*A* 139). The "indifferen[ce]" and "dry heavy dejection" remained unchanged throughout the "melancholy winter of 1826–7" (*A* 143); whatever he did during this time, he did "mechanically, by the mere force of habit," with no "delight in virtue or the general good, but also just as little in anything else" (*A* 143). As a result, he felt himself adrift: "I was thus, as I said to myself, left stranded at the commencement of my voyage, with a well equipped ship and a rudder, but no sail" (*A* 143). Mill's entrance into self-consciousness may resolve the problem of free will, but the passages immediately following that entrance suggest something else is at stake in his recovery, as well.

What first begins to move Mill forward is the experience of reading Marmontel's *Memoires*:

> I frequently asked myself, if I could, or if I was bound to go on living, when life must be passed in this manner. I generally answered to myself, that I did not think I could possibly bear it beyond a year. When, however, not more than half that duration of time had elapsed, a small ray of light broke in upon my gloom. I was reading, accidentally, Marmontel's *Memoires*, and came to the passage which relates his father's death, the distressed position of the family, and the sudden inspiration by which he, then a mere boy, felt and made them feel that he would be everything to them—would supply the place of all that they had lost. A vivid conception of the scene and its feelings came over me, and I was moved to tears. From this moment my burden grew lighter. The oppression of the thought that all feeling was dead within me, was gone. I was no longer hopeless: I was not a stock or a stone. (*A* 145)

According to many critics, what relieves Mill's depression in this passage is his recognition of—or else his displacement of—the murderous rage he felt toward his father for the artificiality of his education. As A. W. Levi wrote in 1945, and as many critics have echoed since, "Raised in a social milieu where ... the only acceptable attitude toward the father was love or, at the very least, respect," Marmontel's *Memoires* provided a "substitute expression" of feelings that Mill could not articulate in any other way.[62] Although it is impossible to overlook the events described in the passage that so lightens Mill's mood, there is also some evidence that he himself sought to make a more complicated point than that he wished his father was dead.[63] After all, James Mill, too, uses the deaths of a father—and of a son—as important examples of psychological principles in his *Analysis*. At the same time that John Stuart describes the death of a father, therefore, he is also implicitly revising crucial aspects of his father's theory of mind.

The first example in the *Analysis* of the death of a son appears in James Mill's crucial chapter on "The Association of Ideas" as a way to illustrate how antecedent feelings tend to be forgotten when consequent feelings are of greater importance:

> A friend arrives from a distant country, and brings me the first intelligence of the last illness, the last words, the last acts, and death of my son. The sound of the voice, the articulation of every word, makes its sensation in my ear; but it is to the ideas that my attention flies. It is my son that is before me, suffering, acting, speaking, dying. The words which have introduced the ideas, and kindled the affections, have been as little heeded, as the respiration which has been accelerated, while the ideas were received.[64]

It is striking that James chose such a loaded example to make such a generalizable point: after all, one can never focus on sensations in understanding language. So why turn to the example of the dead child? My suspicion is that the answer simply has to do with his desire to underscore the imaginative transport involved in this scene. Here, the father imagines something he has not experienced, but the strength of the associations he has with his son and with his son's death are so strong as to make him feel almost as if he had: "It is my son that is before me." What is being forgotten or repressed are not the words, but instead all the real-world circumstances that stand between him and the body he most desires to see.

The second example from the *Analysis* that is relevant to John Stuart's experience of reading Marmontel appears in an equally prominent place, in James Mill's chapter on "Memory":

> After a lapse of many years, I see the house in which my father died. Instantly a long train of the circumstances connected with him rise in my mind: the sight of him on his death-bed; his pale and emaciated countenance; the calm contentment with which he looked forward to his end; his strong solicitude, terminating only with life, for the happiness of his son; my own sympathetic emotions when I saw him expire; the mode and guiding principles of his life; the thread of his history; and so on. In this succession of ideas, each of which is an idea of memory, there is not a single link which is not formed by association; not an idea which is not brought into existence by that which precedes it.[65]

As in the previous instance, the materiality of the prompt—in this case, the house—is quickly obscured by the train of associations attached to it, and the pathos of the circumstances serves to underscore the profundity of that erasure. But other similarities pertain, as well. In both cases, for example, the relation between subject and object is resolutely maintained: James Mill describes no sympathetic identification or attempt to imagine the feelings of anyone else. His feelings remain resolutely his own. Yet at the same time, the relation between the real and the imagined or remembered is almost wholly obscured: while in the first instance, the father has a vivid conception of what he would have felt were he to have been by his son's side while he died, in the second, the son has a vivid memory of what he did feel when he watched his father die. In both cases, feeling is involved, but it is of a kind that in no way confuses the relation between persons. Rather than sympathy, therefore—a term ordinarily used to describe one person's entrance into the feelings of another—James Mill's feelings here remain resolutely attached to himself and extend only to an imagination of what he felt or would have felt in another place and time.

John Stuart's description of his experience of reading Marmontel both echoes his father's examples and departs from them in important ways. On the one hand, there is a similar clarity in terms of relative subject positions: he does not imagine he *is* any of the characters about whom he reads. Moreover, as in his father's case, his experience is described as involuntary. John Stuart does underscore his passivity more than his father: he does not "imagine"; instead, "a vivid conception ... *came over* me, and I *was moved* to tears." Already we seem to be in a more Romantic mental landscape in which feelings have an agency independent of the persons who feel them. Because he is not himself involved in the scene he reads, however—unlike James Mill, he is neither father to the son, nor son to the father—his relationship to that scene remains that of a spectator, invested in what he reads about by neither proximity nor causality, but only by interest. This demonstrates the extent to which emotional responsiveness need not be bound up with selfishness. Further, the revisions John Stuart made to the passage in the *Autobiography* prior to publication suggest that he wished to underscore the fact that he was not simply identifying with the son who replaces the father—a move that would have reintroduced a suggestion of self-regarding feelings. Instead, he emphasizes that he was moved by a set of social relations—a set to which he has no obvious tie. Thus, while James Mill imagines being moved by precisely those relations he experiences as most deeply connected to himself—that of a father to a son or a son to a father—John Stuart imagines those relations without inserting himself into one of the available positions. Thus, what in James Mill's account is implicitly directed toward self, for John Stuart becomes not just unselfish in the sense that he is not involved but also in the sense that he closes down the possibility that the pleasure of the scene arises from his ability to imagine himself as any one of the key players. Thus, the first version of the passage in which he begins to weep reads: "A vivid conception of *his and their feelings* came over me, and I was moved to tears"—a formulation that retains some sense of his relation to differentiated persons. The second version reads, "A vivid conception of *this scene* came over me, and I was moved to tears"—"this scene" removing those persons and replacing them with something like a theatrical tableau. The final version reads, "A vivid conception *of the scene and its feelings* came over me, and I was moved to tears"—which seems almost to personify that tableau and so make it the potential object of identification or emotional attachment (*A* 144–45, all emphases added).[66] Mill thus ultimately describes himself as moved by a set of social relations.

John Plotz has recently pointed out the way Mill uses the experience of reading as a way to evade the uncomfortable immediacy of direct personal address. Mill embraces reading, Plotz claims, because it gives him access to feelings that are not but might be his own in a context that seems to mitigate the coercive potential of the face-to-face encounter. "Only when poetry has opened up the reader's own feelings as belonging, antecedently, to another person can that reader begin to delineate his or her discrete self," Plotz explains. "Only in his *indirect* or mediated encounter with the highly wrought feelings of others can Mill discern his own."[67] This seems both right and important. Yet, in Mill's relation to the scene Marmontel describes, he takes the indirection Plotz describes several steps further: rather than feeling the feelings of another person that are also his own, he feels feelings generated by a social relation—and then, too, the feelings generated by those feelings. Mill's experience of reading Marmontel thus ultimately seems to be less about identification than a first step toward social sympathy—that is, sympathy felt toward a collective rather than just an individual.

Wordsworth's Lament

In *The End of the Line*, Neil Hertz describes the experience of the sublime in terms that closely resemble those Mill uses to describe his crisis. According to Hertz, in moments of what he calls "sublime blockage," "Typically the poised relationship of attenuated subject and divided object reveals its inherent instability by breaking down and giving way to scenarios more or less violent, in which the aggressive reassertion of the subject's stability is bought at some other subject's expense."[68] The minimal difference within the divided object that Hertz describes could easily be that between Mill before and Mill after his self-interrogation—that is between "dullness" and "indifference." And, as Hertz predicts, the resulting blockage or stasis seems to be resolved by an act of violence—against Marmontel's father, or perhaps against James Mill. Mill's initial response to that violence is one of enormous relief. Yet in the *Autobiography*, he describes quickly descending back into a paralysis even more terrifying than that which preceded it. This is an eventuality that Hertz does not necessarily anticipate, but then, Mill represents a threat that is somewhat alien to the psychoanalytic frame with which Hertz is working: that of dissolving into the social in a way that leaves no remainder of self at all. Mill's problem, in other words, is that of maintaining an internally differentiated sense of self that also mandates a differentiated relation to the social.

The full terrors involved in self-identity are only fully manifest *after* Mill describes his experience of reading Marmontel: clearly, whatever therapy that writer provided was ultimately insufficient. Immediately after he describes the relief he felt upon weeping, Mill offers a particularly vivid account of the anxiety and despair he continued to experience. After his encounter with Marmontel, he explains, he was once again able to enjoy some music. However, this pleasure was attended with enormous psychic risks:

> I at this time first became acquainted with Weber's *Oberon*, and the extreme pleasure which I drew from its delicious melodies did me good, by shewing me a source of pleasure to which I was as susceptible as ever. The good however was much impaired by the thought, that the pleasure of music ... fades with familiarity.... And it is very characteristic ... of my then state ... that I was seriously tormented by the thought of the exhaustibility of musical combinations.... This source of anxiety may perhaps be thought to resemble that of the philosophers of Laputa, who feared lest the sun should be burnt out. It was, however, connected with the best feature in my character, and the only good point to be found in my very unromantic and in no way honourable distress. For though my dejection ... could not be called other than egotistical ... yet the destiny of mankind in general was ever in my thoughts, and could not be separated from my own. I felt that the flaw in my life, must be a flaw in life itself. (*A* 149)

The speed with which Mill moves from his pleasure in Weber to his horror at the idea of the "exhaustibility of musical combinations," to his anxiety that, were "every person in the community ... free and in a state of physical comfort, the pleasures of life ... would cease to be pleasures," makes this passage worth quoting at length. The overall impression it conveys is of a kind of Escheresque claustrophobia, as it slides vertiginously from one horrifying vision of overdetermination to another. Yet in Escher, anxiety is generated by the impossibility of determining the relation between surface and depth—a state of affairs akin to the mathematical sublime in which the mind is checked by its confrontation with a series it cannot bring under "some sort of conceptual unity."[69] Here, by contrast, the claustrophobia is generated by very nearly the opposite state of affairs: the concern that relations are all too knowable, musical combinations are all too exhaustible, and the pleasures of life are all too easily depleted. Mill has once more fallen into a deterministic landscape, in which all possible combinations are depleted in anticipation. The consequence is to lock him into a hall of mirrors in which every image he sees is of himself. He thus describes reading "through the whole of Byron ... to try whether a poet, whose peculiar department was supposed to be that of the intenser feelings, could rouse any feeling in me" (*A* 149). His disappointment, he explains, arises from the fact that "the poet's state of mind was too like my own. His was the lament of a man who had worn out all pleasures, and who seemed to think that life, to all who possess the good things of it, must necessarily be the vapid uninteresting thing which I found it. His Harold and Manfred had the same burden on them which I had" (*A* 149–51). The sheer ludicrousness of Mill's identification with Byron, Harold, or Manfred suggests the extent to which Mill's blockage is less one of self-division than of self-unity or narcissism. There is no difference between self and self, self and other, present and future: all collapse into a single undifferentiated mass.

This is a problem Mill elsewhere attributes to his father's model of mind. As Janice Carlisle and others have noted, and as the foregoing account suggests, despite his encomium to James Mill as "the second founder of the Associationist psychology"—David Hartley was the first—John Stuart's notes are often highly critical of his father's claims.[70] John Stuart challenges James Mill on a number of bases, but most consistent is his insistence that his father obscures the role of "belief" in tethering us to our own experiences, and hence, too, the role that self-consciousness plays in all mental experience. This insistence is particularly apparent in his critique of his father's account of memory. While James Mill claims that "it will not be doubted [that] the whole of that state of consciousness which we call memory" is comprised of "1, the idea of the thing" combined with "2, the idea of my having seen it," John Stuart insists that this does not begin to capture the complexity of the situation:[71]

> The doctrine which the author thinks "will not be doubted" is more than doubted by most people, and in my judgment rightly. To complete the memory of seeing the thing, I must have not only the idea of the thing, and the idea of my having seen it, but the belief of my having seen it; and even this is not always enough; for I may believe on the authority of others that I have seen a thing which I have no remembrance of seeing.[72]

In addition to the idea of the thing, the idea of one having seen it, and the belief of one having seen it, he goes on to explain in another note, one also needs a sense of that "inexplicable tie" that connects "a long and uninterrupted succession of past feelings going as far back as memory reaches, and terminating with the sensations I have at the present moment.... This succession of feelings, which I call my memory of the past, is that by which I distinguish my Self."[73] Moreover, it also distinguishes that self "from the parallel successions of feelings which I believe, on satisfactory evidence, to have happened to each of the other beings, shaped like myself, whom I perceive around me."[74] In making these claims, John Stuart underscores his father's inability to account for the idea of "self"—a gap that Carlisle describes as endemic to associationist philosophy: "Impressions are like beads on a string, except that, as the associationist would argue, the presence or absence of the string that holds them together can never be ascertained."[75] The resulting skepticism about "the integrity of human identity," Carlisle continues, constitutes one of the key problems John Stuart sought to resolve.[76] He may not have been successful—even in the passage quoted above, he rhetorically throws up his hands. Aside from being able to identify the fact of a bond, he cannot specify identity any further: "Here, I think, the question must rest, until some psychologist succeeds better than any one has yet done in shewing a mode in which the analysis can be carried further."[77] According to Alan Ryan, this failure is only that—a failure.[78] But rather than regarding the inexplicability of self-consciousness *solely* as a problem, at least in the context of Wordsworth, it can also be understood to serve some more positive function. As such, the tenuous tether between self and experience suggests the role internal self-differentiation plays in opening up the possibility of external relationship as well. The result may not be an intuitively self-evident model of the self, but it is a model that involves sufficient self-differentiation to enable both a critical relation to self and also an emotional investment in others.

It is worth noting the extent to which even the apparently innocuous exercise of turning to poetry in a moment of distress can be understood as a rejection of Bentham's philosophy. In his discussion of Bentham's lack of interest in poetry, Mill writes, "Words, he thought, were perverted from their proper office when they were employed in uttering anything but precise logical truth."[79] As F. Parvin Sharpless explains, Bentham was particularly concerned that poets may distort rational pleasure-pain valuations: "In order to serve ambitious and selfish ends these spokesmen brand activities as painful which are really not so, or deny the pain which exists in actually painful conditions."[80] For Mill, however, this possible revaluation is itself a site of possibility:

> I needed to be made to feel that there was real, permanent happiness in tranquil contemplation. Wordsworth taught me this, not only without turning away from, but with a greatly increased interest in, the common feelings and common destiny of human beings. And the delight which these poems gave me, proved that with culture of this sort, there was nothing to dread from the most confirmed habit of analysis. At the conclusion of the Poems came the famous Ode, falsely called Platonic, "Intimations of Immortality": in which, along with more than his usual sweetness of melody and rhythm, and along with the two passages of grand imagery but bad philosophy so often quoted, I found that he too had had similar experience to mine; that he also had felt that the first freshness of youthful enjoyment of life was not lasting; but that he had sought for compensation, and found it, in the way in which he was now teaching me to find it. The result was that I gradually, but completely, emerged from my habitual depression, and was never again subject to it. (*A* 151–53)

Perhaps the most striking aspect of this passage is the ostentatious implausibility of his identification with Wordsworth. It may not be quite as bizarre as his attempt to compare himself with Byron. Yet, before this point in the

Autobiography, we have been given no sense that Mill had a happy childhood, that his unselfconsciousness was in any way pleasurable, or even that he had any especially strong tie to nature, despite his very belated claim that "the love of rural objects and natural scenery" constituted "one of the strongest of my pleasurable susceptibilities" (*A* 151). Nevertheless, when Mill insists that he, too, "felt that the first freshness of life was not lasting," the difficulty of locating anything in the *Autobiography* resembling "first freshness" cannot, I think, be regarded as simply an accident. Rather than wishful thinking, this implausibility seems part of his insistence that he is being "educated" by the poet. He is learning something, in other words, and the first thing he learns is not how to achieve compensation, but instead that compensation is, in fact, appropriate. In other words, Mill learns that the unselfconsciousness he can now imagine that he experienced as a child can be understood as "first freshness," that his subsequent entrance into self-consciousness constitutes a source of sorrow or grief, and hence, that now amends need to be made. Wordsworth is thus credited with stabilizing self-consciousness by describing that state in terms of loss. He is also credited with identifying it not just as something all persons share, but as something we can only ever share, since in the absence of social relationship, Mill had no way to identify what he (may or may not have) felt as painful. Wordsworth may not have exactly caused Mill's self-consciousness, but he has provided a model for it and a name for what it involves: suffering.

In this passage, then, Mill identifies Wordsworth as educating him in how to differentiate between present and past (and hence, too, between present self and past self), a differentiation that he defines in terms of loss. At the same time, the exact content of that loss—and the resulting compensation—remain interestingly underspecified. The key passage of the poem describing the compensation the poet finally receives comes in the final stanza of the poem where Wordsworth proclaims:

> What though the radiance which was once so bright
> Be now for ever taken from my sight,
>   Though nothing can bring back the hour
> Of splendour in the grass, of glory in the flower;
>   We will grieve not, rather find
>   Strength in what remains behind,
>   In the primal sympathy
>   Which having been must ever be,
>   In the soothing thoughts that spring
>   Out of human suffering,
>   In the faith that looks through death,
> In years that bring the philosophic mind.

(LINES 178–89)

This passage is usually described in terms of the poet's acceptance of the passing of an immediate, intuitive, unselfconscious relation to nature as the price he must pay for the "primal sympathy" that enables him to appreciate "the soothing thoughts that spring / out of human suffering." This self-consciousness means he no longer has the status of a natural object: he is no longer able to "trip[]" as "lightly" as the "brooks" themselves, but as a result, he is able to "love" them "even more" (l. 197–98)—love being a relational emotion that requires some kind of distance between self and other.[81] What Wordsworth describes, in other words, is the opening up of a series of intervals or gaps—between self and other, present self and past self—that constitute losses as well as the bases of relationship. As Geoffrey Hartman explains, although "the recognition that restores Wordsworth is elusive," what matters more than content is the "dialogue of the soul with itself in the presence of nature" that the poem performs.[82] "Human suffering" thus comes to seem a universal human condition not simply in the obvious sense that we all have vulnerable bodies and so must eventually die, but in the sense that, insofar as we are all recognizable subjects, we all identify subjectivity with the fact of suffering. We are bound together by this suffering insofar as it is only within that collective context that it comes into existence at all: suffering is thus inextricably linked to the possibility of compensation.

As I mentioned at the beginning of this chapter, one way to understand my claim is as a way to reframe a longstanding debate over whether Mill regards the subject as primarily isolated or primarily social. Rather than opposed alternatives, in Mill's account, privacy—or the recognition of individuation with its concomitant loss of "primal freshness"—is something like the condition of the language game of pain. This model of the subject does considerable work for Mill. Most importantly, it begins to explain how assumptions about the privacy of sensation can coexist with a connection felt toward others. It is not, however, entirely devoid of problems of its own. Most importantly, it raises a question regarding the limits of the language game, or the extent to which the very idea of a language game might close down the possibility of radical transformation.

Debates over whether or not Wittgenstein's notion of the language game is conservative are longstanding and ongoing. For my purposes, the most important question this debate raises is that of the extent to which it holds open a space for radical forms of disagreement. As Christopher C. Robinson explains, Wittgenstein's "focus on agreement" can seem to render his "philosophy blind to disagreement and incapable of conceiving of criticisms of social practices while we are engaged in them."[83] In both "Thoughts on Poetry and Its Varieties" (1833) and *On Liberty* (1859), I think we can see Mill working out precisely this problem—in the one text, in the positive terms of underspecification, and in the other, in the negative terms of the defense against overspecification. In both texts, Mill examines how the social definition of the subject can coexist with the possibility of radical transformation. In both cases, the answer he gives is that of underspecification as a state of affairs that opens the possibility of endless renegotiation.

In "Thoughts on Poetry," that underspecification is made to seem constitutive of poetry in the first place. As M. H. Abrams explains, one of the more innovative aspects of Mill's theory of poetry is its "inver[sion] [of] the neo-classic ranking of the poetic kinds."[84] By contrast with Aristotle and neo-classical critics for whom the plot represents the "soul" of poetry, for Mill, "plot becomes a kind of necessary evil"—one with which he consistently seeks to dispense. Rather than tragedy or epic, therefore, lyric represents the highest form of poetry because "other forms are all alloyed by non-poetic elements, whether descriptive, didactic, or narrative."[85] Thus, for Mill, not only does poetry not *have* to be about anything in particular, it *should* not be about anything in particular. Poetry is "the expression or uttering forth of feeling," he writes—a situation that leaves the content almost wholly undefined.[86] "Feeling," after all, covers a great deal of ground. Nor is this all, for an additional question arises regarding whose feelings are ultimately felt in poetry. "The poetry is not in the object itself," Mill writes, "but in the state of mind in which [it] may be contemplated."[87] Instead of the objects, or even the poet, therefore, the poetry of poetry appears to be inherent as a kind of latent possibility in the mind of the person who reads it. "Poetry, which is the delineation of the deeper and more secret workings of human emotion, is interesting only to those to *whom it recals* what they have felt, or whose imagination it stirs up to conceive what they could feel, or what they might have been able to feel had their outward circumstances been different."[88] Poetry is not available to all, and it in no way depends on any particular circumstance; instead, it is something like a permanent possibility of feeling to which only certain subjects have access.[89] No correspondence between the feelings of the poet or speaker and those of the reader is here mandated. Instead, the poetry simply recalls or suggests something for at least some few, privileged readers.

Mill's *On Liberty* addresses the problem of underspecification much more straightforwardly, for here the goal is less to define the nature of the objects that can serve as sources of pleasure and self-definition than to address how to stave off the tyranny of social life. "Society can and does execute its own mandates," Mill writes,

> and if it issues wrong mandates instead of right, or any mandates at all in things with which it ought not to meddle, it practises a social tyranny more formidable than many kinds of political oppression, since, though not usually upheld by such extreme penalties, it leaves fewer means of escape, penetrating much more deeply into the details of life, and enslaving the soul itself.[90]

The language of penetration and enslavement here suggests a deep concern regarding limits that exist on what can be thought, said, or even felt in the context of any given language game. As Michael Kober explains of Wittgenstein's notion of a "world picture," although the picture contains "all the kinds of knowledge a community may share," and so serves as a "basis, a foundation of a community's looking at the world," not "everything contained [in that picture] need be true."[91] "Above all," Kober quotes Wittgenstein claiming, "it is the substratum of all my enquiring and asserting."[92] As such, it may or may not be available to challenge. For Mill, however, membership in a community of "native speakers" need not preclude self-development. It constitutes its precondition, but that may in fact be all. What we share is a vocabulary of pain, a communal acceptance of its privacy; but that shared knowledge does not exhaust it any more than it offers a solution for it. It provides merely a starting point. This state of underspecification still poses problems: it is the task of *On Liberty* to warn us of them again and again.

As I discuss in the introduction, Stanley Cavell claims that one "moral" of Wittgenstein's *Philosophical Investigations* might be that "the fact, and the state, of your (inner) life cannot take its importance from anything special in it. However far you have gone with it, you will find that what is common is there before you are. The state of your life may be, and may be all that is, worth your infinite interest. But then that can only exist along with a complete disinterest toward it. The soul is impersonal."[93] In the *Autobiography*, this impersonality is made to seem like *both* a loss and a gain. Coming as Mill is from a context in which universal interiority is *not* a given, but instead a hard-won fact, the "common-ness" of his soul may seem lamentable. At the same time, however, his discovery that he can speak of a pain that he possesses as distinctively his own, yet is also possessed by all those around him, constitutes a source of literally unutterable satisfaction, a condition of human sociability, and hence, too, an inexhaustible resource for both a sense of self and social life.

CHAPTER TWO

Harriet Martineau and the Impersonality of Pain

HARRIET MARTINEAU OPENS her *Autobiography* (1877) with sensations. "My first recollections," she writes,

> are of some infantine impressions which were in abeyance for a long course of years, and then revived in an inexplicable way,—as by a flash of lightning over a far horizon in the night. There is no doubt of the genuineness of the remembrance, as the facts could not have been told me by any one else. I remember standing on the threshold of a cottage, holding fast by the doorpost, and putting my foot down, in repeated attempts to reach the ground. Having accomplished the step, I toddled (I remember the uncertain feeling) to a tree before the door, and tried to clasp and get round it; but the rough bark hurt my hands.[1]

For a woman writer renowned for the strength of her political and philosophical convictions, the power of her intellect, and the intensity of her ambition, this is a somewhat surprising way to begin her autobiography. Most importantly, it provides no intimation of the "remarkable[ness]" of her life—the principal reason she gives for regarding her autobiography as one of the "duties of [her] life" (*A* 34). Nevertheless, it does foreground the qualities of mind that she claims qualify her for the work: "a strong consciousness and a clear memory in regard to my early feelings" (*A* 34). Most of us have gone through some version of Martineau's experience of learning to walk. Yet probably relatively few are able to recall the "uncertain feeling" involved in being a toddler with such specificity. Martineau thus begins to introduce a pattern that recurs throughout the two volumes of her *Autobiography*: not just of concerted effort rewarded but of the incredible precision with which she remembers the sensations involved in both the effort and the reward. We are apparently being prepared for a narrative of the inevitable triumph of this acute little toddler.

As the paragraph continues, however, the status of Martineau's infant sensations becomes more complicated.[2] While the opening initially emphasizes achievement related to perceptual accuracy, the passage goes on to underscore just how misguided sense impressions can be—even, or perhaps especially, when those sensations are painful.

> My bad health during my whole childhood and youth, and even my deafness, was always ascribed by my mother to [the inadequacy of her wetnurse]. However it might be about that, my health certainly was very bad till I was nearer thirty than twenty years of age; and never was poor mortal cursed with a more beggarly nervous system. The long years of indigestion by day and night-mare terrors are mournful to think of now.—Milk has radically disagreed with me, all my life: but when I was a child, it was a thing unheard of for children not to be fed on milk: so, till I was old enough to have tea at breakfast, I went on having a horrid lump at my throat for hours of every morning, and the most terrific oppressions in the night. Sometimes the dim light of the windows in the night seemed to advance till it pressed upon my eyeballs, and then the windows would seem to recede to an infinite distance. If I laid my hand under my head on the pillow, the hand seemed to vanish almost to a point, while the head grew as big as a mountain. (*A* 39–40)

Illness here is couched as the product of ignorance and thoughtless habit: the fact that "it was a thing unheard of for children not to be fed on milk." But error is also made to seem like the *product* of Martineau's illness, part of its phenomenology. Thus, physical suffering is cast as a problem in and of itself, and also as a cause of her horrified misrecognition of her own body, as well as the world around her. Rather than a medium for seeing, the dim light becomes a threatening object, able to impinge upon her body. Meanwhile, that body, too, is massively distorted as "the hand" (no longer "my" hand) seems to "vanish," and "the head" grows.[3] Nor is this all: perceptual errors only multiply as the passage goes on, leading to yet more terrors. "Sometimes I was panic struck at the head of the stairs," she continues,

> and was sure I could never get down; and I could never cross the yard to the garden without flying and panting, and fearing to look behind, because a wild beast was after me. The starlight sky was the worst; it was always coming down, to stifle and crush me, and rest upon my head. I do not remember any dread of thieves or ghosts in particular; but things as I actually saw them were dreadful to me; and it now appears to me that I had scarcely any respite from the terror. (*A* 40)

With the exception of the "wild beast" that she imagines might be chasing her, Martineau does not claim she suffered from hallucinations or visions: she was not afraid of imaginary "thieves or ghosts." Instead, it was simply "things as I actually saw them" that terrified her. She saw and heard only what was there, yet the way she perceived or experienced those things was nevertheless misguided, inaccurate, and exaggerated. Her sensations were at fault rather than anything she imagines about them. The paragraph reaches its climax, ironically enough for one who eventually lost her hearing, with a sound:

> In the wide area below, the residents were wont to expose their feather-beds, and to beat them with a stick. That sound,—a dull shock,—used to make my heart stand still: and it was no use my standing at the rails above, and seeing the process. The striking of the blow and the arrival of the sound did not correspond; and this made matters worse. I hated that walk; and I believe for that reason. (*A* 40)

Unable to understand the lack of correspondence between what she sees and what she hears, Martineau's underlying illness makes even this mundane experience horrifying.

In turning from John Stuart Mill to Harriet Martineau, we remain on close terrain. Like Mill, in her political and economic writings, Martineau was committed to bringing a utilitarian commitment to the greatest good together with a liberal commitment to justice and equality. And like Mill, in her autobiographical writings, Martineau attempts to achieve that goal—or at least to imagine achieving it—through a meditation on the nature of aversive physical experience. Thus, for Martineau, as for Mill, pain and suffering constitute important ways to question the nature of subjectivity, the relations between subjects, and the relation between the subject and the social. The differences between these two writers are at least as striking as the similarities, however, especially in their ideas on education. For Mill, as we saw in the previous chapter, there is no way for education to eradicate the divergence between individuals' interests, and hence, too, every individual's primary attachment to her sensations as her own. Martineau, by contrast, rejects the notion that human interests may ultimately not be fully compatible. The problem she addresses, therefore, is that of how to experience such compatibility: how to experience interdependency. She attempts to achieve this goal, I argue, by casting sensations *themselves* as available to education—a state of affairs that offers some hope of loosening the bonds between the subject and her own pain.

Pain in Martineau's account remains indubitably painful: it cannot simply be educated or philosophized away. "When extreme pain seizes on us," she writes in *Life in the Sick-Room* (1844), "down go our spirits, fathoms deep; and, though the soul may yet be submissive and even willing, the sickening question rises,—'How *shall* I bear this for five minutes? What *will* become of me?' "[4] Pain is clearly an aversive experience for Martineau, but this does not mean that it is wholly self-evident. Working with a radical version of Hartleyan psychology, Martineau insists on the consistency with which all sensation is liable to error, as well as the way all sensation—and especially painful sensation—has the potential to be attached to new associations. Combined with the solitude and the freedom from responsibility that she associated with invalidism, the consequence is to place Martineau's sufferer in a privileged position to free herself from the local attachments—to friends, to family, and even sometimes to self—that stand in the way of the impersonality to which she imagined all persons should aspire.[5] The sufferer from pain thus emerges in her account as the ideal legislator—and hence, as the ideal citizen—albeit one whose condition prohibits her from acting in the world.

This account of Martineau's understanding of pain and its sufferer has consequences for how we understand the work of one of the most important political thinkers and illness writers of the early Victorian period.[6] Martineau's 24-volume *Illustrations of Political Economy* (1832-34), an attempt to disseminate the political theories of Malthus, Ricardo, and James Mill by "illustrating" them in the form of fictional tales, was enormously popular and transformed her nearly overnight into an authority on a staggeringly wide range of issues, despite her sex.[7] She continued her political work throughout her life, writing on everything from poverty to slavery to tax reform to postal rates.[8] But Martineau also had serious health problems for most of her life. As a child, she suffered from digestive difficulties, anxiety attacks, and a progressive hearing impairment. In her mid-thirties, she was diagnosed with "prolapse of the uterus and polypous tumors," for which no medical cure was possible.[9] As a consequence, she spent over five years confined to her sickroom —much of that time in tremendous pain—before undergoing a course of mesmerism that she believed led to a full recovery. In 1855, she became ill again, and although she lived an additional twenty-one years, she spent much of that time confined to her home by her infirmity. As Alison Winter has argued, Martineau's gynecological problems, in particular, meant that "one of early Victorian England's most active public figures risked being transformed into the epitome of delicate femininity, immobilized and cloistered by her illness."[10] Nevertheless, she never sought to conceal her illnesses, and many of her writings address issues of sickness, health, and disability in explicitly personal terms. Her "Letter to the Deaf" (1834), *Life in the Sick-Room, Letters on Mesmerism* (1845), and *Autobiography* (1877), written when she thought she was dying in 1855, but not published until after her death in 1876, all clearly identify her as a sufferer from the maladies she describes and address readers as actual or potential fellow sufferers. In addition, many of her other writings—including several of the tales that made up the *Illustrations of Political Economy* (1832); her introduction to what we now call sociology, *How to Observe* (1838); her novel for adults, *Deerbrook* (1839); her novel for children,

The Crofton Boys (1841); and the essays she wrote for *Once a Week* in the late 1850s and 1860s—focus on issues of health and wellness. None of these texts was as popular as the *Illustrations*, but *Life in the Sick-Room* was particularly well received, with at least some reviewers going so far as to identify the slender volume as second in importance only to the *Illustrations*.[11]

Although critics have occasionally considered Martineau's political and illness writings together, such accounts tend to focus most consistently on how the writer used her illness as a source of power.[12] For example, Trev Lynn Broughton argues that Martineau constitutes a prominent example of how "politically deft women" in the Victorian period often "appeal[ed] to an ethos of self-denial and self-sacrifice in order to justify extraordinary acts of self-promotion, interference and defiance."[13] Anka Ryall suggests that Martineau "repeatedly used her bodily experiences to contest medical authority."[14] And Laura Stef-Praun points out how Martineau claims that "since the sickroom is a space that disables existing social hierarchies, it can also efface gender inequalities."[15] Such work has been extremely helpful in beginning to answer Roy Porter's call for a "medical history from below," in challenging Michel Foucault's claims regarding the disappearance of the patient's perspective from medicine in the nineteenth century, and in calling into question assumptions of Victorian women's passivity and disempowerment in the face of pathologization.[16] At the same time, however, its focus on how Martineau defines the identity of the invalid means that it tends to overlook the terms she uses to describe the experience of the sufferer. As a result, there has also been a tendency to obscure or minimize the extent to which Martineau's illness writings are bound up with philosophical questions about the nature of sensation, the specificity of pain, and perhaps most importantly, the relation between the individual subject and the social, all of which she engages throughout her work. In this chapter, I argue that part of what makes Martineau's writing so strange, in fact, is the extent to which, rather than regarding one's own pain as the thing one cannot help but recognize, and pain experienced by the other as the thing we can only aspire to understand—the usual problem skepticism confronts—she takes the suffering of the other as relatively self-evident, and one's own pain as relatively opaque. One result of this reversal is a peculiar version of liberalism in which the principal barrier to social justice is less a primary attachment to self (as in Mill) than a nearly ineradicable attachment to those to whom one is closest. What needs to be overcome is less selfishness, therefore, than something like parochialism: an irrational tendency to privilege the near over the distant.

This chapter continues the work of chapter 1 by thinking through the relation between liberal subjectivity and pain. As in the previous chapter, my concern here is with how Martineau seeks to redefine pain as a way to reimagine the relation between the individual and the collective. In the context of Martineau, however, the materiality of the body comes much more clearly to the fore. In *Living Liberalism: Practical Citizenship in Mid-Victorian Britain*, Elaine Hadley argues that in the mid-nineteenth century, an (implicitly healthy) "manly body" was imagined to be a necessary condition in order to achieve the "disinterestedness, objectivity, reticence, conviction, impersonality, and sincerity" identified with liberal subjectivity.[17] Mill's implied body clearly fits this description, at least insofar as it remains unmarked by gender, class, illness, or disability. For Martineau, by contrast, the invalid's very exclusion from active participation in civic life enables her to inhabit the subject position that she identifies with the ideal legislator, or even the deliberative citizen: one freed from the pressures of local attachments. Meanwhile, the healthy and vigorous body is cast as inherently less capable of impersonality. It is disadvantaged by its very ability to act in the world, to engage actively with others, and to fulfill responsibilities that distinguish between those who are closest and those who are furthest away. This chapter thus invites us to consider the many implications of the fact Martineau took as her starting point the disabled, implicitly feminized body of the invalid, and specifically, the new possibilities it raises for thinking about the conditions, nature, and consequences of the impersonality of liberalism.

Feeling Pain

As we have already begun to see, Martineau makes clear throughout her illness writings that being sick involves a host of distortions and inaccuracies. Illness and pain are, first of all, the products of error: indications that we do not yet fully understand the workings of the body and its interactions with the environment. As she explains in her *Autobiography*, "Pain and untimely death are, no doubt, tokens of our ignorance, and of our sins against the laws of nature. I conceive our business to be to accept these consequences of our ignorance and weakness, with as little personal shame on the one hand as vanity or pride on the other" (*A* 433). Thus, suffering is the product of ignorance and therefore error. It is also, however, the cause of it, leading to all kinds of misunderstandings of one's own experience: the menacing light, the vanishing hand, and so forth. The sufferer may be especially liable to make mistakes because of a general ignorance about the body, yet Martineau suggests that the general problem her invalid self represents in these passages is by no means specific to her illness. *All* sensations are liable to produce perceptions that distort their causes; the goal of education is to minimize those distortions as much as possible. As Martineau explains in *Household Education* (1848), even our most basic perceptions stand in need of training: to the "new-born infant ... objects before the eyes can hardly be said to exist. The blue sky and a green tree beside a white house are not seen but as a blotch of colours which touches the eye."[18] However, the power to "receive the images, and perceive" the objects is inherent in the infant and so develops "by degrees"

(*H* 17). Nevertheless, "it depends much on training whether objects and thoughts remain for life indistinct and confused before the perceptive power, as before infant vision, or whether all is clear and vivid as before a keen and practised eye" (*H* 18). Training possesses the awesome responsibility of shaping the most basic aspects of a child's understanding—and an adult's, as well. The sufferer is thus not atypical: all sensations are susceptible to misunderstanding. Illness and pain simply tend to be less common occasions for education or training.

Martineau's vision of the educability of perception was influenced most directly by David Hartley's revision of John Locke's sensationalism—a revision of great importance to Jeremy Bentham, James Mill, and John Stuart Mill, as well. Martineau first became acquainted with Hartley's *Observations on Man, His Frame, His Duty, and His Expectations* (1749) in Joseph Priestley's 1775 edition of the text. According to Priestley, Hartley had "thrown more useful light upon the theory of the mind than Newton did upon the theory of the natural world."[19] And as R. K. Webb and others describe, for many of Priestley's Unitarian followers, the *Observations* was second in importance only to the Bible.[20] Martineau's faith in Unitarian doctrine was beginning to waver by the time of her illness of the early 1840s, yet in *Life in the Sick-Room* she still refers to the "holy Hartley" (*L* 56). Even after she moved away from his teachings in the later 1840s, her work continues to bear clear traces of his influence.[21]

For Locke, sensations naturally give rise to ideas, and ideas lend themselves to associations. As Jad Smith points out, Locke by no means discounts the effects of "custom and education."[22] Nevertheless, "sensation provides the raw materials and basis of all knowledge," while "its associative by-products, formed largely by chance, threaten to diminish the competencies of the understanding."[23] Ideally, it might be possible to imagine each of us able to invent our own language as we go along, abstracting from the unmediated experience we have of a concrete universe:

> The Senses at first let in particular *Ideas*, and furnish the yet empty Cabinet: And the Mind by degrees growing familiar with some of them, they are lodged in the Memory, and Names got to them. Afterwards, the Mind proceeding further, abstracts them, and by Degrees learns the use of general Names. In this manner the Mind comes to be furnish'd with *Ideas* and Language, the Materials about which to exercise its discursive faculty.[24]

Locke admits that this is a fantasy of how language might or should work rather than a description of how it does, yet the notion that in a perfect world language would arise naturally from ideas nevertheless remains intact.

In contrast with this model of a highly personal, private, and individual encounter with a world that gives rise to sensations, which then give rise to ideas, which then are articulated in language, Hartley underscores the social nature of both language and perception. As Richard Allen explains, according to Hartley, "we have ideas because we use language, in concrete social interactions; we do not create language to express the ideas we, as lone individuals, already have."[25] He thus "describes a process whereby, as children, we burble and cry and listen—and gradually gain motor control of our burbling and crying, associate it with what we hear and handle and do, and eventually learn the meaning of what we say."[26] Rather than imagining that we have ideas first and then names for them, therefore, Hartley claims that children use language even before they fully understand what they are saying: "Children first get an imperfect knowledge of the meaning of the words of others; then learn to speak themselves; then to read; and, lastly to write."[27] Such an understanding of language's role in the process of association is bound up with a significant shift in how we think about sensation and perception, as well. Sensation, per se, remains personal and private for Hartley, but it is also transitory and largely inchoate. As a result, our "ideas" come to seem as much the product of association as they are of direct experience. "How would sensations generate ideas," Hartley asks,

> or vibrations generate miniature vibrations, unless parts of the sensations or vibrations, which are infinitely divisible in respect of place and time, did cohere together through joint impression, i.e. association? Further, there is need of an association, that is to say a cause, which will make the brain lean successively in this or that direction, i.e., that will make one part or another of the very complicated miniature vibrations ... especially prevail over the rest.[28]

Associations here precede not just ideas but sensations. As a result, what we feel is made to seem less like the product of a direct encounter with the world than the consequence of preconceptions and learned categories that are brought to bear on the amorphous material of sensory experience.

This understanding of the differences between sensation and perception, and the vastly greater significance of the latter, is clearly reflected in the passages from the *Autobiography* in which Martineau describes her childhood experience of illness. The suffering Martineau describes clearly occurred, was felt, and was felt to be painful. At the same time, the way she perceives it and the emotional responses she has to it are also apparently inaccurate. To return to the passages with which this chapter begins: although she may have felt the dim light from the windows pressing on her eyeballs, it is not quite right to claim that it actually was. Similarly, her hand did not vanish and her head did not grow just because this is what she felt. The sensations themselves may be indubitable, but the way they are perceived is highly liable to education, albeit an education her parents failed to provide.

In *Life in the Sick-Room*, Martineau provides a more expansive account of the theory behind her description of the evanescence of sensory experience.

Even as she claims that "during the year looked back upon, all the days, and most hours of the day, have had their portion of pain," she also insists that the experience of pain is so amorphous as to be impossible to locate or remember (*L* 44).

> During the year looked back upon, all the days, and most hours of the day, have had their portion of pain.... Where are these pains now?—Not only gone, but annihilated. They are destroyed so utterly, that even memory can lay no hold upon them. The fact of their occurrence is all that even memory can preserve. The sensations themselves cannot be retained, nor recalled, nor revived; they are the most absolutely evanescent, the most essentially and completely destructible of all things. Sensations are unimaginable to those who are most familiar with them. Their concomitants may be remembered, and so vividly conceived of, as to excite emotions at a future time: but the sensations themselves cannot be conceived of when absent. This pain, which I feel now as I write, I have felt innumerable times before; yet, accustomed as I am to entertain and manage it, the sensation itself is new every time; and a few hours hence I shall be as unable to represent it to myself as to the healthiest person in the house. Thus are all the pains of the year annihilated. (*L* 44–45)

Despite the fact that she has felt the "same" pain day after day, once it has passed, she is as unable to "recall" the sensation as one who has not experienced it.[29] All she can remember is the fact that it was felt. She is left only with the things with which the sensation is associated: the "concomitants" that are able to "excite emotions at a future time."

The ephemeral nature of pain does pose some problems for the sufferer, for it makes her liable to doubt the fact of her own experience. Laboring under the double burden of a "sense of present and permanent uselessness, and of overwhelming gratitude for services received from hour to hour," the invalid is haunted by anxiety regarding the legitimacy of her invalidism (*L* 112). "In the context of such self-doubt and dissatisfaction," Martineau writes, positive pain comes as a relief:

> The sufferer's spirits rise in proportion to the pain he experiences. He is never so happy as when he feels his paroxysms coming on,—not only because pain of body acts as relief from the gnawing misery of his mind, but because every tangible proof that he is under chastening and discipline, conveys to him a sense of his dignity—reassures him, as a child of Providence. From this may follow too naturally [the invalid's] learning to regard pain as a qualification for ease—as a purchase-money of future good. (*L* 113)

Martineau regards this way of thinking about pain as a perversion to be avoided, "a superstition as low and depraving as almost any the mind can entertain" (L 113); however, she admits it to be an almost inevitable consequence of the evanescence of sensation, and as such, something to which very few invalids are wholly immune. Nevertheless, the transitory nature of pain is regarded principally as an opportunity—for education.

As I have mentioned, Bentham, James Mill, and John Stuart Mill all took Hartley's thinking very seriously, John Stuart going so far as to describe his father's *Analysis of the Phenomena of the Human Mind* (1869) as having been written for the "purpose of following up Hartley's leading thought, and completing what that thinker had begun."[30] Martineau was therefore in no way unusual in maintaining a strong commitment to the power of education.[31] She was, however, unusual among *inheritors* of the utilitarian tradition for her insistence on the extent to which the happiness of the individual can, in fact, come to be bound up with that of the collective. Thus, while John Stuart claims the impossibility of educating children to identify their own pleasures and pains with those of humanity as a whole, Martineau regards this goal as relatively easily achieved.

Such optimism might seem surprising in one who was not only well versed in Malthus's theory of population, but regarded him as a close personal friend. According to Martineau, however, although his observations were correct, "In my opinion, recent experience shows that it does attack a difficulty at the wrong end. The repeal of the corn-laws, with the consequence [*sic*] improvement in agriculture, and the prodigious increase of emigration have extinguished all present apprehension and talk of 'surplus population,'—that great difficulty of forty or fifty years ago" (A 170). Martineau did not discard all concern regarding population growth. For example, one of the more famous of her *Illustrations of Political Economy*, "Weal and Woe in Garveloch," is explicitly dedicated to encouraging the "preventive check."[32] Yet Martineau's conviction that all interests *can*, in fact, be adjudicated enables her to discard Mill's commitment to the self-evidence of the distinction to be made between pleasures that pertain to oneself and those that are bound up with others.[33] She thus disposes with both skepticism and any distinction between natural and artificial associations. In her account, all associations are effectively the product of some sort of education. As she explains in *Household Education*, "Before man can feel pleasure or pain from outward objects or from thoughts, he must perceive them" (H 17), and perception necessarily requires education. Thus, all one need do to guarantee the child will become ideally benevolent is make sure that she or he receives pleasure from the proper objects. If what one wants is a child who will devote herself or himself to the common good, simply train her or him to identify pleasure with "labour[ing] at great and eternal thoughts, in which lies bound up the happiness of a whole nation and perhaps a whole world," rather than with "putting brandy into his stomach, or in any other way gratifying his nerves of sensation" (*H* 16). Particularly in the wake of Mill's critique of such an identification, Martineau's blithe conviction cannot help but be striking.

It might seem to help matters that Martineau regards our natural faculties as predisposed in the right direction, and that she assumes children are endowed with an innate sense of sympathy. But even that predisposition stands in need of training; sympathy alone is no guarantee of socially productive feelings or actions, and can often work against them. Hence, the little girl's wish to protect her doll may be "a pretty thing to witness," but it reflects "the lowest form of human affection till it is trained into close connection with the higher sentiments" (*H* 89). In its original state, sympathy all too easily results in "the young mother who spoils her child ... the aged mother, who loves her manly son as a bear loves its cub;—only with more selfishness ... [and] the man who gives his mind to the comfort of his horse; and never a look or a word to a hungry neighbor" (*H* 90). Sympathy is so selective in its objects, so local in its attachments, and so idiosyncratic in its preferences, as to be not just limited but actually dangerous in its natural form. It thus needs to be "linked on to other and higher kinds of love, and especially to that which is the highest of all, and worthy to gather into itself all the rest,—benevolence" (*H* 90). Happily, in Martineau's account this is a relatively straightforward project. The whole of *Household Education* is dedicated to explicating the details of the task, but in principle the process is fairly simple. First, the child "must be led to desire the good of the cat, or bird, or doll, to the sacrifice of its own inclinations" (*H* 90). Then, "from home, the affection may next be led a little further abroad" (*H* 91). This sequence continues until finally the child has moved on to "benevolence which has no fondness in it, but desires the diffusion of happiness, and acts independently of personal regards" (*H* 91).

Difficult as ideal benevolence might be to imagine, Martineau's *Autobiography* offers a series of examples of what it might look like. Again and again, she describes feeling herself to be of no greater significance than anyone else, and her own actions to be the product not of her desire for her own happiness but instead of her investment in the happiness of all. Such descriptions might seem to be appeals to martyrdom, and yet in context, they rarely seem simply or solely as self-aggrandizing.[34] So, for example, when she claims that "authorship has never been with me a matter of choice," it is difficult to say whether the assertion is the product of incredible arrogance or self-deprecation (*A* 155). "Things were pressing to be said; and there was more or less evidence that I was the person to say them" (*A* 155). Part of what is so strange about this comment is the way it suggests her ability to stand outside herself and weigh the evidence as if she has absolutely no investment in the outcome. A similar form of impersonality is apparent in her startling claim that "there were times when I was sorry that I was not the victim of the [abolitionist] struggle, [because the] murder of an English traveler would have settled the business of American Slavery (in its federal sense) more speedily than perhaps any other incident" (*A* 367). What matters to Martineau is a cause that has potential consequences for hundreds of thousands, if not millions, of lives. Her own life would be a small price to pay. The sentiment may be familiar, but the tone of casual and blithe self-disregard is not: there is no obvious desire to be a martyr here; her death is simply the sensible thing to wish for under the circumstances. The basic commitment underlying such assertions is made especially explicit in her assertion that "I feel no reluctance whatever to pass into nothingness, leaving my place in the universe to be filled by another. The very conception of *self* and *other* is, in truth, merely human, and when the self ceases to be, the distinction expires" (*A* 473). As in the previous instances, here Martineau attempts to achieve a kind of impersonality that regards the self as if it was equivalent to any self—and hence, as if its pain had no greater relevance than if it was that of someone else entirely.

The Invalid's Privilege

However straightforward a task Martineau may make it seem to embrace impersonality, as she complains repeatedly, it is nearly impossible to maintain, if only because our local attachments consistently drag us from the universal to the hopelessly personal. In the *Autobiography*, these attachments are personified in Martineau's mother, whose demands on her time and attention consistently distract her from the important work at hand.[35] For example, despite her desire to remain in America, "working in the cause [of the abolition of slavery] which I believed then, and which I believe now, to be the greatest pending in the world," Martineau explains that "while my mother lived, my duty was clear—to remain with her if she and the family desired it" (*A* 387). This "duty" does not make her mother happy, Martineau points out. Nevertheless, "she and the others wished things to go on as they were; and I never thought of objecting" (*A* 387). In addition to preventing her from remaining in America, Martineau's mother endangers her daughter's work and health by refusing to allow her to "have a maid, at my own expense, or even to employ a workwoman" (*A* 434), and by "daily getting out into the crowded streets by herself, when she could not see a yard before her" (*A* 435)—a situation so distressing to Martineau that her friends "urged my leaving home as frequently as possible" (*A* 435). Martineau ultimately even blames her illness on her mother: throughout this period, she writes, a "tumour was forming of a kind which usually originates in mental suffering" (*A* 435). To have familial obligations and sympathies—the local attachments that work against impersonality—thus becomes not just as disabling as physical debility: it also, in some sense, causes it.

Even as the local impediments involved in sympathy may cause pain and illness, pain and illness provide a nearly unique escape from sympathy's snares. For what invalidism justifies above all else—what Martineau claims made it a blessing in her own life and a potential boon to those who are similarly oppressed—is a justification for being left alone.[36] As she admits in her descriptions of her first experience of illness, at the time her life was "so charged with troubles"—primarily in the form of familial obligations—"that when I lay down on my couch of pain in my Tynemouth lodging, for a confinement of nearly six years, I felt myself comparatively happy in my release from responsibility, anxiety and suspense. The worst sufferings of my life were over now" (*A* 431). Invalidism may involve enormous pain, suffering, and a guilt-inducing inability to act, but it also enables a particular perspective on the world blissfully devoid of the local ties of sympathy.[37]

Despite her critique of the demands that sympathy placed on her, in her transformation from caregiver to one who is cared for, it might seem reasonable to expect Martineau's opinion of fellow-feeling to change, as well. No longer called upon to act on behalf of others, as an invalid Martineau was newly placed in a position to benefit from the compassion and care of others. Yet despite the incidental lip service she pays to sympathy as "a heavenly solace to the soul" (*L* 49), she ultimately makes sympathy seem as much a problem for the invalid as a solution. Martineau was not alone in her doubts regarding the value of sympathy: nineteenth-century illness writers often emphasized the futility of seeking sympathy, the difficulty of finding persons able to understand or imagine their experiences, and the despair to which failures of sympathy can give rise. As I discuss in the introduction, this is particularly true of religious commentators who tend to underscore the futility of seeking consolation from human sources.[38] So for example, in *Sickness, Its Trials and Blessings* (1859), Priscilla Maurice claims that although all who suffer seek sympathy, mere human beings are limited in their power to understand one another's experience: "One comes near and says words of sympathy for one part of the trial; another for some other part; a third sees no trial in it at all; a fourth thinks it must be much less trying than some other form of suffering, or than his own. No one but the sufferer sees it in all its bearings and forms of inward suffering; no one else feels the acute pain of heart and all its throbbings."[39] There is only one who can truly understand the invalid's pain in this account, and that one is God. James Hinton offers a similarly religious perspective on the problem of pain in *The Mystery of Pain: A Book for the Sorrowful* (1866). Acknowledging that pain cannot simply be regarded as punishment for sin, he encourages the sufferer to take a wider view of the problem:

> While we look only at that which directly concerns the individual who suffers, no real explanation of suffering, no satisfaction that truly satisfies can be found. But if we may look beyond, and see in our own suf-

ferings, and in the sufferings of all, something in which mankind also has a stake, then they are brought into a region in which the heart can deal with them and find them good. And if the heart, the reason also. For here it is the soul that is the judge; and if the heart is satisfied, the reason also is content.⁴⁰

Like Maurice, Hinton discounts human sympathy as a solution to the problem of pain. However, while Maurice focuses on the importance of the individual sufferer's resignation and trust in God's sympathy, Hinton underscores the meaningfulness of pain in a larger religious context. Pain may be alleviated in this account less as a result of our faith in God's compassion than our trust in pain's ultimate significance, or even utility. As Hinton explains, "When we look into this subject farther, we see that it is a law of our experience that our own mental condition controls and even alters our feelings. Though we speak of pleasure and pain as fixed and definite things, yet they are truly by no means fixed."⁴¹ Hence, recontextualizing pain as part of God's plan may ultimately alter not just how we understand it, but how we experience it, as well.

While these and other writers tend to emphasize the problems that arise as a result of the *failure* of understanding, Martineau underscores the difficulties that arise from its success. These difficulties are of two kinds: first, sympathy diffuses suffering and so should be employed only when it can be productive; second, any form of social engagement traps the sufferer in a social identity that is itself an effective source of pain. The first of these problems is the simpler to explain, but no less intractable on that account. Eighteenth- and nineteenth-century philosophers were fascinated by the apparent perversity at the core of sympathy with pain—the way it effectively disseminates the suffering we ordinarily seek to avoid. Even Adam Smith insists, "It is agreeable to sympathize with joy; and wherever envy does not oppose it, our heart abandons itself with satisfaction to the highest transports of that delightful sentiment. But it is painful to go along with grief, and we always enter into it with reluctance."⁴² According to Smith, this reluctance can be overcome under certain conditions, but the basic problem remains, for if persons are designed to pursue happiness, there is no obvious reason why they should increase their unhappiness by sympathizing with suffering. For the sentimental philosophers who followed Smith, this tendency to sympathize largely constitutes a given they sought to explain rather than a possibility they felt the need to encourage or discourage. As we have already begun to see, for Martineau, by contrast, very few feelings are so self-evident as to be exempt from training. For her, all feelings are desirable only insofar as they can be attached to concrete and productive action. Even our experience of a sunrise should be turned to account: "The glories of a sunrise, the sublimity of the stormy ocean, the radiant beauties of the night, awaken spontaneous emotions: but it is our duty to perpetuate their influence by looking 'through Nature up to Nature's

God.'"[43] Sympathy is no exception to this rule. Hence, as she explains in her essay, "On the Agency of Feelings in the Formation of Habits" (1836):

> These feelings [of sensibility to others' pleasure and pain] are, in themselves, evanescent, and if not connected with action, are worse than useless; as excitement causes a waste of energy which can only be repaired by increased vigor of action. But if they be made the immediate impulse to some effort of benevolence, they have answered the purpose for which they were bestowed, and in departing, have left behind something more than equivalent to themselves in their utmost intensity and depth.[44]

Sympathy is desirable only when it is connected to some "effort of benevolence." In the absence of such "effort," it is worse than useless, for the "excitement" causes a "waste of energy" which serves solely as a drain on the sympathizer's system.[45]

The problem sympathy poses for the invalid, then, is that she cannot be helped by it in any meaningful way. The consequence, Martineau claims, is all too often unproductive action on the part of those who wish to help. "Many [sympathizers] give their best thoughts to provide alleviations," she explains, while others feel impelled "to cast about for relief, [and] to speak of hope to the sufferer who has no hope, or none compatible with the kind of consolation they attempt" (*L* 50). Such "offers of consolation must be purely irritating to one who was not feeling better," the passage continues, "nor in a state to be cheered by any speculation as to whether his pain would, or would not become more endurable with time!" (*L* 51). Describing her own efforts to cheer friends laid low by illness before her own experiences with invalidism, she admits,

> Exactly in proportion to the zeal with which such considerations were pressed, must have been the sufferer's clearness of perception of the disguised selfishness which dictated the topics and the words. I was ... trying to console myself, and not my friend; indulging my own cowardice, my own shrinking from a painful truth, at the expense of the feelings of the sufferer for whom my heart was aching. (*L* 51)

When trained on one whose condition is not likely to improve, sympathy as the desire to relieve pain can lead to a species of selfishness: a desire to relieve the second-order pain incurred by feeling with and for one who suffers. This is a state of affairs that is only compounded as a result of sympathy's recursiveness: the fact that the sufferer who is confronted with a sympathetic friend stands to have her suffering intensified by the knowledge that she is the cause of her friend's suffering, too. "When welfare of body is out of the question," Martineau explains in defense of her recommendation that the invalid sequester herself when in pain, "peace of mind becomes an object of supreme importance; and this is unattainable when we see any whom we love suffering, in our sufferings, even more than we do: or when we know that we have been the means of turning any one's day of ease and pleasure into sorrow" (*L* 60). Here, the sympathy an invalid feels toward her friend's sympathy with her own suffering constitutes a source of suffering in and of itself. Touched on in *Life in the Sick-Room*, this is a problem that Martineau returns to almost obsessively in her letters. Again and again, she insists on the needless suffering caused by her knowledge of her friends' useless sympathy with her plight. At best, therefore, the sympathy the invalid generates serves only to disseminate suffering to the sympathizer who wishes to help and cannot; at worst, the invalid's suffering actually increases as a result of the sympathizer's misguided attempts to console her and the knowledge she is the source of suffering her friend would otherwise be without.

To the potential sympathizer, therefore, Martineau counsels something like humility: an acceptance of the limitations of knowledge and hence, too, the impossibility of fellow-feeling. Instead of seeking a greater comprehension of the invalid, Martineau advocates that the invalid's friend or caregiver recognize the futility of such an attempt. As the suffering attendant on extreme pain is "peculiar and transient," she explains,

> there could be no use in mentioning it, except ... that attendants, on witnessing a sudden abasement of high courage, on seeing horror of countenance succeed a calm determination, may remember, at the right moment, that there is that passing within of which they can have no conception, and certainly no right to judge. (*L* 116)

Rather than sympathy, compassion, or even care, Martineau emphasizes an acceptance of one's inability to understand and a respect for that which lies outside of one's experience. What no sufferer can fully recognize, except in the very "moment of anguish" itself, certainly no bystander can conceive: the most she or he can hope to offer is a passive act of witnessing and affirmation.

While the negative critique of sympathy has to do with the way the circulation of painful feelings between persons increases suffering without any benefit, Martineau's concern regarding the problems posed by the limiting effects of any social engagement opens up a vision of a positive alternative characterized by an imaginative freedom unavailable in the presence of others. In her account, the problem with society for the invalid is not just that other people's sympathy is a source of pain but also that social existence itself serves as a barrier to the power of ideas, in general, and to the power of the imagination, in particular. Simply by virtue of interacting with other people, the invalid is forced to be aware of herself as an invalid, and hence, of the suffering that constitutes this identity. When alone, by contrast, she has a unique freedom to forget herself, to roam imaginatively, and to profit from her perceptions and experiences. Martineau opens her defense of solitude for the suffering with an insistence on the recursive structure of sympathy: "The experience of years qualifies me to ... declare that I know of no comfort, at the end of a day of suffering, comparable to that of feeling that, however it may have been with one's self, no one else has suffered" (*L* 60). As the passage goes on, however, it becomes clear that something rather different is also at issue: the freedom from self-consciousness that solitude affords and the peculiar subjective relation to others attendant on that freedom. Thus, in explaining her preference to spend anniversaries and holidays alone, Martineau insists,

> When one is alone ... there is nothing ... to prevent my being in the world again for the day; no human presence to chain me to my prison. When ... I am alone with my ... memories of old years, I can flit at will among the family groups that I see gathered round many fire-sides.... By means of that inimitable telescope we carry about in us, (which acts as well in the pitch-dark as at noon, and defies distance and house-walls,) I see in turn a Christmas tree, with its tapers glittering in a room full of young eyes, or the games and the dance, or the cozy little party of elderly folk round the fire or the tea-table; and I hear, not the actual jokes, but the laughter, and "the sough of words without the sense," and can catch at least the soul of the merriment. If I am at ease, I am verily among them: if not, I am thankful not to be there; and at all events have, from life-long association, caught so much of the contagious spirit of sociability, that, when midnight comes, I lie down with an impression of its having been an extraordinary day,—a social one, though ... the face of my maid is, in reality, the only one that has met my eyes. (*L* 62–63)

While the presence of other people simply reminds her of her deprivation—"chains her to her prison"—and so intensifies her pain, the invalid is happiest, and in a sense most social, when left alone. Because the invalid is not always in pain, she can sometimes forget that such pain effectively defines her existence. Further, even when she is in pain, she may mentally wander, and her actual solitude will at least protect her from the interpellating gazes of others. Finally, because she may ultimately recall pain's "concomitants" more vividly than the pain itself, this wandering may enable her to turn even her sufferings to some kind of account: those concomitants may be recalled instead of, or at least in addition to, her actual sufferings. In solitude, she is able to travel, socialize, and surround herself with the people she loves best while still maintaining the relative unselfconsciousness that comes from being alone.

The term Martineau offers for this mental escape is "natural magic," which she defines as "the power of ideas [which] furnish[] an implement ... which may possibly operate at the most hopeless times" (*L* 142).[46] Such a description might sound highly abstract, but in the examples she offers, this "magic" consistently attaches itself to scenarios like the one just cited, in which solitude enables an encounter with others, whether real or imagined, that yields an affective profit. As such, it comes at many moments to look like a version of reading, another practice that can involve watching others who cannot watch us in turn, "socializing" in ways that are, at best, ambiguously social. The passage above bears a marked resemblance to the famous passage from *Dombey and Son* (1846–48) in which the narrator calls for "a good spirit who would take the house-tops off, with a more potent and benignant hand than the lame demon in the tale, and show a Christian people what dark shapes issue from amidst their homes, to swell the retinue of the Destroying Angel as he moves forth among them!"[47] It bears a similarly strong resemblance to Scrooge's experience in "A Christmas Carol" (1843) of peeping in at the Christmas revels of his friends, past and present. In both examples, the ability to watch those who are unable to watch us in turn is more or less explicitly identified with the power of the novel. At the same time, however, Martineau's experience also differs from these other examples because it dispenses so wholly with personalities.[48] This is her fantasy, so one might think she could specify it as highly as she likes. Yet rather than individualized encounters, what Martineau seems to value is a kind of abstraction of particularities. The "family groups" that Martineau gestures toward remain strangely featureless, the "young eyes" do not necessarily seem to belong to anyone in particular, the games and dances are generic, and most importantly, the laughter she hears involves "the sough of words without the sense." She enjoys qualities, characteristics, dynamics, or kinds of actions, but not their specific content.

One way of understanding this de-individuating perspective is in terms of the ideal of impersonal "benevolence" that I described in the first section of this chapter. For the subject who sees herself as interchangeable with others— who "feel[s] no reluctance whatever to pass into nothingness"—it seems especially appropriate to regard others as something other than highly particularized, psychologized subjects. The sense that others possess a nonfungible value that one does not possess oneself would turn benevolence into mere masochism. The truly benevolent gaze, by contrast, might involve something like the impersonal and depersonalizing perception of qualities, characteristics, gestures, and situations suggested in this passage. Thinking about such a perspective in terms of "benevolence" might seem strange if only because it is by no means even clearly social, let alone socially productive. The "encounter," insofar as it can even be called that, depends on the material absence of other people; it takes place wholly in the imagination, and perhaps most importantly, it has no concrete effect in the real world. The perspective it involves thus holds the threat of quietism, a simple retreat from the world of people into the relatively unproblematic and undemanding realms of fantasy or reverie. The ethical questions that might arise from such a stance are of course nullified in the case of the invalid, part of whose suffering inheres in the fact of her inability to provide assistance to others. They do, however, pose obstacles to imagining Martineau offering it as any kind of a model to those who are not in pain.

In other passages that describe related phenomena, a more complicated picture emerges, which might seem more readily compatible with, if not "benevolence," per se, then with the impersonality and freedom from skepticism that Martineau identifies as benevolence's precondition. Consider, for example, an excerpt from one of the most commonly quoted passages from *Life in the Sick-Room*, in which Martineau describes "one particular night of severe pain, which made all rest impossible":

> I ... wandered, from mere misery, from my bed and my dim room, which seemed full of pain, to the next apartment, where some glimmer through the thick window-curtain showed that there was light abroad. Light indeed! as I found on looking forth. The sun, resting on the edge of the sea, was hidden from me by the walls of the old priory: but a flood of rays poured through the windows of the ruin, and gushed over the waters, strewing them with diamonds, and then across the green down before my windows, gilding its furrows, and then lighting up the yellow sands on the opposite shore of the harbor, while the market-garden below was glittering with dew and busy with early bees and butterflies. Besides these bees and butterflies, nothing seemed stirring, except the earliest riser of the neighborhood, to whom the garden belongs. At the moment, she was passing down to feed her pigs, and let out her cows; and her easy pace, arms a-kimbo, and complacent survey of her early greens, presented me with a picture of ease so opposite to my own state, as to impress me ineffaceably. I was suffering too much to enjoy this picture at the moment: but how was it at the end of the year? The pains of all those hours were annihilated—as completely vanished as if they had never been; while the momentary peep behind the window-curtain made me possessor of this radiant picture for evermore.... An inexperienced observer might, at the moment, have thought the conditions of my gain heavy enough; but the conditions being not only discharged, but annihilated long ago, and the treasure remaining forever, would not my best friend congratulate me on that sunrise? Suppose it shining on, now and forever, in the souls of a hundred other invalids or mourners, who may have marked it in the same manner, and who shall estimate its glory and its good! (*L* 45–46)

Several important details differentiate this passage from the previous one. Perhaps most importantly, while the persons described in the first passage were supposedly remembered, here the woman is seen. Yet the value of the latter scene does not inhere in the moment of perception—"I was suffering too much to enjoy this picture at the moment," Martineau explains—but instead in the vision as remembered or imagined. As a result, it comes to seem nearly as much the product of the imagination or memory as the Christmas tree, games, and tea-table. What matters is less what is seen, than what is later recalled. Further, as in the other example, those memories are populated less by personalities or individuals than by characteristics or qualities. Martineau lived in Tynemouth for nearly six years; *Life in the Sick-Room* was written toward the end of that time. She can thus be fairly certain to have known the name, circumstances, and personality of the neighbor she sees through her window. Yet rather than attending to these specifics, Martineau focuses on the traits that can be abstracted from her, traits that are legible on this woman's body: her pace, the position of her arms, and the posture of her body as she surveys her garden tell Martineau everything she needs to know about her "ease" and "complacen[cy]." Jealousy of this healthy body is unmistakable here, but so is the writer's attempt to convey what she possesses as a result of her invalidism: a vision of a sunrise that strews "diamonds" on the waters, that "gilds" the furrows of the green down, and that lights up the yellow sands of the harbor. Further, she possesses the power to share this treasure with others: "Suppose it shining on, now and forever, in the souls of a hundred other invalids or mourners, who may have marked it in the same manner, and who shall estimate its glory and its good!"

In comparison with the concrete achievements of Martineau's health, such a boon may seem meager, but Martineau herself does not seem to have considered it this way. On the contrary, in her letters, she makes particularly clear that she experienced *Life in the Sick-Room* as a way to turn her illness to account. As she wrote to Richard Monckton Milnes in 1843, "It is years since I clearly felt & declared my deafness ... was the happiest thing that ever befel me, as turning out to be the most peculiar & evident means of being of service [in the form of her "Letter to the Deaf"]. Never once did it occur to me till within the last fortnight that here was the same privilege over again. Suddenly —as if between night & morning, my lot is wholly converted & lifted up,— from being ministered to to ministering."[49] Writing about her illness allows her to turn her impersonality into concrete action on behalf of others—a gift she can give to the world. In her letters, she additionally alludes to the benefit she received from an analogous kind of gift. In the letter she wrote Ralph Waldo Emerson to thank him for the volume of essays he had sent her, she describes the benefit she received from it in terms that resonate powerfully with her descriptions of "natural magic" in *Life in the Sick-Room*:

> It has come to me more like a visitation of health than any thing that has happened to me these two years....
>
> ... It is, as far as I know, about the first book in our language which unconsciously conveys (instead of boasting of) the serenity (as well as freedom) which comes of forsaking all description, & yielding solitarily

> to the influences of the Great Spirit.... Your book carries one up to be a sort of Isis, or a message from the gods, poised among the aerial currents, so secure that every faculty is at liberty for looking out. Think what this must be to one who has no prospect whatever of crossing the threshold in the body, & of changing moods by the natural method of changing scene & objects, & you will be glad that you sent me this book.[50]

While illness is identified with the self-consciousness that comes from being trapped in a body and personality one is hard-pressed to forget, "yielding solitarily to the influences of the Great Spirit" transforms self-consciousness into the impersonality that Martineau consistently values so highly. Emerson's essays do not simply enable her to imagine she is someone she is not, to lose herself in the experience of another, or even simply to forget about herself for a moment, but instead to make contact with something that exists beyond the personal—what Emerson in his essay, "The Over-Soul" (1841), calls the "common nature" to which "tacit reference is made" in "all conversation between two persons."[51] "That third party or common nature is not social," Emerson continues, "it is impersonal; is God."[52] In her critique of Emerson, Sharon Cameron claims that each of us cannot help but feel ourself to be "a discrete separate entity whose personal identity matters."[53] But this impersonal God is precisely what seems to attract Martineau to Emerson's work. Freed from local attachments by her illness, and resolutely indifferent to her own possible priority to others, Martineau's invalid is free to "fall[ ] in love with the world," "eyes happily shut [to] the [threat] of skepticism."[54] This is a subjective position that Stanley Cavell, like Cameron, regards as unachievable. It is one that Martineau herself steadfastly, joyfully embraces. The consequence might seem to pull directly against liberalism, with its emphasis on the unique value of every individual, but it represents Martineau's attempt to reconcile liberalism with a commitment to social justice—a dual commitment that she regards as wholly within human reach.

Writing Impersonality

> As I write this, I cannot but wonder when and how you will read it, and whether it will cause a single throb at the idea that it may be meant for you. You have been in my mind during the passage of almost all the thoughts that will be found in this book. But for your sympathy—confidently reckoned on, though never asked—I do not know that I should have had courage to mark their procession, and record their order. (*L* 39)

Everything about this passage from the dedication of *Life in the Sick-Room* seems to contradict the argument I have been making thus far regarding Martineau's rejection of sympathy as a practical aid to the invalid, coupled with her insistence on the value of solitude and imaginative transport as the most effective means to alleviate the invalid's suffering. Here, sympathy is confidently relied upon (although unasked for) and grounded in the understanding available to "fellow-sufferer[s]" alone. The passage thus seems to ignore the epistemological problems Martineau identifies elsewhere regarding experiences that can never be fully remembered. As the passage goes on, however, something strange happens:

> It matters little ... that we have never met—that each of us does not know, except by the eye of the mind, with what outward face the other has encountered the unusual lot appointed to both. While I was as busy as any one on the sunny plain of life, I heard of you laid aside in the shadowy recess where our sunshine of hope and joy could never penetrate to you; and it was with reverence, and not pity, that I inquired of those who could tell whether you had separate lights of heaven, such as there are for retreats like yours. (*L* 39–40)

The fact that Martineau never met the object of her dedication may not be especially striking: as a prolific letter writer, she corresponded with many people she had never encountered in person. The passage raises a question, however, as to whether she *ever* communicated with this person prior to this anonymous address. Martineau says only that she "inquired" about her addressee of mutual friends, not that she ever contacted her herself. Even the book is addressed to this friend in only the most indirect of ways: "I shall not direct [this book] to your hands," Martineau explains, "but trust to the most infallible force in the universe,—human sympathy,—to bring these words under your eye" (*L* 42).

However "infallible" Martineau may have taken this force to be when she wrote this passage, the fact is that "human sympathy" was not completely reliable in the matter of the dedication. Martineau describes her mortification upon hearing that Elizabeth Barrett Browning imagined herself to be its object, for example, insisting that it should be clear she was addressing a much older woman. The other main candidate for the honor, Florence Nightingale, poses the same problems as Barrett Browning, since she was younger than Martineau by several years. The very fact that the identity of Martineau's addressee remains unknown, combined with the questions that remain about whether the two ever communicated at all, suggests the possible irrelevance of questions of identity to the mission of the dedication. It seems significant, after all, that rather than a personal letter written from one named, known person to another, these passages are to an anonymous addressee from an anonymous dedication (*Life in the Sick-Room* was initially published with no author's attribution) in a book meant to be read by thousands of persons other than that addressee. This double anonymity, combined with the breadth of the actual intended audience, suggests that we consider less the local relationship the passages describe, than the larger ethical, social, and literary work they perform. When considered in these terms, the dedication offers something akin to a fictional narrative of friendship, one that might temporarily take us out of ourselves, inspirit us, and enable us to return to our ordinary existences refreshed and revived. Such distraction does an enormous amount of work in Martineau's account. As she writes of travel writing, for example,

> We are insatiable in regard to this kind of book. To us it is scenery, exercise, fresh air. The new knowledge is quite a secondary consideration.... On we go till stopped by the fluttering and distress,—the familiar pain, or the leaden down-sinking of the spirits, and wonder that our trying time has come so soon.... It has not come soon;—it is only that some hours of our penance have been beguiled,—that we have been let out of our prison for a holiday, and are now brought back to our schooling. But the good does not end here. We see everything with different eyes,—the chest of drawers,—the walls,—the bookshelves, and the patterns of the rug. (*L* 74–75)

I suggest that Martineau's dedication seeks to serve a similar function to the travel writing she so admires, offering the invalid a glimpse of a relationship that is distracting and inspiriting, but that is not necessarily a model for experience, except of a virtual kind. Such relations are not necessarily socially productive, except insofar as one person's relief from pain contributes to the general sum of happiness. They are not even clearly relations, despite Martineau's claims to the contrary, since engaging with persons who have only a virtual existence is not exactly a social encounter. They do, however, relieve the terrible pressure of self-consciousness that plagues the invalid, even if only momentarily. Writing of this kind can thus be understood as a species of labor, just as reading of this kind can be conceived of as contributing to a form of impersonality.

Ultimately, of course, Martineau came to embrace a very different form of impersonal relationality: that suggested by mesmerism's commitment to corporeality not as the basis of our individuation, but instead as the condition of our connectedness. Bodies communicate with one another in mesmerism in ways that only secondarily have anything to do with understanding or interiority; they transmit energies or intensities that oftentimes bypass cognition entirely.[55] Even as mesmerism pulls in the direction of impersonality insofar as it dispenses with the personality of the operator, it might seem also to pull away from it, as a result of its dependency on physical proximity. Mesmerism thus seems as if it might bring us right back to Bentham's indictment of sympathy as involving an irrational privileging of the near over the distant. However, in her *Letters on the Laws of Man's Nature and Development* (1851), coauthored with her mesmerist friend, Henry George Atkinson, Martineau insists on the way that proximity in mesmerism merely constitutes a convenient means to the greater end of dispensing not just with the illusion of distance, but with the illusion of forms altogether: "Nothing in the experience of my life can at all compare with that of seeing the melting away of the forms, aspects and arrangements under which we ordinarily view nature, and its fusion into the system of forces which is presented to the intellect in the magnetic state."[56] Mesmerism may go so far toward the dissolution of forms as to do away with social relations from a different direction entirely. It nevertheless clearly brings us closer to the recognition that lies at the core of Martineau's social vision: the illusory nature of the distinction between selves. Hence, again, the strangeness of the claim: "I feel no reluctance whatever to pass into nothingness, leaving my place in the universe to be filled by another. The very conception of *self* and *other* is, in truth, merely human, and when the self ceases to be, the distinction expires" (*A* 473). This is precisely the insight that mesmerism, in Martineau's account, ultimately yields.

In *A Theory of Justice*, John Rawls claims that utilitarianism offers no way of thinking about justice other than those associated with sympathetic identification. Such a perspective, Rawls argues, leaves us unable to "take seriously the distinction between persons" since it generalizes on the basis of the observer's perspective.[57] As an alternative, he famously offers the "original position" as a way of imagining that one's situation within the social order has yet to be decided. The form of impersonality that Martineau seeks to identify with the person in pain—and then with the mesmeric subject—cannot, I think, exactly be assimilated to the "original position." Instead, what Rawls's critique helps us identify is just how far Martineau's privileged perspective is from the hedonistic individualism so often associated with utilitarianism, with its unit-driven calculations of pleasure and pain. Martineau values pleasure, happiness, and freedom from pain. At the same time, she embraces a particular form of impersonality that seems to help her think beyond, and even experience beyond, the unit of the individual.

CHAPTER THREE

Pain and Privacy in *Villette*

READING *VILLETTE* (1853) often feels like prying. The narrator, Lucy Snowe, consistently baffles our curiosity, misleading us, mocking us, and teasing us with partial glimpses or vague outlines of states of affairs that she also identifies as critically important.[1] Many texts hold secrets, and as readers of the Victorian novel, we are well used to ferreting out what is not spoken. What makes *Villette* especially strange, however, is that its secrets are never revealed, and yet the novel never suggests that they *cannot* be spoken. Instead, the narrator very deliberately informs us that she simply chooses not to describe them. Rather than suspenseful or neurotic, therefore, Brontë's novel can feel simply passive-aggressive, implying as it does that the reader is not worthy of the story it has to tell. As the narrator explains of her reluctance to reveal her identity to Dr. John, "Where we can never be rightly known, we take pleasure, I think, in being consummately ignored. What honest man on being casually taken for a housebreaker, does not feel rather tickled than vexed at the mistake?"[2] Like Dr. John, it appears that we have been deemed unable to "rightly know" Lucy Snowe: our sensibilities are too gross, our imaginations too limited. As a result, *Villette* can seem like a test that readers have already failed.[3]

Villette may be unusual among Victorian novels for refusing to tell us what happened to its heroine. Yet it is not, of course, the case that it tells us nothing at all about the events toward which it gestures: on the contrary, the allegories of physical pain that are so often offered in place of the information that is withheld serve to convey at least some sense of what those events might have entailed. Again and again in *Villette*, rather than being told what horrible fate befell Lucy, what disappointment or loss she endured, we are instead given extraordinarily vivid images of physical pain, oftentimes attached to allegorical figures or personifications. It is not simply that we are told that the unspecified event *felt like* physical pain, although that is implied. Instead, when Lucy suffers, that suffering seems to proliferate into multiple registers and modes of representation through which that suffering is conveyed to the reader. In other words, we are made to feel something, and that feeling has some relation to whatever happened to Lucy. By 1853, when the novel was published, the novel form offered a well-established and highly developed set of strategies for describing emotional suffering. My question in this chapter is why Brontë chose not to use them: what claim about emotional and physical anguish she sought to make that required her to go to such lengths. Ultimately, I argue, the allegories of physical pain that are used to convey experiences of mental suffering serve two principal functions in *Villette*: first, they indicate the novel's resistance to and critique of the normalizing tendency of sympathy; and, second, they serve as the basis of an alternative form of interpersonal connection, grounded less in understanding than in the ability to feel pain. The fact that characters are not people and yet elicit emotional responses may be such a given by now as to no longer generate much interest. And yet, Brontë gives this problem new ethical life by insisting on the way fictions make us feel, not for other people, but within ourselves. When seen through the lens of its allegories of pain, *Villette* comes to seem almost wholly antisocial. It rejects the notions of community and collectivity within which Mill and Martineau positioned their models of pain, and conceives of interpersonal relation in only the most minimal possible terms. In *Villette*, pain is "social" only in the sense that it testifies to the existence of other people, not in the sense that it holds out hope for any substantive relation to them.

Several recent critics have indicated the extent to which Brontë writes squarely within a liberal tradition. Amanda Anderson, in particular, has argued that the novel's commitment to women's practices of "moral discernment, impersonal judgment, and even self-crafting" leads to an interest in the "promises and dangers of cultivated distance," which she argues are central to conceptions of liberal ethos in the nineteenth century.[4] This chapter, too, sees *Villette* as engaged with questions pertaining to liberalism; however, while Anderson emphasizes Lucy's "ongoing attempt to appropriate and transform what otherwise operate as disabling or negative modes of detachment: crippling psychological and emotional exile, instrumental and self-interested forms of surveillance, and complacent stoicism," this chapter attends to both the character's and the novel's ambivalence over the consequences of such appropriations and transformations.[5] This chapter thus argues that *Villette* marks a departure from the relative optimism toward the problem of skepticism that characterizes both Mill and Martineau. At its core, it explores the minimal forms of social life that might be possible in the context of radical doubts about the humanity of both the other and oneself. Despite the substantial differences between Mill and Martineau, their shared project uses pain to determine some sustainable relation between the individual and the collective. In Mill's case, pain serves as a way to enter the language game that constitutes the basis of sociability: pain is felt alone because of the way it is also felt by others. For Martineau, pain represents the limit that produces sufficient distance from the collective as to enable an enlightened relation to it. But for both, their liberalism involves both a respect for the irreducible specificity of individual experience and also a sense that this specificity is something shared. For Brontë, by contrast, specificity is everywhere under threat from sympathy as well as from other forces of normalization. Thus, what Mill describes in *On Liberty* (1859) as "the tendency of society to impose . . . its own ideas and practices as rules of conduct on those who dissent from them," here becomes a source of terror.[6] For what is at stake in homogenization is not simply the loss of individuality but the loss of truth and one's relationship with God. Solitude is described as excruciatingly painful, yet it is also posited as infinitely more desirable than its alternative: the self-betrayal that involves becoming one of the many. Rather than something simply to be overcome, therefore, skepticism becomes something to be embraced—not in the sense of holding on to the belief that others may not be persons like oneself, but instead in the sense that it remains to be seen if *anyone* qualifies as a person in the first place.

This chapter is divided into three sections. The first examines the prohibition on relationship in Brontë's world that gives rise to a generalized state of hypochondria—"hypochondria" for Brontë serving to indicate the irreducible specificity of individual experience that takes the place of Adam Smith's *sensus communis*. The second section examines how this specificity gives rise to grotesquely violent allegories of emotional experience. These allegories, I argue, serve as a challenge to and an assault on the reader who seeks to understand what the narrator has endured according to ordinary protocols of understanding and sympathy. The third section explores drowning as a privileged example of aversive physical sensation that is able to establish connections not just between vulnerable bodies but also between the living and the dead, the believer and the doubter, the fictional character and the living person. My ultimate goal is to consider not just Brontë's strange language of physical suffering and what it tells us about how the novelist understood the relations between pain and language, or between mind and body, but also to think about the counterintuitive compromise the novel seeks to make in relation to skepticism. In its attempt to make the reader feel something—or really almost anything—*Villette* also seeks to offer a way to think about one's own pain in reading as if it testified both to one's ineradicable solitude and also, however paradoxically, to the existence of another whose presence, absence, or suffering can be understood to cause it.

Lucy Snowe, Hypochondriac

Purporting to describe the experiences of its anonymous author and narrator, *Confessions of a Hypochondriac; or, Adventures of a Hyp. in Search of a Cure* (1849) details both the mental torments to which the hypochondriac is prey, and the medical chicaneries to which he is all too often subjected. The unnamed narrator is treated with anesthetics, ether, chloroform, homeopathy, hydropathy, hypnosis, probably opium (the exact cause of his hallucinations is never made clear), magic, and something that closely resembles modern "rebirth" therapy: he is forced to crawl through "a pipe or tube ... lined with hedgehogs, or porcupines, or something harder" on the sides, and covered with fur on the bottom.[7] "It was like going through a funnel," he recounts, "and at the extreme extremity, the squeeze was terrific; and how my tiresome body got out, by dint of labour, without being squashed, or elongated, is more than I can divulge."[8] None of these treatments is ever more than fleetingly effective. The narrator is only permanently cured once he finds a doctor who both understands and feels compassion for the psychological aspect of his illness: its origin not just in idleness, as was sometimes claimed of hypochondria, but in the lack of meaningful connection with other people to which idleness can give rise.[9] As the narrator explains, "There was no permanency of ease till the discipline of Goodly [the doctor who cures him] led me to take an interest in the enjoyments, affairs, and duties of life.... The conversation, the chosen amusements of the moment ... dissipated entirely the depraved anxieties of the croaking invalid."[10] Finally freed from the torments of self-absorption, the narrator is able to take his rightful place as a member of a larger community. By the end of the narrative, he is fully restored to mental and physical health: "I read, I criticise, I discuss, I hunt news, and relate it like another man, and have established a small farm in the west of England, which is let in allotments to the labourer and artisan. To watch their progress, to weigh the honey of these bees, to register their efforts and successes, is my singular pastime. It is one that will last."[11] Health here is equated with an evaluative and benevolent relation to others in which the self is fully integrated into a social, literary, and economic world.

This text offers a useful contrast to the way hypochondria functions in *Villette*. While the narrator of *Confessions* seeks compassion, community, and a way to redirect his attention toward the world rather than the sensations of his own body, Lucy's hypochondria indicates a desire to move in exactly the opposite direction: *toward* isolation, solitude, and a skeptical commitment to the uniqueness of one's own sensorium. While the narrator of *Confessions* regards hypochondria as a pathology to be cured, in other words, Lucy seems to regard it as both a way to guarantee her distinctiveness and also a gift from God that would be sacrilege to counter or cure. Hypochondria thus becomes nearly synonymous with independence, freedom of thought, and a commitment to truth-telling, even as it also makes its victim prey to incredible suffering.

Lucy Snowe has rarely been discussed in relation to her self-identification as a hypochondriac, despite the fact that she implicitly embraces the diagnosis on at least three occasions: when she accepts Graham's apology for his inability to help her because his "art [as a doctor] halts at the threshold of

Hypochondria" (*V* 205); when she asserts her privileged power to diagnose the king's ailment: "Ere long, however, if I did not *know*, at least I *felt*, the meaning of those characters written without hand.... Those eyes had looked on the visits of a certain ghost—had long waited the comings and goings of that strangest spectre, Hypochondria" (*V* 238); and when she explains the impossibility of conveying her sufferings to others by comparing her descriptions to the "dark sayings in that language and mood wherein Nebuchadnezzar, the imperial hypochondriac, communed with his baffled Chaldeans" (*V* 303). Perhaps even more importantly, throughout the novel, she consistently embraces not just the term "hypochondria" but the key attributes of the illness as it was understood in the nineteenth century. As I discuss in the introduction, in the nineteenth century, "hypochondria" did not mean exactly what it does today: it rarely indicated simple "pathophobia," or the fear that one is or will become ill.[12] Instead, it was an illness that could originate in either mind or body, whose principal symptom involved an unusual sensitivity to physical sensation—a sensitivity that sometimes but not always correlated to a conviction of the existence of a physical lesion where none could be detected. Despite disagreements regarding the illness's origin and symptomatology, therefore, hypochondria nevertheless had a distinct and identifiable profile: medical professionals almost always agreed that the suffering of the patient is real, even if it does not indicate any visible lesion (although lesion was sometimes identified as an effect of hypochondria); and they assumed that hypochondria was a product, as well as a cause, of isolation. One is isolated and therefore one attends overmuch to the sensations of one's body—or else one attends to one's sensations and so does not engage with others. In either case, hypochondria is cast as a profoundly social ailment: one that serves as an index of the failure of social life.

The relation between isolation and illness seems wholly relevant to Lucy Snowe. Lucy may not exactly think she is sick, but she does feel more than most people, and those feelings are linked to her solitude both in the sense that what she suffers from *is* her solitude, and in the sense that in the absence of other people, her feelings become increasingly acute. "The world can understand well enough the process of perishing for want of food," she laments at one point: "perhaps few persons can enter into or follow out that of going mad from solitary confinement. They see the long-buried prisoner disinterred, a maniac or an idiot!—how his senses left him—how his nerves, first inflamed, underwent nameless agony, and then sunk to palsy—is a subject too intricate for examination, too abstract for popular comprehension" (*V* 303). Solitude here acts directly on the nerves, first irritating them and so making them a source of pain, and then making them incapable of proper functioning. Regardless of the state of his health prior to his internment, the narrator suggests, solitude is enough to rob the poor prisoner of his senses. Solitude is thus described in the novel as both a source of suffering in itself and as leading to acute mental and physical distress. At the same time, however, this solitude is so profoundly overdetermined—and even to some extent sought after—that it is difficult to see it as a condition that could be, or perhaps even should be, remedied. In *Villette*, rather than an error to be corrected, the distinctiveness of the hypochondriac's sensations constitutes a cross to be borne: the cost of being an independent woman, a truthful writer, and a Christian.[13]

Lucy's loneliness is very clearly a product of the triviality of the social world: she is poor, friendless, "inoffensive and shadowlike," and bereft of any family that might support her. As a result, it is far too easy for those around her to overlook her, or to fail to consider her feelings. Yet at the same time, she also goes to extraordinary lengths to guarantee her solitude. At the beginning of the novel, she leaves her native country—where we are led to believe she has at least a few acquaintances—for the fictional Labassecour, a land where she knows no one, where she cannot speak the language, and where her religious difference from the vast majority of the population effectively isolates her from them.[14] Even here, Lucy resists the most basic forms of sociality, rejecting the overtures of the other teachers, running away from M. Paul—one of the few characters in the novel who consistently regards her as worthy of attention—and hiding her identity from Dr. John. This last point is worth underscoring, for it is easy to miss its significance: early on in the novel, Lucy recognizes in Dr. John Graham Bretton, her childhood playmate and the son of a friend of her family. As such, he is already an acquaintance from whom she has every reason to expect kindness. Yet she deliberately conceals her identity from him until a series of accidents reveals it for her. Lucy may be lonely, it seems, but she does not therefore seek the company of others. On the contrary, she very deliberately removes herself from any situation in which she is likely to find herself among friends. Additionally, Lucy invites misunderstanding, apparently taking pleasure in the fact that no two people see her the same way. "What contradictory attributes of character we sometimes find ascribed to us," she exclaims at one point.

> Madame Beck esteemed me learned and blue; Miss Fanshawe, caustic, ironic, and cynical; Mr. Home, a model teacher, the essence of the sedate and discreet ... whilst another person, Professor Paul Emanuel, to wit, never lost an opportunity of intimating his opinion that mine was rather a fiery and rash nature—adventurous, indocile, and audacious. (*V* 334)

According to Mary Jacobus, this variety of opinions suggests that Lucy functions as "a blank screen on which others project their view of her."[15] Although it is certainly true that many of the characters see only what they wish to in Lucy, as Jacobus admits, she herself actively encourages these misunderstandings—and this, even in relation to characters that she purports to esteem: "There is a perverse mood of the mind which is rather soothed than irritated by misconstruction," she claims—but rather than an exception, this is a mood that seems to characterize her most of the time (*V* 109).

In order to understand what Lucy seeks to evade, it is worth considering the precise nature of what others might be able to offer her. For if, on the one hand, sympathy seems to entail understanding, compassion, and consolation, on the other, it involves a normalizing pressure to which Lucy is especially resistant.[16] According to Adam Smith, every experience of sympathy necessarily entails judgment. As he explains in *The Theory of Moral Sentiments* (1759), regardless of the nature of its object—emotion, sensation, aesthetic pleasure, or political conviction—"To approve of the passions of another ... as suitable to their objects, is the same thing as to observe that we entirely sympathize with them; and not to approve of them as such, is the same thing as to observe that we do not entirely sympathize with them."[17] In sympathizing, therefore, we acknowledge our sense of the appropriateness of another's sentiments to a given situation and implicitly confirm that under similar conditions, we imagine that we would feel the same way. This is not to say that we *would* feel the same way: Smith is careful to point out that we consistently underestimate what we feel when placed under duress. Nevertheless, the fantasy of sympathy is that in imagining the feelings of another, we accurately reproduce what we would feel in her place—a significant corollary of this fantasy being that whatever we think we would feel is what we think others *should* feel, as well.

For Smith, the consequence of this hall of mirrors is a socially productive state of self-scrutiny that encourages persons to feel and act as they imagine others would approve. For Lucy, by contrast, such self-consciousness in relation to other people's opinions threatens not just her uniqueness but also her integrity—not least because the people with whom she surrounds herself are so unappealing. For example, although "each of the teachers in turn made me overtures of special intimacy," each is found to be limited. "One I found to be an honest woman, but a narrow thinker, a coarse feeler, and an egotist. The second was a Parisienne, externally refined—at heart, corrupt—without a creed, without a principle, without an affection.... She had a wonderful passion for presents; and, in this point, the third teacher—a person otherwise characterless and insignificant—closely resembled her. This last-named had also one other distinctive property—that of avarice" (*V* 139). The children may occasionally be kind, but they, too, are incapable of becoming her friends, convinced as they are that, as one puts it, her Protestantism means "on ferait bien de vous brûler toute vive ici-bas" (*V* 93). Their mental enslavement to their priests means none of them are worthy of her friendship. To be the object of sympathy from people like these would be horrifying indeed, for it would suggest she had something in common with them—that they shared values or tastes, and hence, that they might be able to share her feelings. Better to remain alone than to receive the sympathy of such as these. This threat is only underscored by the fact that, in a Catholic school in a Catholic country, the feelings of the inmates are continually being monitored and corrected. Surveillance, discipline, and the unfettered flow of sympathy all come to seem like related but different ways of encouraging a fundamental emotional and sensational uniformity among the inhabitants. In such a context, idiosyncrasy, with its corresponding skeptical insistence on one's uniqueness, comes to look like a form of self-preservation, even if the penalty is loneliness with all its concomitant horrors.

In Brontë's own writings, solitude comes to seem crucially necessary to mental independence, for nearly *any* form of relationship is regarded as a threat to one's commitment to truth. As Brontë wrote to Elizabeth Gaskell in 1853, for example,

> Do you—who have so many friends, so large a circle of acquaintance —find it easy, when you sit down to write—to isolate yourself from all those ties and their sweet associations—[so] as to be *your own woman*—uninfluenced, unswayed by the consciousness of how your work may affect other minds—what blame, what sympathy it may call forth? Does no luminous cloud ever come between you and the severe Truth—as you know it in your own secret and clear-seeing Soul?[18]

Isolation may be painful, but it may also be required "to be [one's] own woman, uninfluenced" not only by other people but even by "the consciousness of how [one's] work may affect" them. Any attachment to one's fellows is all too prone to stand between the writer and "severe truth." So committed is Brontë to the value of solitude that she seeks to ward off even Gaskell's answer to her question: "Don't answer the question," she writes. "It is not intended to be answered."[19] She would rather think her own thoughts, it seems, without knowing the potentially distorting thoughts of others. And of course, like Brontë, Lucy is an artist as well as a woman and a Christian: the author of the text we are reading. Personal relations of whatever form constitute a considerable danger to personal honesty, particularly that required of the woman artist.

Thus far I have argued that Lucy's hypochondria may, to a large extent, be regarded as self-induced: the product of a commitment to isolation that seems necessary to mental freedom. Yet, however resistant Lucy may be to human relationship, it is of course not at all accurate to describe her as if she were *only* resistant to connections with others. Particularly with M. Paul, she very clearly allows a relationship to develop and identifies it with extraordinary happiness. What she describes as her "perversity" may mean that the relationship progresses by fits and starts, but by the time he leaves for the West Indies, we are encouraged to believe that upon his return, they will marry. The fact that he dies before they are able to do so seems like little more than a horrible twist of fate. Lucy could have been happy, it seems, but it simply was not meant to be. Such an account suggests that describing Lucy as seeking solitude might be misguided: she is instead thwarted by forces well beyond her control.

Part of what I believe makes *Villette* feel so claustrophobic, however, is that solitude is made to seem *both* like a choice *and* like a necessity: a consequence of the woman artist's need for autonomy *and* of the divine prohibition on idolatry.[20] As Peter Allan Dale points out, throughout her work, Brontë "cannot get round the fear that St. Paul has correctly interpreted our fallen nature, that the desire to love and be loved by the creature is a kind of idolatry that must end in the loss of one's eternal soul."[21] This is a fear that haunts Brontë's personal writings, as well. As she wrote to Ellen Nussey in 1837, "Why are we to be divided? Surely, Ellen, it must be because we are in danger of loving each other too well; of losing sight of the *Creator* in idolatry of the *creature*."[22] Nussey was a very close friend, but it is still striking that Brontë would regard their relationship as the potential object of God's ire. In 1850, she wrote in a similar vein to Amelia Ringrose, advising her not to be too attached to her sister Rosy: "You and Rosy must indeed feel comfort in one another but when I read the expression of your mutual affection, a warning voice seems to whisper 'Rejoice with trembling[.]' You may, and I trust will, long be spared to one another—but we know that it may be otherwise."[23] Such a claim suggests not just that one should not love too much because people die, but that excessive attachment may itself be the *cause* of the beloved's death. Brontë's god is a jealous god; it is thus of supreme importance not to incur his wrath. In this context, the fact that M. Paul dies at the end of *Villette* only confirms what Brontë herself so clearly believed: that human love is all too likely to be thwarted—and hence that "hypochondria" constitutes both testimony to one's valuable autonomy and also a necessary consequence of the curse under which all labor, albeit some more visibly, self-consciously, and painfully than others.

Allegories of Suffering

However strange Lucy's commitment to—and resignation to—solitude may seem in the context of Victorian understandings of hypochondria, it appears even more anomalous in the context of the Victorian novel. While it is certainly common for novels of this period to begin with a protagonist's isolation, ordinarily the narrative movement is toward social integration, most often in the form of marriage. In *Villette*, by contrast, not only does Lucy begin the novel alone, end it alone, and resist nearly all overtures of friendship that are made along the way, she consistently refuses the one source of solace and companionship to which nearly every first-person narrator eventually appeals:

the reader. Raymond Williams has described *Villette* as an example of "the fiction of special pleading," by which he claims to mean "that fiction in which the only major emotion, and then the relation with the reader, is that exact stress, that first-person stress: 'circumstanced like me'. The stress is this really: the world will judge me in certain ways if it sees what I do, but if it knew how I felt it would see me quite differently."[24] This seems like an accurate description of *Jane Eyre* (1847), as well as of the many other nineteenth-century narratives in which the reader's sympathy is called upon to compensate for the failures of sympathy between characters within the text: Mrs. Reed might not love Jane, but we do; Mr. Murdstone might reject David, but we understand the boy's value; Casaubon might not trust his wife, but we recognize her loyalty and devotion. Williams's description does not, however, capture the strangeness of *Villette*. For here, rather than encouraging the illusion that while the world misunderstands Lucy Snowe, readers share her thoughts and feelings, the novel repeatedly calls attention to the fact that we do *not* have full access to the character's interiority. She deceives us—in the instance of her recognition of Dr. John, in particular, but in other less significant contexts, as well.[25] She chastises us both implicitly—by withholding information—and explicitly—by mocking us for our conventional assumptions. Most importantly, she shields us from knowledge of specific events, desires, and dreams that she nevertheless identifies as formative. In place of concrete descriptions of Lucy's experiences, we tend to be given elaborate metaphors in which physical pain is made to stand in for some other emotional content. Such metaphors flirt with allegory without taking on all of allegory's qualities: while they often include personifications or other species of allegorical characters, they also consistently resist interpretation. As a result, they tend less to convey a hidden meaning than to communicate a sense of physical pain combined with a strong impression that some kind of important content remains veiled from view.[26]

According to Angus Fletcher, "Allegory is a method of double meanings that organizes utterance (in any medium) according to its expression of analogical parallels between different networks of iconic likeness."[27] Allegorical narratives thus "lead us to imagine a set of meanings on the other side of [a] hermeneutic wall. In political and cultural terms, these meanings lying on the other side of the wall comprise parts of the whole of an ideology—its commentary and interpretation."[28] Allegory establishes not just correspondences between representations and meanings; it also implies a system of meaningfulness that encodes its own beliefs and commitments. In his book on allegory, Fletcher describes the movement away from allegory and toward realism as a move toward "stories told merely for the sake of the plot," which purport to "correspond to [nothing] except perhaps life itself."[29] In his essay, "Allegory without Ideas," however, he details a further development that he claims is characteristic of postmodernism: while Early Modern allegory sought to create the impression of a relatively stable system of ideas, he explains, postmodern fiction uses allegory precisely to baffle our desire for order and meaning. The idea of these allegories, Fletcher writes, is very often "to show that the incomprehensible is incomprehensible": "Our allegory without ideas asks how the idea can be situated and placed in a sea of ambiguous and vague possibilities."[30]

Fletcher's account of the way fictions can gesture toward the definite ideas they refuse to deliver is suggestive for *Villette*. Yet, if the images Lucy offers us as substitutes for her experiences are not exactly allegories in the Early Modern sense—because we are never allowed fully to understand either their referent or their system of referentiality—nor are they "allegories without ideas" in the postmodern sense: they do not seem to want to tell us that the incomprehensible is incomprehensible. Instead, they both invite interpretation and balk it: they intimate meanings only to insist that we do not have enough information to understand them. As a result, what we as readers are left with is nothing much more than the literal contents of the allegories themselves, which almost invariably revolve around scenes of violence and physical suffering.

The clearest example of the way *Villette* uses and abuses allegory appears quite early in the novel, when the narrator first taunts us with our conventional assumptions about what women's plots can look like, and then taunts us in a different way with her refusal to explain how exactly her own story deviates from that supposed norm:

> It will be conjectured that I was of course glad to return to the bosom of my kindred. Well! the amiable conjecture does no harm, and may therefore be safely left uncontradicted. Far from saying nay, indeed, I will permit the reader to picture me, for the next eight years, as a bark slumbering through halcyon weather, in a harbour still as glass—the steersman stretched on the little deck, his face up to heaven, his eyes closed: buried, if you will, in a long prayer. A great many women and girls are supposed to pass their lives something in that fashion; why not I with the rest?
>
> Picture me then idle, basking, plump, and happy, stretched on a cushioned deck, warmed with constant sunshine, rocked by breezes indolently soft. However, it cannot be concealed that, in that case, I must somehow have fallen overboard, or that there must have been wreck at last. I too well remember a time—a long time—of cold, of danger, of contention. To this hour, when I have the nightmare, it repeats the rush and saltness of briny waves in my throat, and their icy pressure on my lungs. I even know there was a storm, and that not of one hour nor one day. For many days and nights neither sun nor stars appeared; we cast with our own hands the tackling out of the ship; a

heavy tempest lay on us; all hope that we should be saved was taken away. In fine, the ship was lost, the crew perished. (*V* 39)

Clearly something happened that is not being specified: shipwreck stands in for some other kind of disaster. Yet not only is there no way to identify the nature of that disaster here, we are *never* told what happened—and this despite the sense in the text that it is crucially important to Lucy's later life. Instead of the events themselves, all we are given is a horrifyingly vivid sense of what they felt like: drowning. In fact, they felt so much like drowning, we are asked to believe, that when Lucy herself dreams of those events, her nightmares reproduce not the events themselves, but instead "the rush and saltness of briny waves in my throat, and their icy pressure on my lungs." She, too, drowns in her dreams, and this despite the fact that "drowning" initially constitutes only a metaphor that purports to convey some other form of experience.[31]

In the next section, I will return to the strange slide in literary registers that takes place at the end of this passage. My primary concern here is the basic structure of the pseudo-allegory: the way it calls attention to the fact that some content is not being communicated to the reader, along with the way it uses a horrifyingly vivid image of physical suffering to stand in for that content. The consequence is that the reader is left with a physical sensation that is all too easy to imagine—so vividly are the "saltness" and "icy pressure" of drowning described—along with a sense that this sensation corresponds in some way to emotional suffering, the precise nature of which remains concealed. That structure establishes the terms for nearly all the pseudo-allegories that follow. Moreover, although not every pseudo-allegory in *Villette* clearly claims that something is being concealed from the reader's view, they almost always make it *feel* as if something is being obscured or hidden. For example, when reading her description of her feelings while immured at the Rue Fossette, one can easily imagine that all the narrator is trying to convey is what she explicitly identifies as the source of her suffering: her need to repress any futile hope for the future. Yet, the images used to describe that repression are so much in excess of this content that, combined with the training provided to the reader by the shipwreck passage, they at least suggest that something else is going on that the narrator could reveal to us if she wished to. "About the present," the narrator explains, "it was better to be stoical; about the future—such a future as mine—to be dead. And in catalepsy and a dead trance, I studiously held the quick of my nature." The passage continues:

> At that time, I well remember whatever could excite—certain accidents of the weather, for instance, were almost dreaded by me, because they woke the being I was always lulling, and stirred up a craving cry I could not satisfy. One night a thunder-storm broke; a sort of hurricane shook us in our beds: the Catholics rose in panic and prayed to their

saints. As for me, the tempest took hold of me with tyranny: I was roughly roused and obliged to live. I got up and dressed myself, and creeping outside the casement close by my bed, sat on its ledge, with my feet on the roof of a lower adjoining building. It was wet, it was wild, it was pitch-dark. Within the dormitory they gathered round the night-lamp in consternation, praying loud. I could not go in: too resistless was the delight of staying with the wild hour, black and full of thunder, pealing out such an ode as language never delivered to man— too terribly glorious, the spectacle of clouds, split and pierced by white and blinding bolts.

I did long, achingly, then and for four-and-twenty hours afterwards, for something to fetch me out of my present existence, and lead me upwards and onwards. This longing, and all of a similar kind, it was necessary to knock on the head; which I did, figuratively, after the manner of Jael to Sisera, driving a nail through their temples. Unlike Sisera, they did not die: they were but transiently stunned, and at intervals would turn on the nail with a rebellious wrench: then did the temples bleed, and the brain thrill to its core. (*V* 120–21)

The first paragraph of this passage is relatively straightforward, describing as it does the intense "delight of staying with the wild hour" and of enjoying the sublime spectacle of the thunderstorm. The thunderstorm has a material reality that does not appear to stand in for anything else. It is simply a source of excitement and pleasure. The second paragraph is more mysterious: the image used to describe how Lucy represses her feelings is so grotesque, and the cast of characters so vivid as well as strange, as to nearly obscure the circumstances and sensations they are supposedly being used to describe. The biblical reference, in particular, spins dizzyingly out of control. In the original story, Jael is the heroine: her murder of Sisera gives a crucial victory to Israel. In Brontë's revision, however, the gruesomely vivid imagination of Sisera's suffering, combined with the fact that he does not die when Jael "sm[ites] the nail into his temples," seems to alter the meaning of the story, albeit in ways that are not immediately available to interpretation. On one level, Sisera's failure to die simply conveys the way Lucy's desires effectively constitute enemy forces that refuse to accept defeat. Yet the violence and suffering involved are so excessive as to make it seem as if something else might be being conveyed. It is difficult not to feel compassion for Sisera, despite our knowledge that he is the enemy.[32] As a result, what we are left with, first, is a sense of opacity: a sense that we are being given the outlines of some content, experience, or meaning to which we have no direct access; and second, a horrifying sense of just how painful that experience is for Lucy. The metaphor does not exactly line up this way, since Lucy is positioned as both Jael *and* Sisera—aggressor *and* victim. Nevertheless, the impression it leaves is that for Lucy, repressing her desires feels like having a nail driven through her temples and yet failing to die. It feels like having her temples bleed as she turns on the nail, and having her "brain thrill to its core."[33]

It is hard to imagine reading that "thrill," in particular, without an inward cringe. As Marit Fimland writes, the image is so "strong and violent ... that it is tempting to put the novel aside with revulsion."[34] As in the drowning passage, here the language of aversive physical experience forces us to register Lucy's experience while preventing us from evaluating it. To return to Smith for a moment, it effectively enables Lucy to demand that we register her feelings, even as she calls attention to the fact that, because we have little or no knowledge of their cause, we cannot evaluate those feelings' appropriateness, and so also cannot sympathize with them. In both passages, then, the language of physical suffering does not invite sympathy so much as it replaces it with something far less cognitive, and far less normalizing. All we can do is feel—or at least imagine feeling—some faint echo of the suffering described, suffering that overrides questions of appropriateness precisely because of the extreme way in which it is couched as in and of the body.

Drowning

In *The Claim of Reason*, Stanley Cavell explains that "empathetic projection is to other minds what seeing is to material objects"—a state of affairs that means "'seeing' others as human beings is as much like dreaming them as it is like *seeing* them."[35] Cavell's account offers a moving way of thinking about the problem of skepticism. In place of the epistemological question of how one can know the pain of the other, Cavell asks us to consider what is at stake in attending to the inevitability of our doubt. Yet in this section of the chapter, I want to suggest that *Villette*'s practices of embodiment offer a corrective to the way he identifies sentience with "empathetic projection" on the one hand and "human beings" on the other. For I suggest that what most centrally concerns the novel is not so much the problem of how to distinguish between humans and nonhumans—those who are sentient and so deserving of care, and those who are not—but instead the way that something like physical pain might float free of that distinction.

Elaine Freedgood has recently argued for the consistency with which the Victorian novel confuses the distinction between the diegetic and the extradiegetic. "Novels are strange, generically," she writes, "because they do not, and cannot maintain a stable diegesis—because there cannot, ontologically speaking, be any such thing when a narrator can perform feats like free indirect discourse, or when historical and fictional characters can have dinner."[36] Freedgood's point is well taken. Even in this context, however, *Villette* stands out as exceptionally difficult to parse in terms of what constitutes part of the plot and what is better understood as metaphorical, allegorical, or otherwise figurative. The pseudo-allegories in this text are consistently disorienting and obscure, not just in terms of the external content to which they presumably refer but also in terms of the fictional story they seek to tell. It is not just that the reader is left unsure of the meaning of the allegory, or the nature of the thing it is allegorizing; it is also often easy to lose track of the fiction itself. Figures that seem allegorical blur almost imperceptibly with figures that seem realistic. In a review published in *Putnam's Monthly Magazine* in 1853, for example, the reviewer objects to the "personifications of passion" in the text on the grounds that they are "unnatural, and clumsily patched upon the tale," and so make the reader "aware that it is a drama and not a fact; that it is an author writing a very fine book, and not scenes of life developing themselves before you."[37] The reviewer then singles out the portrait of Vashti for particular censure—"Rachel is sketched in the lurid gloom of the French melo-dramatic style. It partakes of the fault of personification to which we alluded"—even as she identifies the "descriptions of the dreary vacation" as "the finest passages in the book."[38] However true it may be that the passages describing Vashti are especially lurid, and those describing Lucy's fever-dreams over the Long Vacation are especially powerful or resonant, it is worth noting that in both cases the reviewer gets the facts wrong. Vashti clearly appears within the plot of the novel and so cannot exactly be understood to constitute a personification: Lucy goes to see her perform with Graham, describes her own responses to her acting and compares them with her friend's, and so forth. Meanwhile, the passages describing the Long Vacation are populated with an enormous range of personifications that interact with one another in ways that are nearly impossible to parse coherently.

Even though the reviewer clearly made a mistake, one can see how the error arose. Vashti may appear in the plot of the novel, for example, yet the way she is described is all *about* personification.[39] "I have said that she does not *resent* her grief," the narrator explains of the actress:

> No; the weakness of that word would make it a lie. To her, what hurts becomes immediately embodied: she looks on it as a thing that can be attacked, worried down, torn in shreds. Scarcely a substance herself, she grapples to conflict with abstractions. Before calamity she is a tigress; she rends her woes, shivers them in convulsed abhorrence. Pain, for her, has no result in good: tears water no harvest of wisdom: on sickness, on death itself, she looks with the eye of a rebel. (*V* 287)

However difficult it may be to identify our shadowy narrator with this "incarnat[ion]" of "Hate and Murder and Madness," Vashti nevertheless conveys her emotional suffering through physical pain in a way that resembles Lucy's own prose (*V* 286). Both characters embrace personification, or at least embodiment, taking suffering and transforming it into things with which they can violently contend. While Vashti "rends her woes" and "shivers them in convulsed abhorrence," Lucy pounds nails through her desires' temples. In both cases, what is contended with ultimately seems of less significance than the contention itself: the violence is described, although the subject of the grief is not. In Vashti, then, we can see Brontë thinking through the rationale for her own aesthetic, and in Lucy's response to it we can discern our ideal response as well. "The strong magnetism of genius drew my heart out of its wonted orbit," she tells us; "the sunflower turned from the south to a fierce light, not solar—a rushing, red, cometary light—hot on vision and to sensation" (*V* 287). The susceptible, it seems, will respond as the sunflowers do—physically, unconsciously, and without reservation: they will feel the heat of the actress's "cometary" power and be attracted by the light she gives off in dying. However clearly Vashti may constitute part of the plot of *Villette*, then, she can *also* be regarded as a personification of Lucy's (Brontë's) literary practice: a practice that uses personification to make emotional suffering something to be "attacked," as well as a spectacle to which the susceptible cannot help but respond.

An analogous argument can be made about the reviewer's error in relation to the passages describing the Long Vacation, for even as they are rife with personifications, they also offer a horribly "realist" account of what it might feel like to very nearly go mad as a result of solitude. Left alone at the Pensionnat for several weeks, Lucy becomes increasingly nervous. She describes the nadir of her time in the following terms:

> Sleep went quite away. I used to rise in the night, look round for her, beseech her earnestly to return. A rattle of the window, a cry of the blast only replied—Sleep never came!
>
> I err. She came once, but in anger. Impatient of my importunity she brought with her an avenging dream. By the clock of St. Jean Baptiste, that dream remained scarce fifteen minutes—a brief space, but sufficing to wring my whole frame with unknown anguish; to confer a nameless experience that had the hue, the mien, the terror, the very tone of a visitation from eternity. Between twelve and one that night a cup was forced to my lips, black, strong, strange, drawn from no well, but filled up seething from a bottomless and boundless sea. Suffering, brewed in temporal or calculable measure, and mixed for mortal lips, tastes not as this suffering tasted. Having drank and woke, I thought all was over: the end come and past by. Trembling fearfully—as consciousness returned—ready to cry out on some fellow-creature to help me, only that I knew no fellow-creature was near enough to catch the wild summons—Goton in her far distant attic could not hear—I rose on my knees in bed. Some fearful hours went over me: indescribably was

I torn, racked and oppressed in mind. Amidst the horrors of that dream I think the worst lay here. Methought the well-loved dead, who had loved *me* well in life, met me elsewhere, alienated: galled was my inmost spirit with an unutterable sense of despair about the future. Motive there was none why I should try to recover or wish to live; and yet quite unendurable was the pitiless and haughty voice in which Death challenged me to engage his unknown terrors. When I tried to pray I could only utter these words:—

"From my youth up Thy terrors have I suffered with a troubled mind." (*V* 176–77)

The most obvious personifications here are Sleep and Death, but other figures are suggested, as well. Who forces the bitter cup to Lucy's lips? Who are these "well-loved dead," and how do they relate to both Sleep and Death and to her tormentors? The bitter cup additionally suggests some other allegorical reference—the most obvious of which is the vinegar and gall offered to Jesus immediately before his crucifixion. In this context, the bitter cup suggests a taunting intensification of her suffering while on the brink of an inescapable and divinely ordained doom. The image could also refer to the "ordeal of the bitter waters," described in the Book of Numbers, which seems to have even greater relevance to this moment. This is a trial imposed on a woman suspected of adultery. If poisoned by the drink, the woman was judged guilty of betraying her husband. If she survived, she was deemed innocent.[40] What makes this context especially relevant to this passage is Lucy's confusion after having been forced to drink: "Having drank and woke, I thought all was over: the end come and past by." In the wake of her ordeal, Lucy does not know whether she has been judged innocent or guilty, whether she lives or dies. That confusion generates other confusions in turn: between characters, personifications, the living, and the dead. The "real" character Goton comes to seem relatively spectral in a context in which Sleep can be appealed to as if she was a person, and in which the well-loved dead could comfort Lucy if they chose to.[41] Not only does realism come to seem fictive and arbitrary in this passage; it comes to seem even less available to appeal than the fever-dream itself.[42]

As in the previous example, in relation to this passage, the reviewer clearly made a mistake: this passage is rife with personifications. Yet it is also easy to see how the impression it conveys might have less to do with personification, per se, than with the confusions that arise between persons and qualities or conditions, between the living and the dead, in a context in which the speaker is less concerned with whether she has survived than with whether she is loved—a state that the psalm she cites at the end of the passage suggests is ultimately indistinguishable from death. The speaker of Psalm 88 complains that he is "Free among the dead, like the slain that lie in the grave, whom thou remembrest no more: and they are cut off from thy hand." To be alienated from God is to be like the dead—a condition with which the narrator of *Villette* seems all too familiar. Lucy, too, seems perpetually on the verge of exile—from God as a result of her attachment to man, and from man as a result of her commitment to self, truth, and God. She is caught in between and hence remains unavailable to consolation. Like the other passage singled out by the reviewer, therefore, this one implicitly raises the question of how one *can* ultimately distinguish between a personification and a character, between a character and a person, between the living and the dead. What exactly is at stake in doing so? And what do such questions have to do with the problem that troubles Lucy most in her hours of need: not whether she is alive or dead, but instead, whether she is loved or "owned."

Issues like these seem especially pressing in this text, not just because it is a novel that ends with the death of the beloved and so implicitly raises the question of what it means to love, or perhaps be loved by, one who is no longer alive, but also because it is a novel that establishes a very deliberate confusion between the deaths of Paul and Lucy as a result of the way that the physical experience of drowning is attached to both. Consider, once again, that strange passage in which the narrator describes what her unspecified experience as a child felt like: "To this hour, when I have the nightmare, it repeats the rush and saltness of briny waves in my throat, and their icy pressure on my lungs." When we are first offered this image, very early in the novel, it seems relatively arbitrary, if horrifyingly vivid. In the wake of M. Paul's death, by contrast, it takes on an entirely different significance.

> The wind shifts to the west.... That storm roared frenzied, for seven days. It did not cease till the Atlantic was strewn with wrecks: it did not lull till the deeps had gorged their full of sustenance. Not till the destroying angel of tempest had achieved his perfect work, would he fold the wings whose waft was thunder—the tremor of whose plumes was storm.
>
> Peace, be still! Oh! a thousand weepers, praying in agony on waiting shores, listened for that voice, but it was not uttered—not uttered till; when the hush came, some could not feel it: till, when the sun returned, his light was night to some!
>
> Here pause: pause at once. There is enough said. Trouble no quiet, kind heart; leave sunny imaginations hope. Let it be theirs to conceive the delight of joy born again fresh out of great terror, the rapture of rescue from peril, the wondrous reprieve from dread, the fruition of return. Let them picture union and a happy succeeding life. (*V* 546)

The first passage offers a metaphor for Lucy's experience as a child, well before she ever meets M. Paul. The second appears as part of the diegesis of the text and describes what supposedly happened. Further, because the two passages are separated by hundreds of pages, it is difficult to imagine that any reader will connect the scenes except perhaps in rereading. Yet, when placed side by side, it is hard not to feel as if somehow the characters have the same experience, and that Lucy has it first. But what could this possibly mean?[43]

One might, of course, describe the first instance simply in terms of foreshadowing. Since this is a first-person narrative told in the past tense, the narrator knows from the beginning what eventually happens to M. Paul. It may not have happened yet for us, but it has happened for her. When she describes drowning at the beginning of the novel, therefore, she might be both describing what her early experience felt like and also giving us a covert intimation of what is to come. Yet, it is a strange form of foreshadowing that mistakes its victim: the fact that Lucy describes *herself* drowning rather than her lover ultimately makes M. Paul's death seem less like the fulfillment of a prediction than like a repetition of something that has already happened.

The idea that Lucy is the first to drown could signal that *Villette* is a traumatic text and that M. Paul's death is the trauma it is endlessly reenacting. In *Unclaimed Experience*, Cathy Caruth recounts Freud's analysis of the dream of a father who has just lost his child: "After a few hours' sleep, the father had a dream that *his child was standing beside his bed, caught him by the arm and whispered to him reproachfully: 'Father, don't you see I'm burning?'*"[44] After tracing Freud's various attempts to understand the dream—as the father's registration of the fact his son's body had, in fact, caught on fire as a result of the attendant's carelessness; as a form of wish fulfillment that turns the dead child into a live one; as a way to protect the father's sleep and so avoid consciousness itself—Caruth turns to Jacques Lacan's claim: "*Awakening ... is itself the site of a trauma*, the trauma of the necessity and impossibility of responding to another's death."[45] "From this perspective," Caruth continues, "the trauma that the dream, as an awakening, reenacts is not only the missed encounter with the child's death but also the way in which that missing also constitutes the very survival of the father."[46] The father's dream and his subsequent awakening thus constitute "the father's encounter with the otherness of the dead child"—an otherness confirmed by his ability to die while the father lives on.[47]

Caruth's account of the dream of the burning child provides a useful context for thinking about Lucy's relationship to M. Paul's death, for it suggests that rather than registering the trauma of survival—as in Freud's case study—Lucy's death by drowning at the beginning of the novel insists that she died, too, and that she died first. "To this hour, when I have the nightmare, it repeats the rush and saltness of briny waves in my throat, and their icy pressure on my lungs." In Caruth's terms, such an identification with the one who has died serves as a way to memorialize the beloved—to mark his death with one's own body. It serves, too, as a way to keep him alive—so long as he is dying, he has not yet actually died. However, it also serves to obscure the difference between the living and the dead in a way Caruth does not discuss, insofar as both are dying all the time, both in Lucy's nightmares and in the reader's. This "saltness," this suffocating pressure—we may not know what they mean, but the point may simply be to feel, for in feeling we attest not just to the existence of the other but to the existence of the one who feels, as well.

I began this chapter with Adam Smith and his insistence on the evaluative precondition of sympathy: the way sympathy requires a prior moment of judgment in which the appropriateness of the other's feelings is decided. In *Villette*, we can see Brontë using the language of physical sensation to evade or bypass such evaluation by refusing to attach her feelings to any clearly identifiable causes or contexts. Further, by erasing any clear distinctions between characters, persons, abstractions, and allegories, and by refusing any clear demarcation between the living and the dead, Brontë challenges our power to confer personhood—as well as the importance of that conferral. When we imagine saltness and feel icy pressure, or cringe as the brain thrills, I do not think we are making any real evaluation of the appropriateness of someone else's feelings in relation to their causes; nor, following Cavell, are we conferring personhood on another. Instead, we are simply registering in one of the most visceral ways possible, not just the fragility of the human body, or even the extent to which that fragility is something we all share, but the fact that something was felt—by Paul, though dead; by Lucy, though a fiction; by Sisera, though ambiguously a historical personage and a personification of Lucy's desires.

Aside from anything else, the subtle shift from using the densely allusive figure of drowning as a metaphor for her experience, to literalizing it in the form of her own nightmares, to literalizing it in a different way in the context of M. Paul's death, suggests a kind of indeterminacy between real and figurative deaths in this text. To die, and to be wholly unloved and unmourned, are made to seem like not just analogous experiences, but in some sense, the same experience. Such an experience cannot necessarily be understood or sympathized with by an observer, but it can, at the very least, be felt by that observer—and in feeling it, one testifies to the fact that someone or something was there. Rather than simply passive activity that takes place outside the frame of the text, in other words, imagining "saltness" and "icy pressure," cringing at the "thrilling brain" twisting on its nail, and conceiving of the bitterness of the bitter cup, constitute ways of testifying to the existence of some other, even if only in the form of imagining that something must cause one to feel this way. Such registration serves only the most minimal epistemological function. It says nothing about whether the other's feelings of pain are evidence of illness or the product of hypochondria—or even whether that other lives or dies. All it can indicate is that something made one feel in a particular way, and in doing so, one effectively, like Lucy in relation to Paul, helps keep the other alive. The model of pain that sustains these relationships presupposes no truth in suffering; all it does is provide ongoing proof of some minimal form of existence.[48]

It is difficult to see such a model as offering a conception of the social that is in any way as robust as those offered by Mill and Martineau. Pain here is less something that is shared or shareable than a sign of the existence of self, along with something that is not self. *Villette* nevertheless maintains an important relation to liberalism, even if that relation is largely negative. Its resistance to homogenization, its insistence that, to paraphrase Veena Das's terms, our future together is already imperiled, serves as an important counter to the relative optimism of the liberal philosophers with which this project begins.[49] That is because skepticism here constitutes a solution as well as a problem, insofar as it resists any attempt at effacing the irreducible specificity of the individual sufferer. This is a conclusion *Villette* calls into question. Against Wittgenstein's rejection of the possibility of secrecy, therefore, *Villette* embraces the fantasy of a private language, even as the novel is haunted by the terror that such privacy might, in fact, be available.

CHAPTER FOUR

Charles Darwin's Affect Theory

> *We behold the face of nature bright with gladness, we often see superabundance of food; we do not see, or we forget that the birds which are idly singing round us mostly live on insects or seeds, and are thus constantly destroying life; or we forget how largely these songsters, or their eggs, or their nestlings, are destroyed by birds and beasts of prey.*
> —CHARLES DARWIN, *ON THE ORIGIN OF SPECIES* (1859)

THE WORLD DARWIN DESCRIBES is one in which suffering is inescapable and omnipresent. Some may effectively win the "struggle for existence," and not all deaths involve pain.[1] Nevertheless, the threat of pain and the visible signs of its existence are everywhere. The basic problem is simply that which Thomas Malthus diagnosed at the end of the eighteenth century "applied to the whole animal and vegetable kingdoms" (*O* 7): that all living things reproduce too much. As Darwin explains, "Every being, which during its natural lifetime produces several eggs or seeds, must suffer destruction during some period of its life, and during some season or occasional year, otherwise, on the principle of geometrical increase, its numbers would quickly become so inordinately great that no country could support the product" (*O* 51). This excessiveness is useful to the species: it defends against extinction and multiplies opportunities for biological variation. It holds no consolation for the individual, however, for it dictates that some must die prematurely so that others may flourish. According to Malthus, the consequence "among mankind" is "misery and vice."[2] For Darwin, the plight of animals and plants is even more tragic, for "in this case, there can be no artificial increase of food, and no prudential restraint from marriage" (*O* 51). Animals and plants are helpless before their fate, and there is simply nothing to be done about it. Rather than regarding suffering as exceptional, therefore, or even as a problem available to redress, Darwin's theory ultimately suggests that there is, to quote Adam Phillips, by definition, "just the right amount" of pain in the world.[3] Darwin's work was "scandalous," Phillips explains, precisely because it "tak[es] for granted that certain kinds of suffering were just part of life."[4] Suffering is ordinary and inevitable, a necessary by-product of a system to which pain simply does not matter.

This vision of a natural world in pain might make Darwin's presence in this project seem self-evident. After all, there is probably no single writer whose work had a greater impact on the way pain was understood in the nineteenth century, as well as in the twentieth and twenty-first. At the same time, however, as a natural scientist, Darwin might also seem like an outlier in a book that otherwise focuses on pain's role in the adequate description of the social. In the first part of this chapter, however, I argue that Darwin uses pain to dismantle precisely the opposition between culture and nature on which such a distinction relies. Culture and nature are not different things in Darwin's work; instead, they are, in Benedict de Spinoza terms, different "attributes" of the same thing. "The thinking substance and the extended substance are one and the same substance," Spinoza writes, "which is now comprehended under this attribute, now under that."[5] Darwin agrees. He thus uses pain to suggest the extent to which even those sensations we might consider least available to culture or will can be understood under precisely those rubrics. Hence, as in the work of the other writers I examine, here the analysis of pain possesses the potential to alter how the conditions of human life are conceived much more broadly. The only difference is that here the "human" itself comes under particular pressure as Darwin encourages us to rethink our assumptions regarding what constitutes a human being in the first place.

In the second section of the chapter, I suggest that Darwin *also* uses pain to call attention to the non-self-evidence of the object of study. Not only can any given object be understood under the rubric of either nature or culture, it is also subject to nearly limitless redescription as a result of its ability to affect and to be affected. Here, again, Spinoza is useful: "By singular things," he writes, "I understand things that are finite and have a determinate existence. And if a number of individuals so concur in one action that together they are all the cause of one effect, I consider them all, to that extent, as one singular thing."[6] Spinozist "things" are thus defined in terms of their effect, and "individuals" have the potential for nearly endless repurposing. Pain, for Darwin, constitutes a particularly prolific "action," able to redefine the "thing" to which it gives rise again and again. In his account, therefore, not only does pain *not* reify the individual, as is often assumed, it is characterized by extraordinary mobility and fecundity. The result is a conceptual landscape that is as unstable as the ground Darwin describes after an earthquake: "A bad earthquake," he writes in his *Journal of Researches* (1839), "at once destroys the oldest associations: the world, the very emblem of all that is solid, has moved beneath our feet like a crust over a fluid;—one second of time has conveyed to the mind a strange idea of insecurity, which hours of reflection would never have created."[7]

This description could just as easily be applied to Darwin's vision of the world in pain more generally.

In a brief third section, I address what Darwin's ontology contributes to ongoing debates within affect theory. Specifically, I argue that his rejection of any assumptions regarding the self-evidence of his object of study, along with his considerations of affective states untethered to individuals, makes him a potentially useful resource for affect theory. At the same time, reexamining affect theory through the lens he provides calls attention to the paucity of recent engagements with the problem of pain.[8] Hovering ambiguously between body and mind, irreducible to either emotion or sensation, Spinoza's notion of affect as "affections by which the body's power of acting is increased or diminished, aided or restrained" has been used recently to think of feeling (with all the attendant ambiguity of that term) in the absence of personhood. Yet this account of affect as tending toward the redefinition of the individual has not often been used to think about pain. This chapter suggests that this is a serious oversight, and one whose remediation requires a revision of how both "affect" and "pain" have most commonly been defined—as well as requires a rejection of the political optimism with which affect is so often identified. Rather than a foregone political outcome, Darwin's work arises out of the conjunction of epistemology and aesthetics—that is, science, albeit a form of science that refuses to trade in what Bruno Latour calls "prematurely naturalized objectified facts."[9] This is precisely where we need to start, I argue, if affect theory is to have any political purchase beyond wishful thinking.

This chapter represents something of a departure from the previous three insofar as it might seem less interested in subjectivity, skepticism, and the social than in something like the relation between pain and ontology: it tracks Darwin's concern with the ways in which pain calls into question the givenness of our objects of study (human beings, organisms, species, etc.) through its fecundity in relation to things. I suggest, however, such concerns cannot be wholly divorced from problems regarding the social. Spinozist double-aspect monism means that questions of "things" are also inevitably questions of "ends" or actions. Objects are constantly forming and reforming into new "things," including new social orders. Questions regarding subjectivity and social life thus remain central here—as do questions regarding skepticism. However, the question of whether the other is a person like myself is recast in Darwin as a question regarding what exactly constitutes that "self." The problem for Darwin is therefore less whether you feel as I do, than the extent to which my feelings can be understood as mine in the first place, or are better conceived as the proper possession of those organisms, objects, or environments to which I am most proximate.

The Expression of the Emotions

Of all Darwin's works, *The Expression of the Emotions in Man and Animals* (1872) provides the most sustained meditations on the nature of emotional experience, in general, and of pain, in particular. In this text, Darwin seeks to counter the claims of his most notable predecessor in the analysis of emotional expression, Sir Charles Bell, author of *The Anatomy and Philosophy of Expression* (1st ed. 1806).[10] Against Bell's claim that God gave humans specific muscles in order to convey specific emotions, Darwin argues that emotional expressions are incidental consequences of physiological processes, which either serve or once served some function in relation to the organism.[11] As Lucy Hartley explains, Darwin's rejection of "Bell's theological framework for understanding instinctive expressions via transcendental purposiveness" thus lays the groundwork for seeing a basic continuity between human and nonhuman animals.[12] Adrian Desmond and James Moore have extended this claim still further, arguing that Darwin's assertions regarding the universality of human expression, and its origin in processes humans share with nonhuman animals, constituted a forceful intervention into debates over the status and implications of racial difference. Darwin's account of emotion was thus not simply intended to offer naturalistic explanations (i.e., natural selection) in place of supernatural ones (i.e., the divine source of emotional expression); it also represented an attempt to combat the claims regarding racial difference made by many of those who sought to defend slavery on the grounds of supposed biological differences between the races.[13]

In recent years, heated debates have once again flared up around *The Expression*, albeit in a very different register. Now the central question is not the status of racial difference, but instead that of cultural specificity: basically, that of whether emotion is learned or innate. The principal spokesman on one side of the debate is Paul Ekman, editor of the Oxford edition of *The Expression of the Emotions*, founder of the Ekman Group, and the model for the charismatic hero of the television show, "Lie to Me" (2009–11).[14] According to Ekman, the interest of Darwin's text lies in the way it demonstrates that emotional expression is *not* primarily a "communicative signal" designed to convey emotional meaning, but instead a "sign of emotion, related to internal physiological changes."[15] Emotional expression is not rhetorical, in other words, but instead what Charles Sanders Peirce would call an index or a natural sign.[16] As such, it constitutes a reliable guide to emotional states, as well as a guarantee of our ability to understand emotional expression "across generations, across cultures, and within cultures between strangers as well as intimates."[17] The face and body are reliable and universally interpretable guides to emotion; we simply need to learn how to read them. The stakes involved in Ekman's characterization of Darwin's work are extremely high, for the supposed universality of emotion and emotional expression—their grounding in fundamental biological structures—has helped legitimate the Facial Action Coding System (FACS) that Ekman promotes. This system has been invoked by neurologists Antonio Damasio and Joseph LeDoux, among others, and is being relied upon in Homeland Security's attempts to develop procedures for, as Ekman has put it, "Spot[ting] a Terrorist on the Fly."[18] It also provides part of the implicit backdrop to efforts of affect theorists such as Elizabeth A. Wilson, Brian Massumi, and William E. Connolly to insist on a biological grounding for affect.

On the other side of this debate, a number of critics have called attention to Darwin's awareness of the cultural specificity of emotional expression. Daniel Gross, for example, has demonstrated Darwin's self-consciousness regarding the extent to which the perception of emotion is a product of expectations, as well as his understanding that "the very experience of an emotion ... depends upon the social and not the biological situation."[19] While Ekman reduces emotion to a bodily function, Gross continues, Darwin suggests that "a robust account of the social world is essential for our understanding of emotion, and therefore we are led astray by any parsimonious account of the social world where cognition is reduced to a bodily function."[20] Meanwhile, John Plotz has argued that Darwin's "account of expressions implicitly makes the case that we are all raised deciphering emotional evidence, and more importantly that evidence is itself produced by bodies that have developed with an implicit awareness that their actions are going to be read."[21] For Gross and Plotz, therefore, Ekman et al. are simply ignoring evidence in *The Expression* that suggests that, however grounded in the physiological he imagined an emotional expression might be, Darwin was also aware of its cultural aspect.

In this section, I suggest that this disagreement can be at least partially attributed to the fact that in many of Darwin's writings, it is nearly impossible to determine where culture ends and biology begins. This is not to say that Ekman is justified in claiming Darwin's authority for his assertions regarding the universality of his taxonomy of emotional expression, or in describing Darwinian expression as only an index rather than also a signaling system. However, it is to suggest that Ekman exploits an ambiguity that arises repeatedly in Darwin's writing that often makes it difficult to determine whether what he is talking about is best understood as natural or cultural. Rather than an error, however, I argue that this ambiguity constitutes a strategic way to insist on the extent to which the social is always available to redescription in biological terms. Such ambiguity, however, is by no means limited to the biological and the cultural; as I discuss at the end of this section, Darwin also consistently obscures the distinctions between the willed and the involuntary, the felt and the unfelt. Such obscurity, I argue, places considerable pressure on any assumptions regarding the importance of such distinctions. From the perspective of evolution, it simply does not matter what we think we are doing—even as, importantly, this is not the only perspective Darwin admits.[22] Darwin consistently and simultaneously keeps both the first- and third-person perspectives in play. The consequence can be disorienting, distressing, or transcendent, or all of these things at once.

In *The Expression of the Emotions*, Darwin offers three basic principles for the production of emotional expression. The first is that of serviceable associated habits—that is, "complex actions [that] are of direct or indirect service under certain states of mind, in order to relieve or gratify certain sensations, desires, & c."[23] As an example, he describes jumping when startled by a snake: such an action might not be serviceable in every instance—when the snake that does the startling is secured behind glass, for example—but it might be, or might once have been, in some other context. The second principle, that of antithesis, consists of "the performance of movements of a directly opposite nature [to those of serviceable associated habits] ... when a directly opposite state of mind is induced" (*E* 28). Here, the clearest example Darwin offers is shrugging, which, as an indication of helplessness, serves as the antithesis of "the fact that squaring the elbows and clenching the fists" are common gestures when men "feel indignant and are prepared to attack their enemy" (*E* 271–72). Unlike jumping away from a snake, such a gesture might seem useless, and hence, potentially arbitrary or rhetorical. Yet Darwin explicitly states that "though these [expressions] are of no use," the "tendency to the performance of [these] movements" is "strong and involuntary" (*E* 28). Antithesis thus comes to seem just as deeply hardwired as flinching.

The third principle, and the one of greatest interest in relation to pain, is the action of the nervous system, which Darwin describes as follows: "When the sensorium is strongly excited, nerve-force is generated in excess, and is transmitted in certain definite directions, depending on the connection of the nerve-cells, and partly on habit: or the supply of nerve-force may, as it appears, be interrupted. Effects are thus produced which we recognize as expressive" (*E* 29).[24] However involuntary serviceable associated habits and the principle of antithesis may be, the action of the nervous system seems to pose a different kind of problem altogether, for it seems not just mechanical but also *necessary* for the proper functioning of the organism. It might be difficult or even impossible not to jump when startled by a snake, but were one able to exert such self-control, the only potential consequence would be to increase the danger of snakebite. It is much more difficult to imagine the malleability of expressions that arise from "the action of the nervous system," for they seem to serve a biological function so fundamental as to be out of reach of the will. Like salivating, or an increased heart rate—two examples that Darwin himself offers—all the actions of the nervous system come to seem "wholly independent of the will" (*E* 75).[25]

The "action of the nervous system" seems especially relevant to thinking about pain since, like nerve force, it is so often described as a nonnegotiable biological given. It is, in fact, the case that Darwin's most extensive discussions of the expression of pain come under the rubric of nerve force. For example, in accounting for the fact that animals in pain "generally writhe about with frightful contortions; and those which habitually use their voices utter piercing cries or groans" (*E* 69–70), Darwin explains that such actions serve a very specific biological function:

> A sensitive nerve when irritated transmits some influence to the nerve-cell, whence it proceeds.... Why the irritation of a nerve-cell should generate or liberate nerve-force is not known; but that this is the case seems to be the conclusion arrived at by all the greatest physiologists.... As Mr. Herbert Spencer remarks, it may be received as an "unquestionable truth that, at any moment, the existing quantity of liberated nerve-force, which in an inscrutable way produces in us the state we call feeling, *must* expend itself in some direction—*must* generate an equivalent manifestation of force somewhere." (*E* 70–71)

Pain generates an excess of nerve force that then *must* find an outlet: writhing, groaning, gnashing of teeth, staring, sweating—these are all ways to perform that vital physiological function. As a result, such actions come to seem wholly involuntary, the consequence of physical exigency rather than any desire to communicate.

In Darwin's notion of nerve force, it might be tempting to see something akin to Brian Massumi's strongly biological account of affect. In *Parables of the Virtual*, Massumi identifies affect with the "missing half-second" that physiologist Benjamin Libet claimed to identify between the "beginning of a bodily event and its completion in an outwardly directed, active expression."[26] Massumi describes Libet's experiments as follows: when "mild electrical pulses were administered to [cortical electrodes] and also to points on the skin ... the stimulation was felt only if it lasted more than half a second: half a second, the minimum perceivable lapse."[27] A second experiment claimed to give "some hint" as to what happens during that "lapse":

> Brain waves of healthy volunteers were monitored by an electroencephalograph (EEG) machine. The subjects were asked to flex a finger at a moment of their choosing and to recall the time of their decision by noting the spatial clock position of a revolving dot. The flexes came 0.2 seconds after they clocked the decision, but the EEG machine registered significant brain activity 0.3 seconds *before* the decision. Again, a half-second lapse between the beginning of a bodily event and its completion in an outwardly directed, active expression.[28]

According to Massumi, Libet's experiments suggest that the missing half-second is missed "not because it is empty, but because it is overfull," and that "will and consciousness are *subtractive*. They are *limitative, derived functions* that reduce a complexity too rich to be functionally expressed."[29] "This requires a reworking of how we think about the body," Massumi concludes.[30] It indicates a rethinking of the mind, as well, and "affect" is the term Massumi uses to mediate between these terms.

Neuroscientists have pointed out serious problems with Libet's science. Susan Pockett, Shaun Gallagher, Daniel C. Dennett, M. R. Bennett, and P. M. S. Hacker are only a few of the investigators who have pointed out the sloppiness of his experimental design and the dubiousness of his conclusions.[31] In addition, as Ruth Leys has argued, the conclusion that Massumi draws from Libet's experiments—that affect has the potential to "transform individuals for good or ill without regard to the content of argument or debate"— raises considerable theoretical and political questions.[32] "The whole point of the turn to affect by Massumi and like-minded cultural critics," Leys writes, is

> to shift attention away from considerations of meaning or "ideology" or indeed representation to the subject's subpersonal material-affective responses, where, it is claimed, political and other influences do their real work. The disconnect between "ideology" and affect produces as one of its consequences a relative indifference to the role of ideas and beliefs in politics, culture, and art in favor of an "ontological" concern with different people's corporeal-affective reactions.[33]

Affect makes politics a matter of nerves rather than ideas—a state of affairs that Massumi sees as a condition of political possibility. The principle for which the missing half-second has been taken to stand—that affect refers to some biological given that is prior to or outside of consciousness and yet nevertheless plays a determining role in our thoughts, feelings, and beliefs— continues to play a central role in many versions of affect studies.

The similarities between Massumi's notion of affect and Darwin's notion of nerve force are suggestive. In both cases, a physiological given is made to seem as if it produces effects that are in some sense autonomous of the agent who nominally registers or produces them. In Darwin's account of nerve force, as in Massumi's account of affect, in other words, we all seem to occupy the position of the girl that political theorist William E. Connolly describes who was made to laugh when the neurophysiologists seeking to "identify the causes of her epileptic seizures ... hit by chance upon a patch of brain where application of [an electric probe] made her laugh."[34] "The young girl," Connolly continues, "following time-ordered principles of retrospective interpretation, decided that these researchers were extremely funny guys."[35] Nerve force must be expended: like the electric probe, it forces us to produce expressions that require explanation. The potential arbitrariness of those explanations is less anomalous than axiomatic of the way emotional expression functions as a whole.[36]

However neat a potential parallel may exist between affect and nerve force, however, the disaggregation of mind and body that Massumi and Connolly assume is repeatedly challenged in Darwin's work. This is not to say it is ignored, but throughout his writings, it is consistently called into question. For example, in the M and N Notebooks (1838–40) that Darwin used to record his early speculations, he seems to distinguish between (presumably mental) grief and (presumably physical) pain in one place; however, only a few pages later, he obscures the differences between them entirely. "Think," he writes in the first passage, "whether there is any analogy between grief & pain—certain ideas hurting brain, like a wound hurts body—tears flow from both, as when one burns end of nose with a hot razor."[37] Here, he seems to regard the physical and the emotional as distinct, although also potentially comparable or analogous. Yet just a few pages later, he questions the self-evidence of that distinction: "Are not love & hate emotions; what are their characteristics;—they are more truly sensations??, a kind of mental pain & pleasure."[38] When love and hate come to seem like sensations rather than emotions and are equated with "mental pain & pleasure," the difference between a sensation and an emotion appears to be meaningless. The closer Darwin looks at phenomena that might seem self-evidently emotional, it seems, the more they begin to turn into their sensational obverse.

By the time Darwin gets to a late work like *The Expression of the Emotions*, one can see him ignoring or bypassing the distinction between the physical and the mental entirely. Thus, he offers the following description of grief under the same running title—"Action of the nervous system"—that he uses for the account of physical pain just cited.

> When a mother suddenly loses her child, sometimes she is frantic with grief, and must be considered to be in an excited state; she walks wildly about, tears her hair or clothes, and wrings her hands. This latter action is perhaps due to the principle of antithesis, betraying an inward sense of helplessness and that nothing can be done. The other wild and violent movements may be in part explained by the relief experienced through muscular exertion, and in part by the undirected overflow of nerve-force from the excited sensorium. (*E* 80)

Here, the pain would seem self-evidently mental rather than physical, and yet like physical pain, grief appears to generate nerve force that then must find an outlet. Although we might think that walking about, tearing hair or clothes, or wringing hands are conventional, learned behaviors—ways of communicating to others a state of psychic distress—in Darwin's account, they function as aids to physiological needs.

In passages like these, it can seem as if Darwin understands psychological pain on the model of physical suffering, and hence, as unavailable to conscious control. Yet elsewhere, it seems as if exactly the opposite might be the case and that he instead understands physical pain on the model of emotional distress, and thus as susceptible to certain forms of cultural specificity or even willed reconfiguration. He consistently holds up weeping, for example, as an efficient means of liberating nerve force: "By as much as the weeping is more violent or hysterical, by so much will the relief be greater,—on the same principle that the writhing of the whole body, the grinding of the teeth, and the uttering of piercing shrieks, all give relief under an agony of pain" (E 175).[39] Nevertheless, he also calls attention to the fact that not everyone weeps:

> With adults, especially of the male sex, weeping soon ceases to be caused by, or to express, bodily pain. This may be accounted for by its being thought weak and unmanly by men, both of civilized and barbarous races, to exhibit bodily pain by any outward sign. With this exception, savages weep copiously from very slight causes, of which fact Sir J. Lubbock has collected instances.... With the civilized nations of Europe there is also much difference in the frequency of weeping. Englishmen rarely cry, except under the pressure of the acutest grief; whereas in some parts of the Continent the men shed tears much more readily and freely. (E 153–54)

As Darwin narrates the narrowing of what initially seems like a universal prohibition on male tears down to a very specific prohibition on Englishman's tears, what might be imaginable as a product of natural selection quickly comes to look highly cultural—or at least what we ordinarily term cultural. Whatever other men may do, Englishmen do not cry. Thus, despite the fact that weeping constitutes a "primary and natural expression ... of suffering of any kind, whether bodily pain ... or mental distress," it is also the case that "a frequently repeated effort to restrain weeping, in association with certain states of the mind, does much in checking the habit" (E 155). Weeping may discharge nerve force, but that does not mean it is unavailable to cultural specificity, or even to the action of the will.

One way to understand this blurring of the distinction between culture and physiology is to place it in the context of Darwin's necessitarianism, or what we would now call his determinism. One of the consequences of necessitarianism is to make it nearly impossible to maintain any meaningful opposition between what we will and what we do involuntarily. As Darwin writes in his M notebook:

> Thinking over these things, one doubts existence of free will every action determined by heredetary constitution, example of others or teaching of others.... & the others are learnt, what they teach by the same means & therefore properly no free will.—we may easily fancy there is, as we fancy there is such a thing as chance.—chance governs the descent of a farthing, free will determines our throwing it up.—equall true the two statements.[40]

Darwin here performs a highly characteristic blurring of any distinction between what we might ordinarily regard as biological and what we usually describe as cultural phenomena. Hereditary constitution, learning by example, and more formal forms of education are all grouped together, and all are seen as countering any fantasy of free will. Like "chance," "free will" here marks not an actual state of underdetermination or freedom, but instead the absence of sufficient information.

This is not to say, however, that free will is *simply* an illusion. Instead, as Darwin explains a few entries later, certain impulses that we experience as acts of the will may, in fact, be legitimately described in those terms.

> With respect to free will, seeing a puppy playing [one] cannot doubt that they have free will, if so all animals., then an oyster has & a polype (& a plant in some senses, perhaps, though from not having pain or pleasure actions unavoidable & only to be changed by habits). now free will of oyster, one can fancy to be [a] direct effect of organization, by the capacities its senses give it of pain or pleasure, if so free will is to mind, what chance is to matter (M. Le Compte)—the free will (if so called) makes change in bodily organization of oyster, so may free will make change in man.—the real argument fixes on heredetary disposition & instincts.—Put it so.—Probably some error in argument, should be grateful if it were pointed out.—My wish to improve my temper, what does it arise from but organization. that organization may have been affected by circumstances & education, & by choice which at that time organization gave me to will—Verily the faults of the fathers, corporeal & bodily are visited upon the children.[41]

Puppies do have free will, but it is the free will of oysters, plants, and people: that involved in acting on the basis of one's organization. When considered under one aspect, my thoughts, feelings, and desires thus seem like the marks of my freedom; when considered under another, they seem as determined as the movements of the mollusk. The result is to suggest that both those who see Darwin as defending a purely biological account of emotional expression and those who call attention to the ways in which he manifests an awareness of the cultural conditions of emotional expression, reify distinctions between nature and culture that hold little purchase in his work. Culture, psychology, even will, come to occupy the same ontological category as biology.[42]

Pain's "Things"

In the first section of this chapter, I emphasized the extent to which, in Darwin's work, identical phenomena can be described either in terms of nature or culture, depending on the aspect under which they are considered. Even pain, which one might imagine to be unambiguously natural, seems like it can be adequately described in either terms. In this section, I focus on a different locus of redefinition of the object of study: one that has less to do with the question of what is or is not "natural," than with the contours of the object about which such questions can be asked in the first place. The provisionality of species for which Darwin is so famous is only one version of a much more general commitment to perceiving the world as if the "things" that populate it are not, in fact, self-evident or stable. To repeat Spinoza's formulation: "By singular things I understand things that are finite and have a determinate existence. And if a number of individuals so concur in one action that together they are all the cause of one effect, I consider them all, to that extent, as one singular thing."[43] As Peter Garratt explains, what this means is that "objects (or other bodies), described usually as unified things, are actually composites made up of smaller parts and in turn of still smaller parts.... Strictly speaking, the objective reality to which even the simplest perceptual act corresponds will be multiple and complex, an intricate 'union of bodies.'"[44] Throughout his work, Darwin underscores the unpredictability and creativity of such perceptual acts: their power not to see things that do not exist, but instead to see things that might otherwise have gone unremarked.[45] He also calls attention to the pressure they place on any presuppositions regarding the definition of the human being. As I discuss in the introduction, pain would seem to define the subject inescapably, if only because of the tragic impossibility of knowing the physical experience of the other. Darwin challenges this notion, calling attention to the difficulty of making pain stay still. Pain is thus generative; it is not, however, always generative of things that unambiguously resemble human beings.

Perhaps the simplest way to explain what I mean by the fecundity or productivity of pain in Darwin is to take a detour through two of the most influential theorists to understand the naturalist's work in relation to Spinoza: Gilles Deleuze and Félix Guattari.[46] It is not entirely accurate to equate Darwin's ontology and theirs, for they attach a political optimism to what they call "becoming" that Darwin does not. Nevertheless, their account of Darwin helps emphasize the unpredictability, ontological status, and aesthetic pleasure at stake in his understanding of the thing.[47] According to Deleuze and Guattari, "becoming" is about co-implication, but not psychology. It is about change, but not transformation:

> Becoming is not to imitate or identify with something or someone. Nor is it to proportion formal relations.... Starting from the forms one has, the subject one is, the organs one has, or the functions one fulfills, becoming is to extract particles between which one establishes the relations of movement and rest, speed and slowness that are *closest* to what one is becoming, and through which one becomes.[48]

In order to explain what this might look like, Deleuze and Guattari turn to Darwin's account of the interdependency of the wasp and the orchid. "*Epi-*

pactis latifolia seems to be fertilised by wasps alone," Darwin explains in *The Various Contrivances by Which Orchids are Fertilised by Insects* (1862).[49] As a result, "were wasps to become extinct in any district, so probably would the *Epipactis latifolia*."[50] According to Deleuze and Guattari, interdependency of this kind makes wasp and orchid aspects of a single entity that is irreducible to the sum of its parts. "There is a block of becoming," they write, "that snaps up the wasp and the orchid, but from which no wasp-orchid can ever descend."[51] To use Spinoza's terms, wasp and orchid may constitute two individuals, but they have a single "effect," and so, effectively, constitute a single thing.

In Darwin's larger corpus, coevolution of the kind Deleuze and Guattari describe constitutes a particularly interesting and theoretically productive site of "becoming," but it is by no means the only one. Many different forms of coming together challenge any easy prediction of the object of study. The most familiar are those that can be understood in terms of interdependency. For example, the "complex relations" that characterize the interactions of all plants and animals pose particularly complicated questions regarding where a particular thing begins and ends—as in Darwin's description of the relation between cats and flowers, which makes it seem nearly impossible to draw a bright line around his object of study:

> The number of humble-bees in any district depends in a great degree on the number of field-mice, which destroy their combs and nests; and Mr. H. Newman, who has long attended to the habits of humble-bees, believes that "more than two-thirds of them are thus destroyed all over England." Now the number of mice is largely dependent, as every one knows, on the number of cats; and Mr. Newman says, "Near villages and small towns I have found the nests of humble-bees more numerous than elsewhere, which I attribute to the number of cats that destroy the mice." Hence it is quite credible that the presence of a feline animal in large numbers in a district might determine, through the intervention first of mice and then of bees, the frequency of certain flowers in that district! (*O* 59)

Flower populations depend on bees, which depend on mouse populations, which depend, in turn, on cats. Hence cats and flowers come to seem inextricably linked as aspects of a single thing whose precise name is difficult to specify. Here, it might be "district." At the end of the *Origin*, it is, famously, "tangled bank."

> It is interesting to contemplate an entangled bank, clothed with many plants of many kinds, with birds singing on the bushes, with various insects flitting about, and with worms crawling through the damp earth, and to reflect that these elaborately constructed forms, so different from each other, and dependent on each other in so complex a manner, have all been produced by laws acting around us. (*O* 360)

Where we may think we see multiplicity, we do; but we *also* see a single interconnected system, no single aspect of which can be wholly separated from the others. The chain of interdependencies goes on and on. The fact it has no end is a source of both pleasure and terror.[52]

Thanks in part to Darwin's own work, the notion that plants, buds, and insects constitute elements of complex ecosystems from which it is difficult to isolate them has become fairly familiar. Elsewhere in his writings, however, Darwin betrays a fascination with much less obvious forms of what he calls "compound" existence. In the section on "compound animals" in *Journal of Researches*, for example, his often-noted tendency toward anthropomorphism is both evidenced and baffled.[53] "In the Crisia," he writes, "if the bristles were excited to move by irritation in any one branch, generally the whole zoophyte was affected. In the instance where the branch started from the simultaneous movement of these appendages, we see as perfect a transmission of will as in a single animal."[54] Thinking in terms of "will" here both helps in the imagination of the compound animal and makes apparent its strangeness—and that seems to be exactly the point. Referencing the description of trees as compound organisms given by his grandfather, Erasmus Darwin, Darwin continues: "The known organization of a tree should remove all surprise at the union of many individuals together, and their relation to a common body.... It requires, however, a greater effort of reason to view a bud as an individual, than a polypus furnished with a mouth and intestines; and therefore the union does not appear so strange."[55] The Crisia is *both* one and many, a single will and many different individuals, each "furnished with a mouth and intestines." As such, it represents something like a permanent state of becoming—one that is scientifically productive, insofar as it provides us with a way to grasp the "compound status" of something that might be much more difficult to understand in such terms: the tree.[56]

Part of what is remarkable in passages like these is the palpable pleasure involved in witnessing such counterintuitive phenomena—a pleasure of which Darwin himself was well aware. As he writes in his M Notebook as part of his meditation on the "pleasure of the imagination": "I am sure I remember my pleasure in Kensington Garden has often been excited by looking at trees at [as] great compound animals united by wonderful & mysterious manner."[57] At such a moment, Darwin appears to be staging something like what Lorraine Daston and Katharine Park describe as a post-Enlightenment form of wonder, in which wonder constitutes an "expression of the natural ... order of laws."[58] Darwin's work contains many such moments in which we are asked to marvel at the sheer strangeness and beauty of the natural world. Yet the role aesthetic pleasure plays in being able to see differently is also perceptible in instances that seem far afield from Darwin's scientific investigations: those that have nothing to do with evolution, or codependence, but are instead the product of a momentary coming together, repurposing, or transmission of characteristics. In *Journal of Researches*, Darwin describes being appalled by the way the gauchos treat their animals: "Animals are so abundant in these countries that humanity and self-interest are not clearly united," he explains.[59] Nevertheless, he is also enthralled by their ability to come together with their animals. "I was one day watching a good rider," he writes,

> as we were galloping along at a rapid pace, and thought to myself, "surely if the horse starts, you appear so careless on your seat you must fall." At this moment, a male ostrich sprang from its nest right beneath the horse's nose. The young colt bounded on one side, like a stag; but as for the man, all that could be said, was, that he started and took fright, as part of his horse.[60]

"Taking fright" here references both what the horse (and the man) do, and also what he or they feel. Hence, at the moment of "starting," man and horse become the cause of one effect: the man does not move with the horse so much as he literally becomes part of him, as both man and horse become "man on horse starting and taking fright." The pleasure apparent here is not exactly scientific wonder since it exposes no generalizable order or law. Instead, it is simply another version of the "pleasure of the imagination"—imagination here not being devoted to making things up so much as to seeing them as they are.

Examples like these could go on and on: Darwin's writings are replete with instances in which one thing is actually revealed to be two or more, or in which many temporarily or permanently become one. They offer descriptions of how one kind of thing becomes another, as well as descriptions of how a thing we might understand in one set of terms can *also* be understood in radically different, and sometimes contradictory, ones. The palpable excitement around these moments makes it especially tempting to rehearse them. I have described just a few to help underscore the aesthetic pleasure Darwin derives from becoming: the sheer joy he manifests in his own power to perceive and the world's ability to offer endless things for him to reconceive. I have also offered them in the hope that they will help make clear the strangeness of the passages to which I now turn, passages in which the "effect" that makes the thing is not horse riding, or tangled-bank-ness, but instead pain.

The notion that pain is generative in this way might seem strange, not just in relation to Darwin but in relation to Spinoza, as well. Spinoza explicitly brackets aversive physical experience on the grounds that, like "cheerfulness, pleasure, melancholy," pain is "chiefly related to the body" and is "only a species of joy or sadness."[61] "Sadness" here refers to "that *passion by which* [the mind] *passes to a lesser perfection*": it diminishes its power of acting, its power to affect and be affected.[62] Pain, for Spinoza, is thus equated with a *diminished* power to generate new things—an equation that might seem to hold for Darwin, as well. "Pain or suffering of any kind," he writes in his "Recollections" (1876–81, pub. 1887), "if long continued, causes depression and lessens the power of action."[63] Thus, although it "is well adapted to make a creature guard itself against any great or sudden evil," pain over the longer term can only be regarded as destructive.[64] On this point, in particular, Spinoza and Darwin seem to be in agreement. Yet, at least in Darwin's case, this is not the end of the story, for as he explains in *The Descent of Man, and Selection in Relation to Sex* (1871), we are social animals, and the "social instincts lead an animal to take pleasure in the society of its fellows, to feel a certain amount of sympathy with them, and to perform various services for them."[65] On a basic level, what this might mean is that however depressing pain may be for the person who experiences it, it may act as a stimulant to others. It serves as a strange kind of stimulant, however, for in acting on its observer, it also begins to break down the self-evidence of the question of who exactly is the observer and who might be regarded as the one actually in pain.

Darwin uses the term "sympathy" to describe this problem, but that term threatens to make the process he describes seem too familiar.[66] For in the context of his monism, in particular, the entrance into another's feelings ends up seeming as if it has a material as well as a psychological aspect.[67] As a result, what we might call sympathy allows human animals to use one another to fulfill certain biological imperatives, to make themselves many, or many into one, or else to confuse the question of what constitutes a person altogether. Earlier in this chapter, for example, I described how Darwin suggests that the Englishman may be prohibited from weeping on his own behalf because of a cultural perception of the weakness and unmanliness of doing so. In discussing that example, I raised a question about the fate of the nerve force that Darwin suggests must and yet at the same time cannot be discharged. The Englishman does not cease to feel pain; he only ceases to express that pain in ways that might afford him relief. As Darwin goes on to explain, however, the prohibition on male tears is not all-encompassing: on the contrary, the gentleman has access to several conditions under which he is allowed to weep. "It is not a little remarkable that sympathy with the distresses of others should excite tears *more freely* than our own distress," Darwin explains, for example (*E* 216, emphasis added). Nevertheless,

> this certainly is the case. Many a man, from whose eyes no suffering of his own could wring a tear, has shed tears at the sufferings of a beloved friend.... We should, however, bear in mind that the long-continued habit of restraint which is so powerful in checking the free flow of tears from bodily pain, has not been brought into play in preventing a moderate effusion of tears in sympathy with the sufferings or happiness of others. (*E* 216)

It might seem like a bit of a stretch to imagine that the "beloved friend" here serves as a kind of prosthetic for the man barred from weeping on his own behalf. Yet, in a monistic universe, imagination is more than simply a mental activity. It can also be regarded under a material aspect that could serve a concrete function for the sympathizer. The man who weeps for his friend inevitably weeps for himself, as well, for the discharge of nerve force takes place regardless of whose pain is being lamented or expressed.

This, however, is not the only way that men are allowed to weep. Weeping from pain or sorrow for oneself is apparently prohibited, but weeping from pain or sorrow for oneself *as if* one was someone else is not. This becomes particularly apparent in Darwin's attempt to puzzle out why men occasionally weep from joy.

> Many a father and son have wept on meeting after a long separation, especially if the meeting has been unexpected. No doubt extreme joy by itself tends to act on the lacrymal [*sic*] glands; but on such occasions as the foregoing vague thoughts of the grief which would have been felt had the father and son never met, will probably have passed through their minds; and grief naturally leads to the secretion of tears. (*E* 214–15)

Here, tears are not the product of felt pain, but instead of the pain that might have been felt under other conditions. As a result, while in the previous example, one man's sympathy with another may be understood in some sense to make the two men one thing, here two men's sympathy with counterfactual versions of themselves in some sense makes those two men four: the men they are, and the men they are not, but might have been. The very nonsensicality of this conclusion begins to indicate the way that male tears come to seem as if they signal the fact that the weeper is *not* in pain, but that someone else is, even if that someone else in some very real sense does not exist, or is somehow also himself.

The confusion of subjects apparent in the father-son passage is only complicated in what is perhaps the most famous passage of *The Expression*: that in which Darwin describes observing an elderly woman on a train. Part of what is so striking about the passage is how novelistic it seems in its imagination of the other's suffering. The "fiction" he writes here, however, is effectively his own.

> I may here mention a trifling observation, as it will serve to sum up our present subject. An old lady with a comfortable but absorbed expression sat nearly opposite to me in a railway carriage. Whilst I was looking at her, I saw that her *depressores anguli oris* became very slightly, yet decidedly, contracted; but as her countenance remained as placid as ever, I reflected how meaningless was this contraction, and how easily one might be deceived. The thought had hardly occurred to me

when I saw that her eyes suddenly became suffused with tears almost to overflowing, and her whole countenance fell. There could now be no doubt that some painful recollection, perhaps that of a long-lost child, was passing through her mind. As soon as her sensorium was thus affected, certain nerve-cells from long habit instantly transmitted an order to all the respiratory muscles, and to those round the mouth, to prepare for a fit of crying. But the order was countermanded by the will, or rather by a later acquired habit, and all the muscles were obedient, excepting in a slight degree the *depressores anguli oris*. (*E* 193–94)

The child Darwin imagines having died is usually identified as his own daughter Annie, whose death at the age of ten he claimed affected him for the rest of his life.[68] At the moment when Darwin attributes thoughts of "a long-lost child" to the woman he observes, therefore, one can see him momentarily "becoming" the old lady, even if, as the passage goes on, he pulls himself back from such confusion. By the end of the passage, rather than Darwin becoming the old lady, the old lady has become evolutionary. The work required to maintain this distance is notable, however. Pain is powerful—whether one's own or someone else's. One of its effects is to call precisely that distinction into question.

Such confusions become only more complicated and suggestive when Darwin wades into the muddy waters of simulated emotion. For according to his theory, it is difficult to imagine how any simulation would ever remain securely in place, if only because expression has such intense power to generate feeling. As Darwin explains:

> The free expression by outward signs of an emotion intensifies it. On the other hand, the repression, as far as this is possible, of all outward signs softens our emotions.... These results follow partly from the intimate relation which exists between almost all the emotions and their outward manifestations; and partly from the direct influence of exertion on the heart, and consequently on the brain. Even the simulation of an emotion tends to arouse it in our minds. Shakespeare, who from his wonderful knowledge of the human mind ought to be an excellent judge, says:—
>
> > *Is it not monstrous that this player here,*
> > *But in a fiction, in a dream of passion,*
> > *Could force his soul so to his own conceit,*
> > *That, from her working, all his visage wann'd;*
> > *Tears in his eyes, distraction in 's aspect,*
> > *A broken voice, and his whole function suiting*
> > *With forms to his conceit? And all for nothing!*
>
> HAMLET, ACT 2, SCENE 2. (*E* 365)

Darwin does not analyze this passage from *Hamlet*: immediately after this passage, he turns instead to the continuity between human and nonhuman animals. It is thus difficult to know what to do with it: the passage does not exactly speak clearly for itself, nor does it make much sense in context. In the paragraph prior to the long quote, Darwin raises a question regarding the priority of feeling or expression. We may express because we feel, he suggests, but we may also feel because we express. The paragraph from *Hamlet* does not exactly make this point, however, although Darwin cites it as if it does. Instead, Hamlet ruminates on the way the players he hired to reenact the murder of his father were able to express emotions they did *not* feel. We are given no reason to believe the actors themselves *feel* the emotions they mime, in other words—only that they express them. As a result, it is difficult to know how to understand Darwin's claim that the lines demonstrate the way "even the simulation of an emotion tends to arouse it in our minds." Does he mean that we, like Hamlet, respond to others' expressions even when we know they are not the product of real emotions? That is the most obvious interpretation, but it does not actually make sense in the context of the preceding paragraph. Is Darwin instead claiming that the players feel what they perform? Possibly, but since they have no deep relation to the action, that would suggest that the tears they shed are somehow *identical to* feelings, and hence, that expression and emotion are to some extent one and the same thing. If understood in the larger context of the scene, Darwin's use of the passage becomes even more obscure.

> What's Hecuba to him, or he to Hecuba,
> That he should weep for her? What would he do,
> Had he the motive and the cue for passion
> That I have? He would drown the stage with tears
> And cleave the general ear with horrid speech,
> Make mad the guilty and appall the free,
> Confound the ignorant, and amaze indeed
> The very faculties of eyes and ears. Yet I,
> A dull and muddy-mettled rascal, peak,
> Like John-a-dreams, unpregnant of my cause,
> And can say nothing.
>
> (*HAMLET*, ACT 2, SCENE 2, L. 586-96)

As in the example of the father and son who weep for themselves as others, here Hamlet uses the actor as a kind of thought experiment in the emotions he would have—and the actions he would perform—were he the kind of person the actor pretends to be. He then compares that counterfactual with his own "real self": a procedure that in some sense transforms that self into the person he imagines. In such a moment, Hamlet effectively feels the feelings that the actor imitates as well as his own. He is able to compare them and also feel something about the comparison. It may not be possible to say exactly whose feeling he ultimately feels, or even who "he" is, but rather than a problem, that seems to be a condition of the possibility of change. Pain is thus as prolific here as it is everywhere else, even though the "things" it produces are not necessarily stable or easily defined.

Darwin's Affect Theory

"Affect theory" remains a highly contested term whose definition varies widely. There are, however, at least two tendencies in much of the work commonly grouped under this rubric that Darwin helps us examine critically. The first is what Ruth Leys has described as affect theory's commitment to "understanding the affects in biological terms"—a commitment that is itself often explicitly traced back to Darwin.[69] According to Elizabeth A. Wilson, for example, what makes Darwin so important for affect theory has to do with the way his materialism "displaced consciousness (and its cerebral seat) from the center of evolutionary explanation. Darwin's early notebooks on emotional expression locate his curiosity in the nervous body, rather than in the conscious mind-brain."[70] By contrast with someone like Wilson who disaggregates psychology and physiology, culture and nature, in order to show how Darwin describes them as interconnected, the first section of this chapter argues that in Darwin's work, such distinctions fail to gain traction in the first place.[71] Even pain, which might seem as if it should constitute the most wholly biological and hence nonnegotiable of all the "emotions" Darwin examines, ultimately comes to seem either cultural or biological, depending on what Spinoza terms the "aspect" under which it is "considered."

The second tendency in contemporary affect theory that I think Darwin helps us reconsider involves the equation that is so often made between affect and progressive politics. This tendency is extraordinarily common. For example, the editors of *The Affect Theory Reader*, Melissa Gregg and Gregory S. Seigworth, take affect's relation to "a body's perpetual *becoming*" as legitimating affect theory's optimism: "casting a line along the hopeful (though also fearful) cusp of an emergent futurity, casting its lot with the infinitely connectable, impersonal, and contagious belongings to *this* world."[72] Ben Anderson effectively equates affect with hope in that both can be described in terms of an aporia that "anticipates something that has *not-yet become*."[73] Meanwhile, Teresa Brennan suggests in *The Transmission of Affect* that affect is necessarily antiimperialist and antiglobalization, since "globalization, after all, is quite mad in the technical sense ('a danger to oneself and others'), insofar as it is destroying the long-term conditions of human survival."[74] In contrast to these writers, for Darwin, affect as what Spinoza defines as the "affections of the body by which the body's power of acting is increased or diminished" has no value, positive or negative. It is simply a condition of being —and this is as true of "becomings" related to pain as it is to anything else. "That there is much suffering in the world no one disputes," he writes in his "Recollections."

> Some have attempted to explain this in reference to man; by imagining that it serves for his moral improvement. But the number of men in the world is as nothing compared with that of all other sentient beings, & these often suffer greatly without any moral improvement. A being so powerful & so full of knowledge as a God who could create the universe, is to our finite minds omnipotent & omniscient, & it revolts out understanding to suppose that his benevolence is not unbounded, for what advantage can there be in the sufferings of millions of the lower animals throughout almost endless time?[75]

Suffering may reflect the fact of natural selection, but that does not make it meaningful. The only thing it can possibly tell us is the negative lesson of the nonexistence of God. In place of any divine order, or any natural political progressivism, all Darwin can point to is the fact of endless transformation, one name for which might be "affect." Affect may constitute an object of fascination or interest, but it offers no political prescriptions. It is no more nor less than a condition of being.

At the beginning of this chapter, I introduced Darwin's description of the earthquake at Concepcion as an image of the instability of his perspective. This same passage seems, too, like a good place to end, insofar as it points to the political unpredictability of Darwin's affect theory.[76] "I have not attempted to give any detailed description of the appearance of Concepcion [after the earthquake]," he writes in his *Journal of Researches*,

> for I feel it is quite impossible to convey the mingled feelings with which one beholds such a spectacle. Several of the officers visited it before me, but their strongest language failed to communicate a just idea of the desolation. It is a bitter and humiliating thing to see works, which have cost men so much time and labour, overthrown in one minute; yet compassion for the inhabitants is almost instantly forgotten, from the interest excited in finding that state of things produced in a moment of time, which one is accustomed to attribute to a succession of ages.[77]

The earthquake is horrible. Its consequences are appalling. The pain of its victims is in no way redeemable. That does not, however, make the spectacle itself less fascinating and compelling.

CHAPTER FIVE

Wounded Trees, Abandoned Boots

Altruism, or the Golden Rule, or whatever "Love your Neighbor as Yourself" may be called, will ultimately be brought about by the pain we see in others reacting on ourselves, as if we and they were part of one body. Mankind, in fact, may be and possibly will be viewed as members of one corporeal frame.

—THOMAS HARDY, JOURNAL ENTRY (MARCH–APRIL, 1890),
QUOTED IN FLORENCE EMILY HARDY,
THE EARLY LIFE OF THOMAS HARDY (1928)

Suppose I feel a pain which on the evidence of the pain alone, e.g., with closed eyes, I should call a pain in my left hand. Someone asks me to touch the painful spot with my right hand. I do so and looking round perceive that I am touching my neighbour's hand (meaning the hand connected to my neighbour's torso)....

An innumerable variety of cases can be thought of in which we should say that someone has pains in another person's body; or, say, in a piece of furniture, or in any empty spot.

—LUDWIG WITTGENSTEIN, *THE BLUE AND BROWN BOOKS* (1933–35)

ALTHOUGH ALL THE WRITERS I examine in this book take pain as a central problem, none address it with the single-mindedness that characterizes Thomas Hardy.[1] His plots, in particular, have been repeatedly singled out for criticism in this respect: they are relentlessly dreary and only become more so over the course of his career.[2] Such gloom is not unmixed with glimpses of joy, but as Gillian Beer points out, "The urgency of intended happiness, intended perfection, pervades Hardy's text, but its poignancy derives from the failures of perfection, the unfulfilled, skewed, and disturbed."[3] We feel the tragedy so much precisely because we are also made to feel this potential for happiness. Again and again Hardy insists on the consistency with which accident—whether in the form of social convention and inherited belief, the difficulty of communication, or the fragility of the body—thwarts human desires and aspirations. Few plans come to fruition in his works, and even when they do, they are almost always attended by disappointment.[4]

The suffering that is described in—and some readers have claimed also disseminated by—Hardy's work has often been identified with what has been called his "pessimism." The writer himself rejected any notion that he offered a consistent or fully developed philosophy, insisting on his status as an artist rather than a philosopher.[5] Nevertheless, as Mark Asquith explains, many critics have extrapolated from his novels a unified conception of "a world governed by deterministic laws."[6] Critics have attributed this cosmic vision variously to Hardy's encounters with the work of Herbert Spencer, Arthur Schopenhauer, Edward Von Hartmann, Charles Darwin, among others—very different thinkers who have been used to generate very different kinds of readings of his work.[7] Regardless of their emphasis, however, most have accepted the centrality of the writer's sense that the universe lacks any divine plan. As Hardy wrote in a letter to Alfred Noyes (and then reproduced in *The Later Years of Thomas Hardy* [1930]), "my sober opinion—so far as I have any definite one—of the Cause of Things ... [is] that the said Cause is neither moral nor immoral, but *un*moral: 'loveless and hateless' I have called it, 'which neither good nor evil knows'—etc., etc."[8] Although here this unmorality goes unspecified, elsewhere he clearly identifies it with the existence of physical pain. As he wrote in his attack on what he saw as a defense of Maurice Maeterlinck's "vindication of nature's ways though they may not be ours":

> Pain has been and pain is: no new sort of morals in Nature can remove pain from the past and make it pleasure for those who are its infallible estimators, the bearers thereof....
>
> So you cannot, I fear, save her good name except by assuming one of two things: that she is blind and not a judge of her actions, or that she is an automaton, and unable to control them.[9]

The existence of physical pain served Hardy as proof that whatever happiness we achieve requires that we ignore the basic circumstance of our existence: that of inhabiting a universe that places no value on our suffering. To ourselves, that suffering is so intolerable as to constitute one of the basic problems of existence. In the cosmic scheme, however, it makes no difference: it has no meaning, it has no significance.

Hardy's pessimism provides an important background to his work and a crucial point of reference for his aesthetic and ethical project. It does not, however, help explain or relieve many readers' sense of the *excessiveness* of the suffering in his work—the sense that there is something particularly difficult or depressing about his novels, even in the context of the many other fin de siècle writers who were exploring the phenomenology and meaning of what I call in the introduction "modern" or "impersonal" pain in a newly secularized universe. Hardy does not detail great amounts of physical pain: he is no simple antivivisectionist, for example, describing experiments performed on animals, or the screams those experiments elicited.[10] Nevertheless, readers have consistently identified something especially oppressive about his work. In this chapter, I focus not on Hardy's plots, painful though they may be, but instead on a few of those many moments in which the reader is asked to register the fact of pain even when that pain has no clearly identifiable location or source. Pain in Hardy is often "homeless" (to revise Veena Das's term) not just in the sense that it garners no attention or care from other characters, or even in the sense that it is socially unrecognizable, although these too are problems to which he returns continually; it is also often homeless in the sense that it is unclear who or what is supposed to be feeling it. It hovers between person and things; it moves from site to site; and it seems, at times, to be everywhere at once. Such descriptions resist being understood in the instrumental terms oftentimes brought to bear on representations of fictional suffering and instead demand an affective registration that is discomfiting at least in part because of its incompatibility with concrete ameliorative intervention.

A long tradition regards fictional representations of pain and suffering as more or less straightforward goads to action. In this account, literature disseminates knowledge and understanding of others, exposes suffering and its causes, and so encourages readers to sympathize with—and presumably feel some responsibility or concern for—those in pain. The consequence is, ideally, ameliorative intervention. As Thomas Laqueur explains, certain eighteenth- and nineteenth-century texts are particularly effective in these terms. "Anyone who has read about the black death in *Journal of a Plague Year*, the mine explosion in Zola's *Germinal*, or the prolonged death of Clarissa and of frail Paul Dombey is affected by these reports of the death of others."[11] Such texts, he continues, "expose[] the lineaments of causality and of human agency," and so represent "ameliorative action ... as possible, effective, and therefore morally imperative."[12] Representations of pain in this account are clearly instrumental: they seek to work through the emotions in order to get something done.

In this chapter, I describe Hardy as both exploring and undercutting the most basic assumptions of the humanitarian narrative. On the one hand, like the writers Laqueur describes, Hardy relies on suffering to establish a bond between those who suffer and those who read about that suffering. Particularly in his later fictions, the novelist also identifies clear causes of at least some of the suffering he describes so as to make certain forms of amelioration seem possible and even imperative. On the other hand, such descriptions are complicated by their coexistence with accounts of suffering that float ambiguously between or beyond subjects, that are attributed to no malign agent, and that hold no hope of prevention or remediation. Such descriptions do not easily fit the paradigm of the humanitarian narrative, but nor do they adhere clearly to tragic paradigms either, for they provide nothing resembling catharsis. Instead, they tend to be confused and confusing—troubling in their very vividness and beauty, as well as in the profundity of the sorrow they describe and convey. Finally, although they can certainly be called "pessimistic" in the sense that they offer no clear path for either remediation or catharsis, for that very reason they invite us to consider the disposition that might be at issue in the reading practices they encourage—affectively engaged practices that ask us to experience ourselves less as potentially responsible observers of pain than as fellow sufferers: active participants in what we also witness. We are thus implicated in Hardy's fictions, less insofar as we are asked to act on behalf of others than in the ways we are asked to feel ourselves, as the novelist puts it in the first epigraph to this chapter, as "members of one corporeal frame."

The emphasis on the suffering reader links this chapter with my discussion of *Villette*—another text in which sympathy is rejected. However, Hardy's interest in the homelessness of pain—its movement between persons and things, as well as between animals, aspects of the land, qualities of light, states of being, and products of the imagination—connects it, too, with my account of Darwin. Like Darwin, Hardy is committed to the tenuousness of any attempt to naturalize the human being as clearly distinguishable from all other things. As in Darwin, therefore, skepticism is made to seem like an almost secondary problem: Hardy is ultimately less concerned with the recognition of an other, than with a way of experiencing the self as connected to all conceivable suffering, even that which can best be described as residing, as Wittgenstein predicts, in "a piece of furniture, or in any empty spot."[13] This is not an orientation that generates a clear imagination of social life. Nevertheless, it can still be understood as a working through of some of the key issues addressed in the first chapters of this book regarding the forms of subjectivity able to keep the individual and the social in productive tension. While Mill, Martineau, and even to some extent Brontë offer some imagination of what that social existence might look like, in Hardy such an existence is made to seem like an impoverished response to a form of suffering that exists everywhere, all the time.

Wounded Trees

She wrapped round her a long red woollen cravat and opened the door. The night in all its fulness met her flatly on the threshold, like the very brink of an absolute void, or the ante-mundane Ginnung-Gap believed in by her Teuton forefathers; for her eyes were fresh from the blaze, and here there was no street-lamp or lantern to form a kindly transition between the inner glare and the outer dark. A lingering wind brought to her ear the creaking sound of two over-crowded branches in the neighboring wood which were rubbing each other into wounds, and other vocalized sorrows of the trees, together with the screech of owls, and the fluttering tumble of some awkward wood-pigeon ill-balanced on its roosting-bough.

But the pupils of her young eyes soon expanded, and she could see well enough for her purpose.[14]

What are we asked to make of the "wounded" and "sorrowing" trees in this passage near the beginning of *The Woodlanders* (1887)? They occupy very little space in the novel: as soon as Marty South's eyes adjust to the darkness, she continues with her work of carrying the spars she has just made out to the shed, and the trees' troubles seem forgotten. For the reader, however, it may be difficult to leave them entirely behind. The personifying pathos of the language used to describe them suggests that they deserve our attention: "wounds" and "sorrows" are terms we tend not to associate with trees, nor do we ordinarily think of the sounds their branches make as pain cries in the way the passage suggests we should, or at least might.[15] The extent to which their suffering seems to result from overpopulation further underscores their possible status as subjects: it makes them seem to resemble the characters in *Jude the Obscure* (1894–95) as tragic victims of their own fecundity. At the same time, however, this is clearly tree rather than human unhappiness: there is, after all, no exact human corollary for the tree's ambiguous ability to produce so many branches that it wounds itself.[16] Rather than simply being personified, therefore, these trees call attention to the way in which, as William A. Cohen has recently argued, Hardy "*de*-naturaliz[es] ... the human and the environment, [and] solicits our interest by upending a lot of conventional ideas about nature."[17] The trees' feelings may not be human, but their very intensity and resonance with the human makes it seem as if they should be attended to, and the fact that they are not, and perhaps cannot be—since Marty has troubles of her own that require she get back to work—is itself a source of pathos.

The fact that it is Marty who moves on in this way is especially striking. Although a minor character in the novel, she is one of the most ethically exemplary, consistently seeking, although also consistently failing, to further the happiness of the other characters. She attempts to save her father, and he dies, possibly as a result of her efforts; she tries to help Winterbourne, and is thwarted—and then he, too, dies; she even tries to help her rival, Grace, only to be conquered by circumstances far beyond her control. Again and again, she attempts to aid others, and just as consistently, she fails. The attention she gives to the suffering of other people is echoed in her consistent concern for the suffering of the trees. As Grace recognizes after Giles's death, only Marty matched his understanding of "that wondrous world of sap and leaves called the Hintock woods" (*W* 297). Marty, however, surpasses even her beloved in understanding: while he has hands "endowed with a gentle conjurer's touch" for planting trees, only Marty can understand their feelings: while planting young fir trees together, she tells Giles that it seems to her that the reason the trees "sigh directly we put 'em upright" is that "they are very sorry to begin life in earnest—just as we be." "Do they?" he replies. "I've never noticed it" (*W* 59). Even by comparison with the gentle conjurer, Marty's perceptiveness is made to seem extraordinary. The fact that she is the one who hears the trees' suffering in the passage with which this section begins, and yet barely pauses in her labors, thus raises a question as to what exactly it means to be attentive in this way—what purpose it serves or value it yields.

It is not entirely clear that Marty *does* register the trees' pain, however. We are told only that "a lingering wind brought [these sounds] to her ear," not that she necessarily understands their meaning, or even that she hears them (*W* 15). Marty is generally so attuned to the feelings of the trees that it seems likely we are being asked to imagine that she does, in fact, hear what the narrator suggests is there to be heard. Yet, the strangely opaque syntax of the description leaves the question open—so open, in fact, that one can also come to the opposite conclusion: that she is the *only* one who would hear the trees this way. The very subjectivism and lyricism of the description makes it possible to imagine that this might be a moment of unmarked free indirect discourse, and hence, a projection of Marty's own feelings onto the trees.[18] At this early point in the novel, she has good reason for the depressive perspective that would hear the trees as suffering: her father is very ill; once he dies, she will be left bereft of both beloved parent and the home they share; in the meantime, she is making ends meet by making spars for thatching, an occupation that is clearly beneath her. Finally, the object of her love, Giles Winterbourne, is in love with another woman. None of these sorrows *exactly* lines up with the trees' sorrows, even though the wounded branches do recall the "red and blistering" palm that results from her labors, and the overcrowded state of the trees resonates with the sense throughout the novel that there are both too few and too many lovers to go around (*W* 10). Rather than an exact match, therefore, the sense we get is simply a family resemblance between the suffering Marty may or may not hear and that which she so clearly feels. Again, however, such resonances do not suggest that Marty is necessarily distorting what she hears. Instead, the echoes between Marty's and the trees' suffering raise a question as to whose pain is being heard—or whether it even makes sense to ask where Marty's pain ends and that of the trees begins.

Passages like this one, fleeting as it is, are one of the principal, though barely recognized, reasons why readers have claimed to find Hardy's novels so difficult to read.[19] We live in a universe of suffering, it suggests; some of it can be called "tree" and some of it can be called "Marty," but such distinctions may not ultimately make much of a difference. Suffering is everywhere all the time, and there is nothing whatsoever to be done about it. Even Marty's actions are in no way modified by her sense of the trees' suffering. She continues to plant them, despite her impression that they would prefer not to "begin life in earnest." She is one of the "barkers" who leave the oaks "flay[ed]" and "naked-legged" without their bark (*W* 122). In the passage that begins this section, as soon as her eyes adjust to the darkness, she returns to her labors. There is something callous about this failure to pause, but there is also something inevitable about it, insofar as the pain itself is irremediable, and she has work that needs to be done. Nor are the trees the only ones who seem beyond help: in part because of its imbrication with the trees' suffering, Marty's pain seems unavailable to aid, as well. Her father's death might be delayed, her poverty might be relieved, and Winterbourne might come to recognize the value of her love for him. Aside from all these concrete and identifiable sources of sadness and pain, however, there is a strong sense in the text that her suffering is essentially existential: as she says about the trees, "They sigh because they are very sorry to begin life in earnest—just as we be." In this moment, she identifies her own sadness not just with that of the trees, but with that of all living beings. Such inevitability makes it easy to feel as if there is something singularly pointless about recognizing either the trees' or Marty's pain. All it can do is intensify the sense—always available in a Hardy novel—that we exist in a disordered universe in which suffering is as meaningless as it is omnipresent.

Part of what is going on in this passage, then, is an instantiation of suffering: a demonstration of its inescapability and meaninglessness. Yet "instantiation" and "demonstration" fail to fully capture the way this suffering hovers ambiguously between potential sites of consciousness or affect. What is conveyed here is far less concrete and easily defined than such terms suggest, and it involves the reader in ways that are similarly difficult to identify clearly. In this passage, as in so many others in his work, Hardy exploits the resources of literary language in order to ambiguate, proliferate, and disseminate sufferings that refuse to settle into distinguishable categories. Thus, in the passage from *The Woodlanders*, Hardy pushes the possibilities of the speakerlessness of free indirect discourse to a kind of limit. Not only does it remain unclear whose perspective is being described—Marty's or the narrator's—that ambiguity makes it additionally unclear the extent to which we are to credit the description and the terms on which credit might be extended. While it is clearly the case that the branches are crowded together and, as a result, that they are making some kind of sound by virtue of rubbing up against one another, the status of these sounds as "vocalized sorrows" remains impossible to determine, even as the stakes of that determination come to seem extremely high. If this is Marty's depressive understanding of what she hears, that suggests one set of affective and ethically charged responses on our part as readers. If it is the narrator's authoritative claim regarding the implicitly human power of the trees to have sorrows and express them, that suggests another. The way in which Hardy refuses to allow us to choose one perspective or the other suggests yet a third possibility: that to choose one or the other is inadequate, and hence, that we are being asked to hold all these possibilities in suspension simultaneously. The effect is to put us as readers in Marty's position, as subjects who could hear if we chose to. In other words, the effect is to implicate us in a series of choices as readers that are structurally impossible, ethically charged, and affectively fraught.

Tess's Pain

The ambiguous and unresolvable perspective associated with Marty's relations with the trees poses a series of ethical, affective, or subjective challenges that bear further exploration. Most importantly, I want to consider what such a perspective—or perspectives—suggests about the subject able to inhabit it: what does she look like, what kind of relationship does she maintain to herself and to others, and what are the ethical and affective consequences of her experience of suffering? Before pursuing these lines of inquiry, however, it seems important to address an obvious question that arises in any discussion of noninstrumental representations of suffering, but that seems especially pressing in relation to the trajectory of Hardy's career: the problem of remediable pain. Thus far, I have focused exclusively on existential suffering. Yet as many critics have noted, in his last novels, in particular, the writer appears to become increasingly interested in concrete, identifiable, and apparently preventable forms of suffering. As Penny Boumelha points out, with *Tess of the d'Urbervilles* (1891), in particular, Hardy seems to discard what she describes as his "elaborately constructed, resolutely non-controversial public persona" and instead "came to be thought of as a writer with a philosophical-cum-moral axe to grind."[20] Throughout his career as a novelist, he may have manifested concern with the sexual double standard, and particularly with the stigma attached to women who bear children out of wedlock. He may have made reference to the threat of sexual violence and objected repeatedly to the unavailability of divorce. However, most critics have agreed that *Tess* represents a watershed in Hardy's career, marking the point at which he ceased focusing quite so much on suffering in general and instead came to prioritize identifiable and remediable social ills.[21]

Despite the plausibility of this narrative, *Tess of the d'Urbervilles* is a much more vexed case than is sometimes recognized. Tess is clearly a victim of a deplorable and avoidable series of events: Alec is obviously a villain whose failure to recognize Tess as an independent center of consciousness enables him to exploit her as a means to the end of his own pleasure. Angel only compounds Alec's crimes by rejecting and then effectively abandoning Tess after she tells him her story. All this suggests the existence not only of evils in the world, but of evils the novel form seems especially well designed to counter insofar as it holds the potential to both call our attention to and make us feel the ways in which other people feel. Thus, even as *Tess* seeks to call attention to the social evils that ruin its heroine's life, it also seems designed to help eradicate those evils by encouraging the kinds of feelings in readers that would not only prevent us from being complicit with such evils in the future, and might also encourage us to help prevent their occurrence. All this suggests a very different relation to the suffering of others from what I have been describing thus far, and something much more closely resembling the "humanitarian narrative" that Laqueur describes: like the parliamentary reports, autopsies, and sentimental novels on which he focuses, *Tess* seeks to change an existing state of affairs by changing the feelings that have allowed that state to come into existence in the first place.

However plausible a reading this may be of Hardy's novel—and its popularity alone begins to suggest how seriously it should be taken—it remains unclear that it constitutes the *entire* truth of the text, or even the locus of its principal investments, for the material ills the novel describes are not necessarily imagined to be remediable. Alec is the most explicitly and easily identified evildoer in the novel, and yet his thorough-going villainy only contributes to many readers' sense that he exists outside the principal economy of the text. Even his temporary reform as a result of Angel's father's preaching seems designed to insist on the impossibility of truly altering his nature in any of the ways that the humanitarian narrative assumes are possible. As he tells Tess when she appeals to his sense of "loving-kindness and purity," he only changed his ways because of the fear of damnation Reverend Claire instilled in him:

> O no. I'm a different sort of fellow from that! If there's nobody to say, "Do this, and it will be a good thing for you after you are dead: do that, and it will be a bad thing for you," I can't warm up. Hang it, I am not going to feel responsible for my deeds and passions if there's nobody to be responsible to.[22]

Such obduracy suggests nothing so much as that men like him will always exist, and hence that the threat of sexual violence will, as well. There is nothing that can necessarily be done about these facts, except perhaps to seek to mitigate their consequences.

Angel poses a different set of challenges, for the crimes he commits against Tess are subtler than Alec's, although perhaps even more damaging. Ultimately, I think the novel *does* have an investment in preventing the kind of cruelty he commits. Yet, as the novel's ultimate interest in Tess suggests, that cruelty is not of a kind for which the humanitarian narrative offers obvious solutions. Unlike Alec, Angel does not need to learn that Tess suffers like himself. He repeatedly acknowledges the fact of her pain, both in the past, as a result of Alec's actions, and in the present, as a result of his own. Instead, the problem seems to be that he acknowledges her pain in the wrong way, seeing it as hers rather than also as his own. He also sees it as defining her as a particular kind of subject: one to whom such things can happen, and hence, one who is unavailable to the kind of narrative he imagines for himself. In the next section of this chapter, I suggest that Tess, as well as Gabriel Oak from *Far from the Madding Crowd* (1874) and Marty South, offer potential examples for ethically responsible engagement with pain, both one's own and that of others. Before I do, it seems worth exploring the exact nature of Angel's failure as a way to think about the disposition that would enable him finally to "judge[] Tess constructively rather than biographically, by the will rather than the deed" (*T* 392).

One way to understand Angel's failure is in terms of what Veena Das calls the task of making a home for the pain of the other. In her essay, "Language and Body: Transactions in the Construction of Pain," Das describes a story by Sa'adat Hasan Manto in which a father and daughter are separated while traveling from one side of the newly established border between India and Pakistan to the other. The daughter is finally found hiding in the forest, "half crazed with fear," and is brought to a clinic where her father meets her. By the time she arrives, it is not clear whether she is alive or dead. Das's summary of the story continues as follows:

> Reacting to the heat and suffocation in the room, the doctor points to the window and says, "*khol do*—open it." There is a movement in the dead body. The hands move toward the tape of the *salwar* (trouser) and fumble to unloosen (literally, open) it. Old Sarajjudin shouts in joy "My daughter is alive—my daughter is alive." The doctor is drenched in sweat.[23]

In her original reading of this scene, Das writes, she "saw Sakina [the daughter] condemned to a living death" and her father mistaking "the movement in the body as a sign of life whereas in truth it is the sign of her living death."[24] Later, however, she came to rethink her interpretation:

> In the societal context of this period, when ideas of purity and honor densely populated the literary narratives as well as family and political narratives, so that fathers willed their daughters to die for family honor rather than live with bodies that had been violated by other men, *this father wills his daughter to live even as parts of her body can do nothing else but proclaim her brutal violation.*[25]

Das proposes seeing in the father's words an attempt to imagine how "the pain of [a] female body so violated can live in a male body": "In the speech of the father, at least, the daughter is alive, and though she may find an existence only in his utterance, he creates through his utterance a home for her mutilated and violated self."[26] The father is not necessarily either right or wrong: "Although it has the formal appearance of an indicative statement,"

Das explains, the father's cry makes no truth claim but instead constitutes a kind of speech act that "beseech[es] the daughter to find a way to live in the speech of the father."[27]

The relevance of Das's account of Manto's story to Tess's seems self-evident: like Sakina, Tess is the object of sexual violence. Unlike her, however, rather than being offered the shelter of the father's exclamation, "My daughter is alive!", Tess is confronted with Angel's insistence, after she tells him her story, that "the woman I have been loving is not you." "But who?" she asks. "Another woman in your shape" comes the answer (*T* 248–49). Rather than giving his wife the opportunity to "live on" in his words, Angel effectively proclaims Tess's death—a proclamation then literalized in the sleepwalking scene, in which Angel goes through the motions of burying her.[28] "My poor poor Tess, my dearest darling Tess! So sweet, so good, so true!" he exclaims, holding her in his arms, "rolled ... in the sheet as in a shroud." The passage continues:

> The words of endearment, withheld so severely in his waking hours, were inexpressibly sweet to her forlorn and hungry heart. If it had been to save her weary life she would not, by moving or struggling, have put an end to the position she found herself in. Thus she lay in absolute stillness, scarcely venturing to breathe.... "My wife—dead, dead!" he said. (*T* 267)

Angel carries her outside, across a narrow footbridge, to the ruined choir of the Abbey-church, and places her carefully in the "empty stone coffin of an abbot.... Having kissed her lips a second time he breathed deeply, as if a greatly desired end were attained," and he goes to sleep beside the coffin (*T* 268). Tess then gently leads him back to his bed without waking him or telling him what he has done. Angel's refusal to see the Tess he loved in the woman who was raped seems, in a very real sense, to seal her death warrant—not just in this scene, but in everything that happens after this point in the novel. Even her murder of Alec and her execution can be understood as consequences of Angel's failure to make a home for her pain: a way to live on despite all that has happened to her.

It is not entirely clear, however, what making a home for Tess's pain might involve. I do not wish to oversimplify Sakina's story: as Das's invocation of a living death begins to suggest, life and death are not the only possible outcomes. Tess's case, however, is even less straightforward. First, we have no precise understanding of what exactly her pain consists of. We are never made privy to either of her confessions: her accounts to both her mother and Angel of whatever happened with Alec remain securely outside the narrative. Further, Hardy goes to great lengths to obscure whatever happens to Tess in the woods—not just in the sense of failing to describe it, but also in the sense of inviting several competing and incompatible interpretations. Generation after generation of critics have sought to determine the precise nature of the rape or seduction, but as J. T. Laird has shown, Hardy went to great lengths to ensure the impossibility of answering that question.[29] This is not to say it does not matter in the novel. The very fact that our attention is repeatedly drawn to the fact that we do not know suggests it is very important—or, more precisely, that Hardy wants to call attention to the fact that we cannot know, even as he incites our desire for that knowledge. Second, by interposing so much time between the rape and Angel's courtship, Hardy makes clear that by the time Tess marries, whatever pain she experienced as a result of Alec's actions or the birth and subsequent death of her baby have been transmuted into purely social sentiments: a question not of inner sensations, but of social judgments, received stigmas, and irrelevant conventions. Even shortly after the rape, we are told that Tess's unhappiness is social rather than personal. "Alone in a desert island would she have been wretched at what had happened to her?", the narrator demands shortly after her child is born. The passage continues:

> Not greatly. If she could have been just created, to discover herself as a spouseless mother, with no experience of life except as the parent of a nameless child, would the position have caused her to despair? No, she would have taken it calmly, and found pleasures therein. Most of the misery had been generated by her conventional aspect, and not by her innate sensations. (*T* 104)

Although in "harmony with the actual world," she terrifies herself with "phantoms and voices antipathetic to her" that are "based on shreds of convention," and so "mak[es] a distinction where there was no difference. Feeling herself in antagonism, she was quite in accord. She had been made to break an accepted social law, but no law known to the environment in which she fancied herself such an anomaly" (*T* 97–98). By the time of her marriage, even these feelings appear largely to have died out, conquered by "the irresistible, universal, automatic tendency to find sweet pleasure somewhere, which pervades all life" (*T* 119). While at Crick's Dairy, she is described as "even now only a young woman of twenty, one who mentally and sentimentally had not finished growing." As a result, the narrator insists, "it was impossible that any event should have left upon her an impression that was not in time capable of transmutation" (*T* 119). Her principal unhappiness by the time of her marriage, therefore, is the result of her concern for Angel's feelings: how he will react to her confession.

According to Elaine Scarry, what makes Tess such a valuable character in the novel is her refusal to embrace the opportunities afforded by the fact that bodies do, in fact, recover from physical trauma, and hence that by the time Angel meets Tess at the dairy, she no longer bears any visible marks of what has happened to her. "If, as readers have sometimes asserted, Hardy is in love with Tess, surely the attribute that most compels his love is her capacity for self-substantiation in the midst of transformation.... To disown the younger self that rode in a cart carrying beehives one night or rode on a horse a second night is to substitute a different, younger self, to replace the sixteen-year-old Tess with another sixteen-year-old girl."[30] Scarry is clearly correct to claim that we are made to feel as if Tess has no ethical choice but to tell Angel what happened to her. Yet, what Scarry calls "self-substantiation" is offered less as a triumph on her part than as a tragic necessity in a social context that imagines sexual and reproductive history to define the individual. In that sense, Tess's confession, whatever its content, effectively gets as much wrong as it does right. Something obviously happened to her that night in the woods—something that altered her irrevocably. However, the narrator makes clear she was also altered by Prince's death, her departure from her home to Crick's Dairy, and the experience of falling in love with Angel. The privileging of the one event over the others is thus a social necessity rather a reflection of any deep truth about Tess.

One might, then, understand Angel's failure in relation to Tess as that of failing to make a home for Tess's pain, and hence, to say, "you live," as Sakina's father does. One might also claim that his failure inheres in the fact that he effectively makes *too much* of a home for that pain—too concrete, stable, and permanent a dwelling for something that turns out to have constituted only one moment among many that have made Tess who she is.[31] Angel does not, after all, imagine Tess dead with disgust or loathing, as the fathers Das describes do in relation to their daughters: the "archetypical motif" against which Manto's story is written "is of a girl finding her way to her parents after having been subjected to rape and plunder and being told, 'Why are you here—it would have been better if you were dead.'"[32] By contrast with such parents, Angel carries Tess to her tomb gently and lovingly, and insists, even in his sleep, that she was good and true. Angel may simply have read too much Samuel Richardson and so can equate rape only with madness or death. "O you cannot be out of your mind!" he exclaims when Tess first tells him of her experience. "You ought to be! Yet you are not.... My wife, my Tess—nothing in you warrants such a supposition as that?" "I am not out of my mind," she replies (*T* 247–48). He seems unable to comprehend the fact that Tess did not just live on after she was raped; she went on to flourish. Pain of the kind she experienced, he insists, is a prison from which there is no escape. Hence, even in the absence of any visible mark of her suffering, all he can do is see her as a completely different person. "O Tess, forgiveness does not apply to the case!" he tells her, in response to her plea that he "forgive me as you are forgiven! *I* forgive *you*, Angel." "You were one person," he insists, "now you are another. My God—how can forgiveness meet such a grotesque—prestidigitation as that!" (*T* 248). For reasons I will discuss in a moment, it may not be exactly right to say that Tess is *not* in pain at the moment she marries Angel. Nevertheless, the kind of home that Angel offers for that pain—one that is ultimately a tomb—cannot constitute a desirable way to engage it.[33]

Abandoned Boots

In order to begin thinking about what alternatives to Angel's engagement with Tess's pain might look like, it seems useful to consider the ways in which Tess herself engages with the pain of others. Tess has long been recognized as an ethical exemplar. Her sense of responsibility for her siblings, her refusal to blame Angel for her fate, and her responses to suffering: all these attributes have been consistently identified as reasons for the novel's obvious valorization of her character.[34] Especially singled out for commendation is the scene in which she gently wrings the necks of the pheasants wounded by hunters and left to die.[35]

> With the impulse of a soul who could feel for kindred sufferers as much as for herself, Tess's first thought was to put the still living birds out of their torture, and to this end with her own hands she broke the necks of as many as she could find, leaving them to lie where she had found them till the gamekeepers should come, as they probably would come, to look for them a second time.
>
> "Poor darlings—to suppose myself the most miserable being on earth in the sight o' such misery as yours!" she exclaimed, her tears running down as she killed the birds tenderly. "And not a twinge of bodily pain about me! I be not mangled, and I be not bleeding, and I have two hands to feed and clothe me." She was ashamed of herself for her gloom of the night, based on nothing more tangible than a sense of condemnation under an arbitrary law of society which had no foundation in Nature. (*T* 298)

At a moment like this one, Tess puts her own suffering to one side in order to prioritize the more immediate needs of the creatures around her. Foreshadowing Hardy's own mercy killing of Tess, at this moment his character recognizes the conventionality and hence relative triviality of her own suffering, as well as the greater need of those she is also able to aid.[36]

The kind of sympathy Tess manifests at this moment seems relatively straightforward: she imagines the feelings of the pheasants, consults what Adam Smith would call the "impartial spectator" in her breast—and so is able to recognize the speciousness of her own suffering by comparison with theirs—and proceeds accordingly. This all seems fairly recognizable. Elsewhere, however, Tess's ability to imagine others' suffering, and to relate that suffering back to herself, is couched in terms that are far stranger and less predictable than those offered in the scene with the pheasants. Tess consistently thinks in terms of hypotheticals or fictions that serve both to shift her attention away from herself and to call attention to the ambiguous sense of connectedness her pity makes possible. After walking all night to see Angel's parents, for example, Tess hides her walking boots in order to make the best possible impression on her in-laws. Upon finding the Clares are at church, Tess returns to her boots, only to discover they have already been found by Mercy Chaunt, once Angel's sweetheart, and Angel's brothers, who think they were "thrown away ... by some tramp or other.... Some imposter who wished to come into the town barefoot, perhaps, and so excite our sympathies." Tess's response demonstrates the extent of her compassionate disposition. Initially, her pity is for herself: "She knew that it was all sentiment, all baseless impressibility, which had caused her to read the scene as her own condemnation; nevertheless she could not get over it" (*T* 319). Quickly, however, that self-pity is transmuted into pity for the immediate objects of her unwitting antagonists. "As she again thought of her dusty boots she almost pitied those habiliments for the quizzing to which they had been subjected, and felt how hopeless life was for their owner" (*T* 319–20). Once Tess's pity becomes attached to the boots, its quality toward herself shifts: she identifies herself as the owner of the boots, and then subsequently, as the representative of her estranged husband:

> "Ah!" she said, still sighing in pity of herself, "*they* didn't know that I wore those over the roughest part of the road to save these pretty ones *he* bought for me—no—they did not know it! And they didn't think that *he* chose the colour o' my pretty frock—no—how could they? If they had known perhaps they would not have cared; for they don't care much for him, poor thing!" (*T* 320)

Once routed through the boots, even Tess's self-pity becomes relatively impersonal, attaching to herself principally as the owner of the boots and then as Angel's wife—Angel standing in as the one really deserving of a kind of care these people seem to have denied him. At the same time, these vectors of pity—for the boots, for Angel, for herself as the owner of the boots and as Angel's wife—may seem to indict Mercy, Cuthbert, and Felix in a way that establishes an impossibly high standard for concern. In misrecognizing the boots, these people are convicted of not caring about their brother and friend. Such a suggestion expands Jesus' teaching—"whatever you did not do for one of the least of these [brothers of mine], you did not do for me"—to extraordinary limits, making it seem as if in not pitying the boots, we fail Christ, as well. On some level, this conviction seems justified by the fact that in assuming that the boots have been hidden by a tramp who is seeking to play on their sympathies, Mercy, Felix, and Cuthbert demonstrate their skeptical dispositions. On another, the fact that Tess's pity attaches so specifically to her boots suggests that they themselves are in fact appropriate objects of concern. The boots may not be able to feel, but that does not mean she is wrong to pity them, if only because that pity indicates the mobility of her imagination, with its ability to shift so quickly from self to boots, to self as related to boots, to self as related to Angel. The detour through the boots reorients Tess's sense of herself as a self, and what emerges on the other side is importantly different from the sense of self with which she began.

Moments like these do not, it should be noted, involve a confusion of self and world. Nor do they involve the kind of dissolution of self into the landscape that has sometimes been valorized in Hardy's work. Instead, individuation is critical for his vision of ethics. When Tess loses her sense of self in the garden while listening to Angel's music, for example, her absorption in what she hears makes the rest of her effectively disappear into her environment.[37]

> Tess was conscious of neither time nor space. The exaltation which she had described as being producible at will by gazing at a star, came now without any determination of hers; she undulated upon the thin notes of the second-hand harp, and their harmonies passed like breezes through her, bringing tears into her eyes. The floating pollen seemed to be his notes made visible, and the dampness of the garden the weeping of the garden's sensibility. (*T* 138–39)[38]

While a source of extreme aesthetic pleasure for the reader—and a moment of apparent happiness for Tess—the kind of unselfconsciousness signaled at this moment is at best ethically neutral and at worst dangerous, as evidenced in the irresponsibility of the farm-workers as they return home from the market, who "followed the road with a sensation that they were soaring along in a supporting medium, possessed of original and profound thoughts; themselves and surrounding nature forming an organism of which all the parts harmoniously and joyously interpenetrated each other. They were as sublime as the moon and stars above them; and the moon and stars were as ardent as they" (*T* 74). Like Tess in the garden, these workers lose any sense of themselves as subjects separate from the objects they perceive. Rather than serving the cause of love, however, it facilitates only their selfishness: this stupor contributes to their willingness to stand by while Tess is raped in the forest. Instead of simply involving a dissolution into the landscape, then, what Hardy seems to be privileging in Tess's way of seeing her boots is the imaginative capacity necessary to conceive a meaningful relationship to those boots—one that would recast her ownership of them as important for them, rather than simply for herself.

Moments like these punctuate Hardy's fiction. Tess may be a particularly privileged example, but as we began to see in the first section of this chapter, Marty South, too, possesses the power to make us consider what makes something an appropriate object of pity: the extent to which such objects need to be able to feel pain to warrant it. Nor are Tess and Marty isolated examples. Early on in *Far from the Madding Crowd*, for example, Gabriel Oak mourns the ewes and unborn lambs that have been killed as a result of his dog's overzealous "impression that since he was kept for running after sheep, the more he ran after the better."[39] Both his pity and ours move very quickly from one object to another in a way that suggests not just the value of pitying the sheep, but also the value of considering and feeling for all the other actual and potential sufferers in the situation. Oak sees the broken rails and the footprints of his ewes and feels "a sensation of bodily faintness":

> Oak looked over the precipice. The ewes lay dead and dying at its foot—a heap of two hundred mangled carcasses, representing in their condition just now at least two hundred more.
>
> Oak was an intensely humane man: indeed, his humanity often tore in pieces any politic intentions of his which bordered on strategy, and carried him on as by gravitation. A shadow in his life had always been that his flock ended in mutton—that a day came and found every shepherd an arrant traitor to his defenseless sheep. His first feeling now was one of pity for the untimely fate of these gentle ewes and their unborn lambs. (*F* 40–41)

As the narrator points out, the members of Gabriel's flock were always meant for a premature end: they were being raised in order to be killed for food. Rather than making Oak's grief seem inconsistent, however, the "shadow in his life" cast by this recognition makes his current grief seem like only an intensified instance of the grief he carries with him always. The sheep should not have died this way, nor should they have died in the way he intended. Both outcomes are occasions for pity. The fact of his intended betrayal of his flock thus only makes his grief for them remarkable in the sense that it means that their deaths represent a huge financial loss for him. The catastrophe forces him to give up his farm and his dreams of marrying Bathsheba Everdene, the woman he loves. The fact that his pity goes first to the sheep, rather than himself, thus suggests the profundity of his humanity.

Gabriel's attention does eventually turn to himself, but even when he registers what he has lost, his attention still lights on himself only briefly on his way to thinking about others. The passage quoted above continues as follows:

> It was a second to remember another phase of the matter. The sheep were not insured.—All the savings of a frugal life had been dispersed at a blow: his hopes of being an independent farmer were laid low—possibly for ever. Gabriel's energies, patience and industry had been so severely taxed, during the years of his life between eighteen and eight and twenty, to reach his present stage of progress that no more seemed to be left in him. He leant down upon a rail, and covered his face with his hands.
>
> Stupors however do not last for ever, and Farmer Oak recovered from his. It was as remarkable as it was characteristic that the one sentence he uttered was in thankfulness:
>
> "Thank God I am not married: what would *she* have done in the poverty now coming upon me!" (*F* 41)

Gabriel's attention passes to himself for a moment: he registers both the fact of what he has lost and what that loss feels like: the emptiness of whatever reservoir of "energies, patience, and industry" has sustained him for the last ten years. Very quickly, however, he recovers from his stupor and shifts his focus from his own concerns to those of the woman who might have been his wife. There is something strange about this last shift in his attention, not just because his concern is for one who has rejected his love, but also because of the way it suggests a kind of pity for a woman who in some sense does not exist: the wife he does not in fact have. His ability to be thankful he is not married, in other words, suggests his ability to imagine what his wife's experience would have been—to imagine and to some extent even pity a hypothetical—as well as to privilege her happiness above any comfort she might have given him in his distress.

The ambiguity of the relief Gabriel feels at not being married in turn echoes an ambiguity regarding the pity he feels for the sheep, as well. As I have already begun to suggest, that ambiguity is partially a product of the fact that he would have eventually been responsible for their slaughter. It is also a result of the fact that at least some of the sheep in question have yet to be born and so have a somewhat hypothetical existence themselves. The unborn lambs and Bathsheba do have some recognizable status in the world, of course, but not in the way that Gabriel must imagine them in order to pity them as he does.[40]

Both the fictionality of Gabriel's pity—the way it is extended to beings that do not unambiguously exist—and the flexibility involved in its movement from the sheep to the unborn lambs to himself to Bathsheba, not as she is, but as she might have been, echo Tess's relation to the boots. As such, they offer a glimpse of an alternative to "home" as the model for an ethical disposition toward the pain of others. The perspectives Gabriel and Tess embody do not necessarily result in any recognizably practical consequences, even though both characters are clearly identified as valuable in their respective texts. What constitutes this value seems to have less to do with practices—at least as a first aim—than with the kind of disposition that is oriented toward the suffering of others as importantly connected with their own. Hence, if Gabriel's pity for the unborn sheep and the woman who might have been his wife suggests one kind of imaginative capaciousness, one that is willing to entertain hypotheticals alongside existing states of affairs, Tess's compassion for her boots gives the outline of another, one that is able to reconceive of herself as most important or most relevant insofar as she is the owner of boots that might be misunderstood, or insofar as she is the wife of a man whose family does not value him properly. In both these cases, the pity that is felt seems most appropriately directed toward the self that pities, while the essence of the ethical imagination seems to inhere in directing that pity elsewhere.

This is not just a perspective that is described in the text, however; it is instantiated by it, too, and so made available to the reader willing to go along with its ethical program. Repeatedly, the reader is asked to maintain an affective relation to suffering we know does not exactly exist. In a sense, of course, this is what all reading of fiction involves. At moments, however, Hardy redescribes the problems posed by all fiction in ways that seem designed to challenge our willingness to go along with the simple selflessness, the mobility of the imagination able to redefine the self as attached to other things, and the willingness to entertain the possibility of suffering even where it does not or cannot exist. Consider, for example, the following passage from *Tess*:

> It was so high a situation, this field, that the rain had no occasion to fall, but raced along horizontally upon the yelling wind, sticking into them like glass splinters, till they were wet through. Tess had not known till now what was really meant by that. There are degrees of dampness, and a very little is called being wet through in common talk. But to stand working slowly in a field, and feel the creep of rainwater, first in legs and shoulders, then on hips and head, then at back, front, and sides, and yet to work on till the leaden light diminishes and marks that the sun is down, demands a distinct modicum of stoicism, even of valour. (*T* 305)

The sheer vividness of the description of Tess's physical condition places an implicit demand on us as readers to experience her suffering with her. We, too, are battered by the "glass splinters" of rain, depressed by its heaviness and creeping coldness, and deafened by the "yelling wind." How will she get through this? we ask ourselves. How will we? One possible response to such suffering, of course, is to find someone to hold responsible: one might blame Angel for the misunderstanding of his wife that led to their estrangement, the farmer's coldheartedness in allowing his field hands to work outside in such weather, or even Tess herself for her stubborn refusal to ask her husband's family for help. At the same time, however, livestock must be fed, and workers need to be paid. The only solution to both problems is for someone to labor in the rain, even if that someone is not Tess. We might be able to imagine Tess's suffering as the consequence of human error, in other words, but not necessarily the suffering of those who might come to replace her. Combined with the consistency with which she is described as a "nearly typical" farmhand, this passage makes her suffering seem to stand in for that of all field hands—something that cannot easily be remediated.

As the passage continues, however, a shift takes place that makes all our imagined responses seem irrelevant:

> Yet [Tess and Marian] did not feel the wetness so much as might be supposed. They were both young, and they were talking of the time

when they lived and loved together at Talbothays Dairy, that happy green tract of land where summer had been liberal in her gifts; in substance to all, emotionally to these. (*T* 305)

The relative insensitivity described in the second paragraph does not wholly cancel the discomfort of the first: Tess and Marian still feel some discomfort and depression, even if it is not "so much as might be supposed." The way this suffering is obscured by pleasant recollections, however, raises a question about the function of the first paragraph. The intensity of the suffering is so great—but to what possible end? It might be underscored in order to convey the power of the characters' imaginations—to impress on us that even suffering this intense can be relieved by the force of ideas. That does not wholly capture the feeling we take away from the passage, however, for by virtue of making us first imagine the pain of working in the fields and then recognize its inevitability for someone if not for Tess, it seems almost to ambiguate the difference between feeling pain and not feeling it. It thus challenges us to consider what it would mean to claim that Tess is not really suffering at this moment, or that her suffering does not count because she is not paying it proper attention. Putting the problem in these terms may once again seem to raise the bar for compassion impossibly high, making it necessary to imagine suffering as a possibility even when no suffering is being felt. But that is exactly what Hardy often seems to be proposing in his fiction. Not just suffering that is felt, but suffering that cannot be felt—suffering that pertains to objects and situations unable to experience pain—is repeatedly offered as deserving of our attention.

Again, however, the mobility of pity seems at least as relevant as the objects on which it lights. In the larger passage from which these two paragraphs have been taken, the challenge is even more extreme, for it begins to identify Tess with a kind of suffering that she not only does not fully feel, but that she has no way to recognize or understand:

The swede-field, in which she and her companion were set hacking, was a stretch of a hundred odd acres, in one patch, on the highest ground of the farm, rising above stony lanchets or lynchets.... Every leaf of the [turnips] having already been consumed the whole field was in colour a desolate drab; it was a complexion without features, as if a face from chin to brow should be only an expanse of skin. The sky wore, in another colour, the same likeness; a white vacuity of countenance with the lineaments gone. So these two upper and nether visages confronted each other, all day long the white face looking down on the brown face, and the brown face looking up at the white face, without anything standing between them but the two girls crawling over the surface of the former like flies. (*T* 304)

Tess has no way of inhabiting the perspective that sees her as merely a fly crawling on the surface of a face with eyes only for the sky. It is an image even more trivializing than Pip's fever-dreams of being a brick in a wall or a cog in a vast machine, or Esther's nightmares of being a bead in a flaming necklace: Dickens's characters may be haunted by the sense of being parts of assemblages not of their own making, but Hardy's passage takes this nightmare several steps further in depriving the character of the ability even to see the possible triviality of her story and her pain. These things, the images of the two faces suggest, may be nothing more than irrelevant and annoying details of no greater importance than the life histories of the "innumerable flies and butterflies" that, at a happier moment, Tess's skirt brushed up from the grass and "which, unable to escape, remained caged in the transparent tissue as in an aviary" (*T* 158). We may be focusing on the wrong thing in attending to Tess, it seems. The earth, too, has a face—as does the sky. What sorrows, dramas, or experiences might they have to relate, to which Tess is less than irrelevant? Hardy never pursues this suggestion: we have no way to follow up on the idea that the sky and the earth are truly deserving of the attention we have hitherto devoted to Tess. Instead of an actual paradigm shift, therefore, the momentary interruption of perspective seems to seek to generate a suspicion of Tess's ultimate unimportance, a suspicion that serves only to underscore the sorrowfulness of her life.

The scene in the swede-field does not represent exactly the same drama as is involved in Gabriel Oak's feelings for his sheep, Tess's imagination of her boots' pain, or the passage in which Marty's pain is bound up with, and in some sense indistinguishable from, that of the trees. However, they are all importantly related insofar as they suggest the ways in which a mobile imagination of the pain of others serves not just to reorient the way self imagines other, but the way self and other come to seem related. What all these examples share, in other words, is a way of thinking about pain less as something suffered by other people, animals, trees, or life-forms who deserve our pity, than as a condition of possibility for experiencing ourselves as part of a *universe* that suffers. This is a felt disposition that may or may not result in ameliorative intervention, though at the very least it might prevent us from doing unnecessary harm. More important than action—and importantly prior to it—are the modes of seeing, feeling, and imagining that do not exactly blur the boundaries between self and other so much as they enable one to see self and all conceivable others as in relation to each other, as "members of one corporeal frame."

AFTERWORD

The Fantasy of the Speaking Body

THROUGHOUT *VICTORIAN PAIN*, I have examined ways of thinking about pain in the nineteenth century that go well beyond the epistemological models so often taken for granted today. In this afterword, I consider some of the ways in which the nineteenth century *did* engage with an exclusively epistemological model—as well as some of the potential risks involved in that engagement. Elaine Scarry, the twentieth century's most important theorist of this model, cites almost no Victorian literature in *The Body in Pain*. Nevertheless, she was trained and continues to teach as a Victorianist, and certain aspects of her model of pain are themselves deeply Victorian: most importantly, her insistence that the knowledge of the existence of pain necessarily generates the desire to relieve it and her conclusion that the willful infliction of pain constitutes what she calls a form of "moral stupidity."[1] This phrase deliberately echoes George Eliot: "We are all of us born in moral stupidity," the novelist writes in *Middlemarch* (1871), "taking the world as an udder to feed our supreme selves."[2] Eliot, crusader for an ethical model premised on knowledge and oriented toward care, constitutes an important implicit reference point for Scarry's project. As such, the novelist begins to suggest the historical specificity of Scarry's model: its relation to nineteenth-century adaptations of eighteenth-century notions of sympathy as the means by which communities are consolidated; to new humanitarian efforts to use emotional response as an engine of social change; and to new ways of thinking about social life in the absence of divine guarantees and in the context of what was often cast as the atomistic individualism of capitalism and liberalism.[3] Eliot also begins to signal some of the potential dangers of imagining that care must or even can be premised on knowledge: specifically, the fantasy it generates of something like transparent communication. What Eliot helps us see, in other words, is the connection between the demand for knowledge and what I call the "fantasy of the speaking body": the fantasy, that is, of a way to make the body speak in a way that bypasses consciousness with all its distortions. The most common way to achieve that goal is through pain.[4]

According to Page du Bois, the fantasy that pain can force bodies to speak can be traced back at least to Ancient Greece. Since slaves were conceived exclusively *as* bodies, they were considered capable of telling the truth only when physically compelled to do so: "The slave can only produce truth under coercion, can produce only truth under coercion. The court assumes that he will lie unless compelled by physical force to speak truly and that when compelled he will speak truly."[5] Because pain supposedly speaks directly to and through the body, not only could slaves be tortured, they *had* to be tortured in order for their testimony to be legally admissible. The mind may lie, but the body possesses no such choice: it cannot help but speak the truth.

When judicial torture moved into Europe in the twelfth century, the fantasy of the speaking body moved along with it.[6] "Torture inflicted pain," Lisa Silverman writes, "as a means of achieving the spontaneous truth of the body rather than the composed truth of the mind."[7] "The infliction of pain" was thought to "draw truth from the body just as a knife draws blood."[8] By the eighteenth century, this belief in pain's power to elicit truth from the body supposedly no longer held much sway. "Where the [Early Modern] jurists sought the spontaneous utterances of people in pain," Silverman explains, "the [eighteenth-century] philosophes insisted that truth was cultivated in moments of self-control and that people in pain were incapable of the kind of thoughtful reflection necessary to create that truth."[9] According to Cesare Beccaria, for example, one of the most prominent anti-torture activists of the period:

> A man on the rack, in the convulsions of torture, has it as little in his power to declare the truth, as, in former times, to prevent without fraud the effects of fire or boiling water.
>
> Every act of our will is invariably proportioned to the force of the sensory impression which is its source; and the sensory capacity of every man is limited. Thus the impression of pain may become so great that, filling the entire sensory capacity of the tortured person, it leaves him free to choose only what for the moment is the shortest way of escape from pain.[10]

Rather than truth, then, by the late eighteenth century, pain came to be a way to elicit lies. Yet, despite the apparent consensus regarding the demise of the fantasy of the speaking body, it has had a vibrant afterlife since the eighteenth century.

Torture may not have been a particularly live issue in nineteenth-century England. Despite its near-ubiquity in Early Modern Europe, it had never been a common practice in England, and by the nineteenth century, even exceptional uses had largely ended. Nevertheless, the fantasy that pain has the power to impel truth remained surprisingly active—as in discussions of vivisection, a practice that could supposedly reveal truths regarding biological and perhaps, too, psychological phenomena through the infliction of pain. Victorian novels also return to it repeatedly, whether in the form of the scar whose changes enable Rosa Dartle's observers to read her feelings, Heathcliff's "vivisectional" experiments on his adopted relatives that reveal their true feelings toward himself and each other, or Mary Barton's fevered mumblings that threaten to expose those she seeks to protect.

Precisely because of her commitment to an ethic based on an epistemological model of pain, Eliot reproduces a particularly clear version of the fantasy that pain might be able to make the body speak. This is a fantasy one can see in several of her novels, but in both *Middlemarch* and "The Lifted Veil" (1859), what elsewhere emerges as a vaguely discernable pattern is made startlingly apparent. *Middlemarch* is perhaps the less obvious of the two examples. The novel is almost universally read as embracing a relatively straightforward account of knowledge and understanding as the basis of compassion. Despite all her appeal at the beginning of the novel as a brilliant woman who seeks more from life than her provincial environment can provide, Dorothea Brooke still needs to learn a crucial ethical lesson about regarding others as independent centers of consciousness. She begins this education in relation to her unprepossessing husband, Mr. Casaubon, a man she marries in the hope that serving as his helpmeet will give her vague desires a meaningful shape and purpose. After Casaubon dies, Dorothea is put to an even harder test when she witnesses what she thinks is a guilty love scene between the man she loves, Will Ladislaw, and the married Rosamond Lydgate. Dorothea spends a sleepless night wrestling with her jealousy and her profound sense of what she thinks she has lost. Proof of her victory over her egotism comes when she manages to place her own desires to one side and concern herself with the welfare of those more immediately involved in the scene. "She forced herself to think of [her experiences of the day before] as bound up with another woman's life" and decides that "her own irremediable grief ... should make her more helpful, instead of driving her back from effort." As in any humanitarian narrative, this shift in perspective from her own suffering to that of another impels action: Dorothea decides to return to Rosamond to see if she can provide her with aid or advice.

By this point in the novel, Rosamond has repeatedly demonstrated her refusal of any demand for truthful language. A perfect egotist, her flirtation with Will is only one of a long list of her crimes, final proof of her inability or unwillingness to imagine the feelings of others. Upon hearing Dorothea's arrival announced, therefore, Rosamond unsurprisingly "wrap[s] her soul in cold reserve" and "prepare[s] herself to meet every word with polite impassibility."[11]

As Dorothea begins to speak, however, Rosamond's reserve is gradually broken down, until finally the two women reach the following crisis. The speaker is Dorothea:

> "Trouble is so hard to bear, is it not?—How can we live and think that any one has trouble—piercing trouble—and we could help them, and never try?"
>
> Dorothea, completely swayed by the feeling that she was uttering, forgot everything but that she was speaking from out the heart of her own trial to Rosamond's. The emotion had wrought itself more and more into her utterance, till the tones might have gone to one's very marrow, like a low cry from some suffering creature in the darkness. And she had unconsciously laid her hand again on the little hand that she had pressed before.
>
> Rosamond, with an overmastering pang, as if a wound within her had been probed, burst into hysterical crying.[12]

Here, one person breaks down the defenses of an unknowable person first by a touch and then by communicating some kind of energy from her own body to her object's. Under cover of metaphor, the violence of that "communication" is made grotesquely explicit: Dorothea's sympathy makes Rosamond feel as if a "wound within her had been probed." The consequence is that Rosamond is moved to perform her one fully moral act in the novel, confessing that the man she loves, Will Ladislaw, has only ever loved Dorothea.

This scene constitutes a turning point in the novel, both in terms of the plot, and in terms of its ethical agenda. Dorothea's successful act of compassion is fully rewarded in the information she receives as a result, information that paves the way for her to be reunited with Will. From the perspective of Dorothea, therefore, this scene represents a moment in which selflessness is met with selflessness, and a concern for another is rewarded in ways that could never have been predicted. From Rosamond's perspective, by contrast, the scene looks quite different: she is *not* altered by the encounter with Dorothea. After the two women part, she undergoes a brief illness and then lapses once more into selfishness. At the end of the novel, we see her happily married to a fashionable doctor, having worked her first husband into an early grave. Even aside from the consequences of the encounter, the actual nature of the scene is quite different for the two women, for while Dorothea experiences her utterance simply as language, Rosamond experiences it as a kind of violence that forces her, almost mechanically, to produce truthful language. Rosamond thus deserves no real credit for her confession; she had no choice but to make it.

In the context of *Middlemarch*, the demand for knowledge, the infliction of pain, and the production of truthful speech is obscured by metaphor. Eliot's short story, "The Lifted Veil," by contrast, makes the relationship explicit.

The story as a whole is usually read as an allegory of the limits of knowledge to generate compassion. Latimer, the main character and narrator of the story, possesses a supernatural ability to perceive others' thoughts and feelings. Rather than understanding or care, however, this knowledge leads only to a too-intense consciousness of other people's selfishness and egotism. As the character complains, his "superadded consciousness ... became an intense pain and grief when ... the rational talk, the graceful attentions, the wittily-turned phrases, and the kindly deeds [of those who were in close relation to him] ... were seen as if thrust asunder by a microscopic vision, that showed all the intermediate frivolities, all the suppressed egoism, all the struggling chaos of puerilities, meanness, vague capricious memories, and indolent make-shift thoughts."[13] Knowledge may help Latimer understand those he meets, but his response to that understanding is primarily disgust.

As critics have noted, the story as a whole has a great deal to say about Eliot's ambivalent relationship to even the most desirable versions of an ethic of compassion premised on knowledge. A scene at the end of the novel, however, has proven strangely resistant to interpretation in relation to what comes before. In this scene, Latimer gives his friend, the kindly Dr. Meunier, permission to perform an experiment on his wife's recently deceased maid. Meunier opens an artery "in the long thin neck that lay rigid on the pillow," and as the doctor transfuses his blood into the woman's veins, she slowly awakens.[14] Latimer narrates:

> I could see the wondrous slow return of life; the breast began to heave, the inspirations became stronger, the eyelids quivered, and the soul seemed to have returned beneath them....
>
> The dead woman's eyes were wide open, and met [Latimer's wife, Bertha's] in full recognition—the recognition of hate.... The gasping eager voice said—
>
> "You mean to poison your husband.... The poison is in the black cabinet.... I got it for you.... You laughed at me, and told lies about me behind my back, to make me disgusting ... because you were jealous.... Are you sorry ... now?"
>
> The lips continued to murmur but the sounds were no longer distinct. Soon there was no sound—only a slight movement: the flame had leaped out, and was being extinguished the faster.[15]

As in the scene from *Middlemarch*, here one character violates the body of another—here literalized in the incisions Meunier makes so as to enable the transfusion. That violation wakes up the dead object and causes her to speak the truth.

These scenes provide an important reference point for this project, if only because they begin to suggest the extent to which even Eliot, committed as she is to an ethics based on knowledge, can be seen, however ambivalently, to be working out the dangers implicit in that ethics. When isolated from a social medium, the epistemological imperative is dangerous not just because of the risk it runs that it may in fact not be met, but because of the fantasies of transparent communication it implies—fantasies in which the body might be made to speak. This fantasy is replayed every day in American life. The most lurid cases involve representations of torture in which the sudden infliction of pain magically expels truthful speech. Attempts to use MRIs and other imaging technologies to determine pain levels (a practice of particular interest in legal contexts), medical guidelines on how to differentiate between patients who are "really" in pain from those who are "merely" feeding an addiction: these are just a few of the examples of attempts to bypass the consciousness of the one who suffers and so access her supposed truth.[16] No model of pain provides a safeguard against cruelty, of course. Even when we think of pain as a demand rather than a deictic, we are still capable of refusing to respond to that appeal. As Veena Das explains, "The sentence 'I am in pain' ... makes a claim on the other—asking for acknowledgment that be given *or denied*."[17] There are no guarantees.

Victorian Pain starts with attempts to complicate utilitarian assumptions of human atomism in relation to aversive physical sensation. Pain is not self-evident, private, and isolating, John Stuart Mill and Harriet Martineau insist. Instead, it is something we necessarily experience in relation to, and in the context of, others. Charlotte Brontë measures the cost of that recognition, and laments the loss of privacy. Meanwhile, Charles Darwin and Thomas Hardy expand its parameters to include not just other people but all things that do or can be imagined to suffer. Pain in their accounts is something like a condition of existence—something that brings us together at least as much as it separates us. None of these models offer a "solution" to the problem of pain—or to the inevitability of skepticism—but they do begin to suggest the contours of alternative ways of thinking about aversive physical experience, ways that have the potential, at least, to encourage us to ask exactly what we do when we choose to make understanding a prerequisite for care.

NOTES

Introduction: Pain, Subjectivity, and the Social

1. The phrase the "view from nowhere" is from Thomas Nagel, *The View from Nowhere* (New York: Oxford University Press, 1986).

2. Ludwig Wittgenstein, *The Blue and Brown Books: Preliminary Studies for the "Philosophical Investigations"* (1933-35; New York: Harper Perennial, 1960), 50-51.

3. See Lucy Bending, *The Representation of Bodily Pain in Late Nineteenth-Century English Culture* (Oxford: Clarendon Press, 2000); Roselyne Rey, *The History of Pain* (Cambridge, MA: Harvard University Press, 1995), 132-260; David B. Morris, *The Culture of Pain* (Berkeley: University of California Press, 1991), 64.

4. "The Function of Physical Pain: Anaesthetics," *Westminster Review* 40, no. 1 (1871): 198.

5. J. Edgar Foster, *Pain: Its Mystery and Meaning, and Other Sermons* (London: James Nisbet, 1891), 8, quoted in Bending, *Representation of Bodily Pain*, 32.

6. Thomas Robert Malthus, *An Essay on the Principle of Population* (1798; Oxford: Oxford University Press, 2004), 13.

7. Ibid. On Malthus's impact on debates about population growth, see S. G. Checkland, *The Rise of Industrial Society in England, 1815-1885* (New York: St. Martin's Press, 1964), 390-400. For his effect on the abolition of the Poor Laws, see Harold Perkin, *The Origins of Modern English Society 1780-1880* (London: Routledge & K. Paul, 1969), 189-90. For the complicity of Malthusian with Evangelical pessimism, see Boyd Hilton, *The Age of Atonement: The Influence of Evangelicalism on Social and Economic Thought, 1795-1865* (Oxford: Oxford University Press 1992), 3-35.

8. Charles Darwin, *On the Origin of Species* (1859; Oxford: Oxford University Press, 1996), 51.
The passage continues: "It is the doctrine of Malthus applied with manifold force to the whole animal and vegetable kingdoms" (ibid.).

9. Catherine Gallagher, *The Body Economic: Life, Death, and Sensation in Political Economy and the Victorian Novel* (Princeton: Princeton University Press, 2006), 38.

10. Thomas Hobbes, *Leviathan* (1651; Cambridge: Cambridge University Press, 1991), 88-89.

11. Despite taking issue with many of its assumptions, for example, all three of the most important recent histories of pain also acknowledge *The Body in Pain* as the most influential theorization of pain of the twentieth century. See Bending, *Representation of Bodily Pain*, 86; Javier Moscoso, *Pain: A Cultural History* (Basingstoke: Palgrave Macmillan, 2012), 4; Joanna Bourke, *The Story of Pain: From Prayer to Painkillers* (New York: Oxford University Press, 2014), 4.

12. Elaine Scarry, *The Body in Pain: The Making and Unmaking of the World* (Oxford: Oxford University Press, 1985), 4.

13. Ibid., 5.

14. Ibid., 11.

15. Eric J. Cassell makes a subtler distinction between pain and suffering, claiming that "suffering is experienced by persons, not merely by bodies, and has its source in challenges that threaten the intactness of the person as a complex social and psychological entity." "The Nature of Suffering and the Goals of Medicine," *The New England Journal of*

Medicine 306, no. 11 (1982): 639. Throughout this book, I move between the terms "pain" and "suffering" in a way that seeks to reproduce the ambiguities common throughout the nineteenth century.

16. Scarry, *Body in Pain*, 289–90.

17. Ibid., 9. For an account of Victorian strategies for achieving this goal, see Thomas Laqueur, "Bodies, Details, and the Humanitarian Narrative," in *The New Cultural History*, ed. Lynn Hunt (Berkeley: University of California Press, 1989), 176–204.

18. See, for example, Moscoso, *Pain*, 4. Morris additionally claims that Scarry fails to distinguish between chronic and acute pain. *Culture of Pain*, 6. On phantom limb, see Cassandra S. Crawford, *Phantom Limb: Amputation, Embodiment, and Prosthetic Technology* (New York: New York University Press, 2014).

19. Darius Rejali, *Torture and Democracy* (Princeton: Princeton University Press, 2007), 31.

20. The Gate Control Theory of Pain that was first introduced in 1965 and continues to guide much medical research and practice asserts that "psychological factors such as past experience, attention, and emotion influence pain response and perception." Ronald Melzack and Patrick D. Wall, "Pain Mechanisms: A New Theory," *American Association for the Advancement of Science* 150, no. 3699 (1965): 978. Also see Ronald Melzack, "Gate Control Theory: On the Evolution of Pain Concepts," *Journal of Pain* 5, no. 2 (1996): 128–38; Ronald Melzack and Patrick D. Wall, *The Challenge of Pain* (London: Penguin, 1996), 98–99, 165–93. The definition of pain currently posted on the website of the International Association for the Study of Pain reflects this understood complexity: "An unpleasant sensory and emotional experience associated with actual or potential tissue damage, or described in terms of such damage." "Pain," *Taxonomy: International Association for the Study of Pain*, http://www.iasp-pain.org/Taxonomy#Pain. Emotional and sensory, actual or potential, this definition allows for a much greater degree of ambiguity than Scarry suggests.

21. This commitment is related to her understanding of the imagination as capable of producing mental images whose vividness rivals that of actual perceptions. On this issue, see Rei Terada, "Seeing is Reading," in *The Legacies of Paul de Man*, ed. Marc Redfield (New York: Fordham University Press, 2007), 167–69; Geoffrey Galt Harpham, "Elaine Scarry and the Dream of Pain," *Salmagundi* 130/131 (2001): 215–18.

22. Peter Singer, "Review Essay: Unspeakable Acts: The Body in Pain (Scarry) and Torture (Peters)," *The New York Review of Books* (Feb. 27, 1986), http://www.nybooks.com/articles/1986/02/27/unspeakable-acts/. Singer is here summarizing Edward Peters's description of the logic of torture.

23. Scarry, *Body in Pain*, 9.

24. Stanley Cavell, *The Claim of Reason: Wittgenstein, Skepticism, Morality, and Tragedy* (1979; New York: Oxford University Press, 1999), 338.

25. Ludwig Wittgenstein, *Philosophical Investigations* (1953; Oxford: Blackwell, 2001), §297. On Wittgenstein's critique of the idea of private language, see Robert J. Fogelin, "Wittgenstein's Critique of Philosophy," in *Cambridge Companion to Wittgenstein*, ed. Hans Sluga and David G. Stern (Cambridge: Cambridge University Press, 1996), 34–45; Anthony Manser, "Pain and Private Language," in *Studies in the Philosophy of Wittgenstein*, ed. Peter Winch (London: Routledge & K. Paul, 1969), 166–83; Stephen Mulhall, *Wittgenstein's Private Language: Grammar, Nonsense, and Imagination in Philosophical Investigations*, §243–315 (Oxford: Oxford University Press, 2007), 45–53.

26. Cavell, *Claim of Reason*, 335.

27. Also see Stanley Cavell, "The Avoidance of Love: A Reading of *King Lear*," in *Must We Mean What We Say? A Book of Essays* (New York: Charles Scribner's Sons, 1969), 347.

28. It is thus potentially a performance of what Andrew H. Miller has described as "perfectionism." In *The Burdens of Perfection: On Ethics and Reading in Nineteenth-Century British Literature* (Ithaca, NY: Cornell University Press, 2008), Miller uses Cavell to consider how Victorian writers sought to overcome the paralyzing effects of skepticism. Miller and I are engaged with many of the same twentieth-century philosophers, and my work owes a great deal to his. While the texts he examines are concerned with the aesthetic and ethical work of living a "good life," however, those to which I attend are haunted by the possibility that such lives might not ultimately matter. One indication of this difference lies in the fact that in the texts he examines, marriage constitutes the most "prominent form" of the "powerful attachment" able to "supplant" skepticism (xii). Remarkably little romantic love appears in the pages of *Victorian Pain*, and what little does appear is not successful.

29. Arthur Kleinman, Veena Das, and Margaret M. Lock, eds., *Social Suffering* (Berkeley: University of California Press, 1997), ix.

30. Veena Das, *Life and Words: Violence and the Descent into the Ordinary* (Berkeley: University of California Press, 2007), 40.

31. See, for example, Hanna Fenichel Pitkin, *Wittgenstein and Justice: On the Significance of Ludwig Wittgenstein for Social and Political Thought* (Berkeley: University of California Press, 1993); Chantal Mouffe, *The Democratic Paradox* (London: Verso, 2000); Christopher C. Robinson, *Wittgenstein and Political Theory: The View from Somewhere* (Edinburgh: Edinburgh University Press, 2009); and Richard E. Flathman, *Toward a Liberalism . . .* (Ithaca, NY: Cornell University Press, 1989).

32. Cavell, *Claim of Reason*, 361.

33. This is also my reason for not addressing poetry: since poetry is already attentive to the things that cannot be spoken in prose, shifts between registers tend to resonate in different ways. In many of the prose works I examine, there is a self-conscious attempt to approximate at least some of the conditions of poetry.

34. Sharon Cameron, *Impersonality: Seven Essays* (Chicago: University of Chicago Press, 2007), xi.

35. Ibid., ix.

36. Benedict de Spinoza, *Ethics* (1677; London: Penguin, 1996), 32.

37. Ibid., 70.

38. Ibid., 32.

39. See chapter 4 for an extended discussion of affect.

40. Bending, *Representation of Bodily Pain*, 52–53. The literature on nineteenth-century neurology is vast and complex. In addition to the scholars whose work I engage directly, see Rick Rylance, *Victorian Psychology and British Culture 1850–1880* (Oxford: Oxford University Press, 2000); Alan Richardson, *British Romanticism and the Science of the Mind* (Cambridge: Cambridge University Press, 2001); Laura Otis, *Networking: Communicating with Bodies and Machines in the Nineteenth Century* (Ann Arbor: University of Michigan Press, 2001; idem, *Organic Memory: History and the Body in the Late Nineteenth and Early Twentieth Centuries* (Lincoln: University of Nebraska Press, 1994); Nicholas Dames, *Amnesiac Selves: Nostalgia, Forgetting, and British Fiction, 1810–1870* (New York: Oxford University Press, 2001); Edward S. Reed, *From Soul to Mind: The Emergence of Psychology, from Erasmus Darwin to William James* (New Haven, CT: Yale University Press, 1997); Roy Porter, "Pain and Suffering," in *Companion Encyclopedia of the History of Medicine*, vol. 2, ed., W. F. Bynum and Roy Porter (London: Routledge, 1997), 1574–91; Peter Melville Logan, *Nerves and Narratives: A Cultural History of Hysteria in Nineteenth-Century British Prose* (Berkeley: University of California Press, 1997); Robert H. Wozniak, *Mind and Body: René Descartes to William James* (Bethesda, MD:

National Library of Medicine, 1992); H. N. Gardiner, Ruth Clark Metcalf, and John G. Beebe-Center, *Feeling and Emotion: A History of Theories* (Westport, CT: Greenwood Press, 1970); Alison Winter, *Mesmerized: Powers of Mind in Victorian Britain* (Chicago: Chicago University Press, 1998).

41. "What Is Pain?" *The Lancet* (Aug. 13, 1887): 333.

42. Lorraine Daston, "The Theory of Will versus the Science of Mind," in *The Problematic Science: Psychology in Nineteenth-Century Thought*, ed., William R. Woodward and Mitchell G. Ash (New York: Praeger, 1982), 98.

43. Alexander Bain, *The Senses and the Intellect* (1855; London: Longmans, Green, 1868), 52–53.

44. Thomas Dormandy, *The Worst of Evils: The Fight against Pain* (New Haven, CT: Yale University Press, 2006), 282.

45. Ibid., 276.

46. Ibid., 277.

47. John P. Harrison, "On the Physiology, Pathology and Therapeutics of Pain," *The Western Lancet and Hospital Reporter* 9 (1849): 352.

48. Martin S. Pernick, *A Calculus of Suffering: Pain, Professionalism, and Anesthesia in Nineteenth-Century America* (New York: Columbia University Press, 1985), 95, 94.

49. Ibid., 94.

50. General reluctance to use anesthetics could also be exacerbated by convictions of the relative insensitivity of non-Europeans, members of the lower classes, criminals, alcoholics, drug addicts, and infants. See Ibid., 148–70; Bending, *Representation of Bodily Pain*, 177–239; Bourke, *Story of Pain*, 192–230.

51. Bourke, *Story of Pain*, 286.

52. Ibid., 288.

53. Priscilla Maurice, *Sickness, Its Trials and Blessings*, 7th ed. (1850; London: Rivingtons, 1859), 83.

54. G. A. Rowell, *An Essay on the Beneficent Distribution of the Sense of Pain* (Oxford: Published and sold by the author, 1857), 6.

55. James Hinton, *The Mystery of Pain: A Book for the Sorrowful* (1866; New York: Mitchell Kennerly, 1914), 33.

56. Maurice, *Sickness*, 4–5.

57. John Thornton, *A Companion for the Sick Chamber: or, The Uses of Affliction Briefly Stated and Illustrated, with Examples and Prayers* (London: Frederick Westley and A. H. David, 1835), 2, 44.

58. Ibid., 22.

59. Ibid., 126.

60. Revd. George Martin, *Our Afflicted Prince: A Sermon the Substance of Which Was Preached in the Lewisham High Road Congregational Church on Sunday Morning, December 17, 1871* (London: Elliot Stock, 1871), 5, 11.

61. Maurice, *Sickness*, 16–17.

62. H. Cameron Gillies, "The Interpretation of Disease, Part III: The Life-Saving Value of Pain and Disease," *The Lancet* (Aug. 13, 1887): 306.

63. Ibid., 306.

64. Ibid., 307.

65. The difference made by evolutionary theory can be measured by comparing the vitriolic reactions to Gillies in 1887 with the apparent lack of controversy around Roswell's very similar claims in 1857.

66. A. St. Clair Buxton, "Letter to the Editor: Pain and Its Interpretation," *The Lancet* (Sept. 24, 1887): 635.

67. Ibid., 635.
68. Bending, *Representation of Bodily Pain*, 67.
69. W. J. Collins, "Letter to the Editor: Pain and Its Interpretation," *The Lancet* (Aug. 20, 1887): 391.
70. Ibid.
71. E. R. Williams, "Letter to the Editor: Pain and Its Interpretation," *The Lancet* (Sept. 17, 1887): 593.
72. J. Russell Reynolds, "Fashions in Medicine," *British Medical Journal* (Sept. 2, 1871): 256, 257.
73. Michel Foucault, *The Birth of the Clinic: An Archaeology of Medical Perception* (1973; New York: Vintage, 1994), 15. On the distinction between illness as "the innately human experience of symptoms and suffering" and disease as "the problem from the practitioner's perspective," see Arthur Kleinman, *The Illness Narratives: Suffering, Healing, and the Human Condition* (New York: Basic Books, 1988), 3, 5.
74. Mary Fissell, "The Disappearance of the Patient's Narrative and the Invention of Hospital Medicine," in *British Medicine in an Age of Reform*, ed. Roger French and Andrew Wear (London: Routledge, 1991), 93.
75. N. D. Jewson, "The Disappearance of the Sick Man from Medical Cosmology, 1770–1870," *Sociology* 10, no. 2 (1976): 232, 231.
76. Foucault, *Birth of the Clinic*, xviii.
77. Literary critics, in particular, have used Foucault to consider how Victorian novels competed with the modes of observation and narration being developed in the clinic. On the relation between the novel and the case history, see, for example, Lawrence Rothfield, *Vital Signs: Medical Realism in Nineteenth-Century Fiction* (Princeton: Princeton University Press, 1992); Jason Daniel Tougaw, *Strange Cases: The Medical Case History and the British Novel* (New York: Routledge, 2006); Meegan Kennedy, *Revising the Clinic: Vision and Representation in Victorian Medical Narrative and the Novel* (Columbus: Ohio State University Press, 2010). A number of other critics have turned to discourses of medicine to consider how, as Athena Vrettos puts it, illness reconfigures "conceptions of the self." *Somatic Fictions: Imagining Illness in Victorian Culture* (Stanford, CA: Stanford University Press, 1995), 3. Also see Jane Wood, *Passion and Pathology in Victorian Fiction* (Oxford: Oxford University Press, 2001); Helen Small, *Love's Madness: Medicine, the Novel, and Female Insanity, 1800–1865* (Oxford: Clarendon Press, 1996); Miriam Bailin, *The Sickroom in Victorian Fiction: The Art of Being Ill* (Cambridge: Cambridge University Press, 1994); Janis McLarren Caldwell, *Literature and Medicine in Nineteenth-Century Britain: From Mary Shelley to George Eliot* (Cambridge: Cambridge University Press, 2004).
78. On the importance of the hospital to medical training, see W. F. Bynum, *Science and the Practice of Medicine in the Nineteenth Century* (Cambridge: Cambridge University Press, 1994).
79. Anne Digby, *Making a Medical Living: Doctors and Patients in the English Market for Medicine, 1720–1911* (Cambridge: Cambridge University Press, 1994), 77.
80. Lilian R. Furst, *Between Doctors and Patients: The Changing Balance of Power* (Charlottesville: University Press of Virginia, 1998), 31.
81. On invalidism as a potential source of power, see Maria H. Frawley, *Invalidism and Identity in Nineteenth-Century Britain* (Chicago: University of Chicago Press, 2004).
82. Das, *Life and Words*, 39.
83. Esther Fischer-Homberger, "Hypochondriasis of the Eighteenth Century—Neurosis of the Present Century," *Bulletin of the History of Medicine* 46, no. 4 (1972): 391.
84. Other useful histories of medicine that discuss hypochondria include George C. Grinnell, *The Age of Hypochondria: Interpreting Romantic Health and Illness* (New York:

Palgrave Macmillan, 2010); Bruce Haley, *The Healthy Body and Victorian Culture* (Cambridge, MA: Harvard University Press, 1978); Roy Porter, *Mind Forg'd Manacles: A History of Madness in England from the Restoration to the Regency* (Cambridge, MA: Harvard University Press, 1987); Michael J. Clark, "'Morbid Introspection,' Unsoundness of Mind, and British Psychological Medicine, c. 1830–c.1900," in *The Anatomy of Madness: Essays in the History of Psychiatry*, vol. 3, *The Asylum and its Psychiatry*, ed. W. F. Bynum, Roy Porter, and Michael Shepherd (London: Routledge, 1988), 71–101; Sally Shuttleworth, *Charlotte Brontë and Victorian Psychology* (Cambridge: Cambridge University Press, 1996); Jenny Bourne Taylor and Sally Shuttleworth, eds., *Embodied Selves: An Anthology of Psychological Texts, 1830–1890* (Oxford: Clarendon, 1998). Also see Frawley's analysis of *The Confessions of a Hypochondriac*, which emphasizes the connections often made in the mid-nineteenth century between hypochondria and masculinity. *Invalidism and Identity*, 64–112.

85. See, for example, the following articles, all of which define hypochondria in terms of the fear of illness or the conviction on the part of a patient that she is ill in the absence of any physical lesion: Dr. Clutterbuck, "Lectures on the Diseases of the Nervous System," *The Lancet* (April 14, 1827): 550–54; M. Andral, "Lectures on Medical Pathology," *The Lancet* (Jan. 26, 1833): 550–56; John Conolly, "The Croonian Lectures, Lecture III: Description of General Paralysis," *The Lancet* (Oct. 27, 1849): 443–46; W. H. O. Sankey, "Illustrations of the Different Forms of Insanity," *British Medical Journal* (Feb. 13, 1864): 175–76.

86. Thomas King Chambers, "Lecture on Hypochondriasis," *British Medical Journal* (Jul. 5, 1873): 6.

87. "Medical Annotations," *The Lancet* (Jun. 13, 1863): 664.

88. Conolly, "Croonian Lectures," 443.

89. Ibid.

90. Chambers, "Lecture on Hypochondriasis," 6.

91. Ibid., 7.

92. Ibid. This account of the origin of hypochondria is often attributed to Etienne Esquirol: "Hypochondriacs have illusions, which spring from internal sensations. These persons deceive themselves, and have an illusion respecting the intensity of their sufferings, and the danger of losing their life. But they never attribute their misfortunes to causes that are repugnant to reason." *Mental Maladies: Treatise on Insanity* (1838; Philadelphia: Lea and Blanchard, 1845), 112.

93. Clark, "Morbid Introspection," 72.

94. "Hints to the Public and the Legislature, on the Nature and Effect of Evangelical Preaching," *The Quarterly Review* 8 (Nov. 1810): 498. Interestingly, the principal subject of the writer's essay is the religious hypochondria supposedly induced by Evangelicalism.

95. A. D. Hodgkiss observes that recent discussions of chronic pain closely resemble nineteenth-century discussions of hypochondria. "Chronic Pain in Nineteenth-Century British Medical Writings," *History of Psychiatry* 2, no. 5 (1991): 27–40.

96. W. H. Ranking, "Observations on Spermatorrhoea, or the Involuntary Discharge of the Seminal Fluid," *The Lancet* (Oct. 14, 1843): 46–53; John Elliotson, "St. Thomas's Hospital: Clinical Lecture," *The Lancet* (Nov. 3, 1832): 161.

97. "Foreign Department: Hypochondria Politica in Germany," *The Lancet* (Jun. 17, 1848): 669. The first time I read this passage, I assumed it was a satirical commentary. Its seriousness seems demonstrated by its reproduction in the *Boston Medical and Surgical Journal* and the *Buffalo Medical Journal*.

98. Dr. Armstrong, "From Lectures on the Principles and Practice of Physic," *The Lancet* (Jul. 23, 1825): 72.

99. William Withey Gull and Francis Edmund Anstie, "On Hypochondria or Hypochondriasis," in *A System of Medicine*, ed. J. Russell Reynolds (London: Macmillan, 1876), 629.
100. Ibid.
101. Andral, "Lectures on Medical Pathology," 550.
102. Ibid., 552.
103. Bourke, *Story of Pain*, 16.
104. Morris, *Culture of Pain*, 9.
105. Bouke, *Story of Pain*, 16.
106. Moscoso, *Pain*, 6.
107. Das, *Life and Words*, 38.
108. Ibid., 39.

Chapter 1: John Stuart Mill and the Poetics of Social Pain

1. John Stuart Mill, *Autobiography* (1879; *The Collected Works of John Stuart Mill*, vol. 1, *Autobiography and Literary Essays*, ed. J. M. Robson [Toronto: University of Toronto Press, 1981]), 111–13; hereafter abbreviated *A*. In the University of Toronto *Collected Works*, different versions of the *Autobiography* are printed on facing pages. Pages 111 and 113 are therefore consecutive pages of the 1879 version.

2. John Stuart Mill, *On Liberty* (1859; *The Collected Works of John Stuart Mill*, vol. 18, *Essays on Politics and Society*, ed. J. M. Robson [Toronto: University of Toronto Press, 1977]), 263.

3. Jeremy Bentham, *An Introduction to the Principles of Morals and Legislation* (1781; Amherst, NY: Prometheus Books, 1988), 1.

4. Ibid., 1–2.

5. Ibid., 3.

6. See Jeremy Davies's discussion of how pain, for Bentham, becomes "an absolute," able to override all other motivations—and this despite the philosopher's articulated commitment to the nonexistence of such absolutes. *Bodily Pain in Romantic Literature* (New York: Routledge, 2014), 63–66.

7. Ludwig Wittgenstein, *Philosophical Investigations* (1953; Oxford: Blackwell, 2001), §244–50, §300–309.

8. The term "social pain" revises Arthur Kleinman, Veena Das, and Margaret Lock's notion of "social suffering," which they claim suggests how "suffering is produced in societies and how acknowledgement of pain, as a cultural process, is given or withheld." "Introduction," in Arthur Kleinman, Veena Das, and Margaret M. Lock, eds., *Social Suffering* (Berkeley: University of California Press, 1997), xiii. As with nearly all the writers I examine in this project, Mill never clearly distinguishes between mental and physical suffering.

9. Wendy Donner, *The Liberal Self: John Stuart Mill's Moral and Political Philosophy* (Ithaca, NY: Cornell University Press, 1991), 146. Nancy Yousef, *Isolated Cases: The Anxieties of Autonomy in Enlightenment Philosophy and Romantic Literature* (Ithaca, NY: Cornell University Press, 2004), 172.

10. Alexander Bain, *John Stuart Mill: A Criticism; with Personal Recollections* (London: Longmans, Green, 1882), 38.

11. A. W. Levi, "The 'Mental Crisis' of John Stuart Mill," *Psychoanalytic Review* 32 (1945): 94.

12. Ibid., emphasis removed.

13. Janice Carlisle, *John Stuart Mill and the Writing of Character* (Athens: University of Georgia Press, 1991), 51.

14. John M. Robson, "J. S. Mill's Theory of Poetry," in *Mill: A Collection of Critical Essays*, ed. J. S. Schneewind (Notre Dame: University of Notre Dame Press, 1969), 256. Two key exceptions to the tendency to describe Mill's crisis in primarily psychological terms are Jonathan Loesberg and Nancy Yousef, both of whom I discuss later in this chapter. Jonathan Loesberg, *Fictions of Consciousness: Mill, Newman, and the Reading of Victorian Prose* (New Brunswick, NJ: Rutgers University Press, 1986); Yousef, *Isolated Cases*.

15. Carlisle, *John Stuart Mill*, 64.

16. John Durham, "The Influence of John Stuart Mill's Mental Crisis on His Thoughts," *American Imago* 20, no. 4 (1963): 372–73.

17. Bentham, *Introduction to the Principles*, 15, emphasis in original.

18. Ibid., 17–18.

19. Ibid., 17.

20. Frances Ferguson, "Belief and Emotions (from Stanley Fish to Jeremy Bentham and John Stuart Mill)," in *Politics and the Passions, 1500–1850*, ed. Victorian Kahn, Neil Saccamano, and Daniela Coli (Princeton: Princeton University Press, 2006), 231.

21. John Rawls, *A Theory of Justice*, rev. ed. (Cambridge, MA: Harvard University Press, 1999), 118. Rawls's project, he clarifies elsewhere, is not just to achieve justice, but to achieve the *feeling* of justice (73).

22. Charles Dickens, *Hard Times* (1854; London: Penguin, 2003), 9.

23. John Stuart Mill, "Sedgwick's Discourse" (1835; *The Collected Works of John Stuart Mill*, vol. 10, *Essays on Ethics, Religion and Society*, ed. J. M. Robson [Toronto: University of Toronto Press, 1969]), 50.

24. James Mill, *Analysis of the Phenomena of the Human Mind*, vol. 2 (1829; with notes by John Stuart, Alexander Bain, Andrew Finklater, and George Grote, 1869; London: Longmans, Green, Reader, and Dyer, 1878), toc.

25. For a complete overview of motives, see Jeremy Bentham, "Table of the Springs of Action" (1817; *The Works of Jeremy Bentham*, vol. 1, ed. John Bowring [Edinburgh: William Tait, 1843]), 169–94.

26. Mill, *Analysis*, vol. 2, 300.

27. Ibid., 184–85.

28. Elaine Scarry, *The Body in Pain: The Making and Unmaking of the World* (Oxford: Oxford University Press, 1985), 4.

29. Bentham, *Introduction to the Principles*, 3.

30. Mill, *Analysis*, vol. 2, 217.

31. As John Stuart Mill points out, James Mill gets this model of mind from David Hartley, for whom the principle of association is all-determining. "Blakey's History of Moral Science" (1833; *The Collected Works of John Stuart Mill*, vol. 10, *Essays on Ethics, Religion and Society*, ed. J. M. Robson [Toronto: University of Toronto Press, 1985]), 24. I discuss Hartley at greater length in the next chapter.

32. Mill, *Analysis*, vol. 2, 51–52.

33. Ibid.

34. John Locke, *An Essay Concerning Human Understanding* (1689; Oxford: Oxford University Press, 1975), 55. The passage continues: "Afterwards, the Mind proceeding farther, abstracts them, and by Degrees learns the use of general Names. In this manner the Mind comes to be furnish'd with *Ideas* and Language, the Materials about which to exercise its discursive Faculty: And the use of Reason becomes daily more visible, as these Materials, that give it Employment, increase" (ibid.).

35. Mill, *Analysis*, vol. 1, 70.

36. Ibid., 83.

37. James Mill, *The Article "Education" Reprinted from the Supplement to the* Encyclopaedia Britannica (London: J. Innes, 1825), 9. On James Mill's understanding of education, also see W. H. Burston, *James Mill on Philosophy and Education* (London: Athlone, 1973); Elie Halévy, *The Growth of Philosophic Radicalism* (New York: Macmillan, 1928), 455–78; F. W. Garforth, *John Stuart Mill's Theory of Education* (New York: Barnes & Noble, 1979). John Stuart Mill's most extensive commentary on education appears in his "Inaugural Address Delivered to the University of St. Andrews," where he writes, "Whatever helps to shape the human being, to make the individual what he is, or hinder him from being what he is not—is part of his education." (1867; *The Collected Works of John Stuart Mill*, vol. 21, *Essays on Equality, Law, and Education*, ed. J. M. Robson [Toronto: University of Toronto Press, 1984]), 217.

38. Mill, *Article "Education"*, 34.

39. Ibid., 35.

40. Ibid.

41. Undated manuscript, quoted in *Bentham: Selected Writings of John Dinwiddy*, ed. William Twining (Stanford, CA: Stanford University Press, 2004), 49.

42. See Halévy's discussion of the impact of Malthus on utilitarianism. *Philosophic Radicalism*, 490.

43. Ibid., 508.

44. Harold Perkin, *The Origins of Modern English Society* (New York: Routledge, 1969), 257–58. See Catherine Gallagher's account of how Bentham relies on government to close "the psychological gap between particular felicific calculations and general ones." *The Body Economic: Life, Death, and Sensation in Political Economy and the Victorian Novel* (Princeton: Princeton University Press, 2006), 69. Also see Elaine Hadley's account of the *Autobiography* as seeking to balance altruism and self-interest. *Living Liberalism: Practical Citizenship in Mid-Victorian Britain* (Chicago: University of Chicago Press, 2010), 101–3.

45. Mill, *Analysis*, vol. 2, 219.

46. Ibid., 220.

47. Ibid.

48. Ibid., 227.

49. Ibid.

50. Ibid., 278.

51. Mill additionally claims that his father's account ignores the "physiological effect" of sensations, as well as of the ideas, expectation, or memory of sensations. "In whatever manner the phenomena are produced," he writes, "they are a case of the quasi-chemistry of the nervous functions, whereby the junction of certain elements generates a compound whose properties are very different from the sum of the properties of the elements themselves." Ibid., 235. This formulation suggests a relative unpredictability to associationism, a point to which he returns in his claim that "the laws of the phenomena of mind are sometimes analogous to mechanical, but sometimes also to chemical laws." *A System of Logic Ratiocinative and Deductive* (1843; *The Collected Works of John Stuart Mill*, vol. 8, *A System of Logic Ratiocinative and Deductive, Part II*, ed. J. M. Robson [Toronto: University of Toronto Press, 1974]), 853.

52. Mill, *Analysis*, 217.

53. Ibid., 218.

54. Jerome H. Buckley, "John Stuart Mill's 'True' Autobiography," *Studies in the Literary Imagination* 23, no. 2 (1990): 228. Thomas Carlyle, *Sartor Resartus* (1833–34; Oxford: Oxford University Press, 1987), 128–29.

55. Loesberg, *Fictions of Consciousness*, 55.

56. Isaiah Berlin objects that "without the assumption of freedom of choice and responsibility in the sense in which Kant used these terms, one, at least, of the ways in which they are now normally used is, as it were, annihilated." *Four Essays on Liberty* (London: Oxford University Press, 1969), 6. Yet Mill is especially vitriolic on the question of fatalism: "A Fatalist believes, or half believes (for nobody is a consistent fatalist), not only that whatever is about to happen, will be the infallible result of the causes which produce it, (which is the true necessitarian doctrine), but moreover that there is no use in struggling against it.... We are exactly as capable of making our own character, *if we will*, as others are of making it for us." *System of Logic*, vol. 8, 840.

57. Alan Ryan, *The Philosophy of John Stuart Mill*, 2nd ed. (Houndmills: Macmillan, 1987), 104.

58. Loesberg, *Fictions of Consciousness*, 31.

59. Ibid., 56.

60. Ibid., 57–58.

61. Carlyle, *Sartor Resartus*, 129.

62. Levi, "'Mental Crisis,'" 97.

63. The passage in Jean François Marmontel's *Memoirs of Marmontel, Written by Himself* is itself extremely complicated. Rather than simply replacing his father in caring for his mother and his siblings, Marmontel describes himself as collapsing from grief after being haunted by his father's ghost. (1804; London: H. S. Nichols, 1895), 45–47.

64. Mill, *Analysis*, vol. 1, 100.

65. Ibid., 326.

66. For descriptions of the differences between the drafts, see William Thomas, "John Stuart Mill and the Uses of Autobiography," *History* 56, no. 188 (1971): 341–59; and Levi, "'Mental Crisis.'" The Toronto *Collected Works* reprints three different sets of revisions.

67. John Plotz, "Mediated Involvement: John Stuart Mill's Antisocial Sociability," in *The Feeling of Reading: Affective Experience and Victorian Literature*, ed. Rachel Ablow (Ann Arbor: Michigan University Press, 2010), 76. As Yousef puts it, "Mill famously finds relief in the language of poetry, though it is more the dubious comfort of finding one's self-diagnosis confirmed than it is the relief of cure, for the feeling communicated in poetry is nothing other than, nothing more precise than, the feeling of incommunicability itself." *Isolated Cases*, 184–85.

68. Neil Hertz, *The End of the Line: Essays on Psychoanalysis and the Sublime* (New York: Columbia University Press, 1985), 223.

69. Ibid., 40.

70. Mill, *Analysis*, vol. 1, xii.

71. Ibid., 329.

72. Ibid.

73. Mill, *Analysis*, vol. 2, 175.

74. Ibid.

75. Carlisle, *John Stuart Mill*, 22.

76. Ibid.

77. Mill, *Analysis*, vol. 2, 175. John Stuart Mill describes selfhood in almost identical terms in the *Logic*: "There is a something I call Myself, or, by another form of expression, my mind, which I consider as distinct from these sensations, thoughts, &c.; a something which I conceive to be not the thoughts, but the being that has the thoughts, and which I can conceive as existing for ever in a state of quiescence, without any thoughts at all. But what this being is, though it is myself, I have no knowledge, other than the series of its states of consciousness." *System of Logic*, vol. 2, 64.

78. Ryan, *Philosophy*, xxxiii–xxxiv.

79. John Stuart Mill, "Bentham" (1838; *The Collected Works of John Stuart Mill*, vol. 10, *Essays on Ethics, Religion and Society*, ed. J. M. Robson [Toronto: University of Toronto Press, 1969]), 113.

80. F. Parvin Sharpless, *The Literary Criticism of John Stuart Mill* (The Hague: Mouton, 1967), 30.

81. Paul Magnuson is relatively unusual in insisting that the childhood Wordsworth laments is not prelinguistic and therefore unalienated. Instead, he claims that "the precedent of a time in which a significant utterance is difficult or impossible must itself be a time in which sublime utterance came without difficulty." *Coleridge and Wordsworth: A Lyrical Dialogue* (Princeton: Princeton University Press, 1988), 284.

82. Geoffrey H. Hartman, *Wordsworth's Poetry, 1787–1814* (New Haven, CT: Yale University Press, 1964), 273.

83. Christopher C. Robinson, "Why Wittgenstein is Not Conservative," *Theory and Event* 9, no. 3 (2006), https://www.press.jhu.edu/journals/theory_and_event/robinson_sample.html

84. M. H. Abrams, *The Mirror and the Lamp: Romantic Theory and the Critical Tradition* (New York: Oxford University Press, 1953), 23.

85. Ibid., 23–24.

86. John Stuart Mill, "Thoughts on Poetry and its Varieties" (1833; *The Collected Works of John Stuart Mill*, vol. 1, *The Autobiography and Literary Essays*, ed. J. M. Robson [Toronto: University of Toronto Press, 1981]), 348.

87. Ibid., 347.

88. Ibid., 346–347, emphasis added.

89. For a discussion of how Mill addressed the skeptical problem by defining objects as permanent possibilities of sensation, see Alan Ryan, Introduction to *The Collected Works of John Stuart Mill*, vol. 9, *An Examination of William Hamilton's Philosophy and of The Principal Philosophical Questions Discussed in his Writings*, ed. John M. Robson (Toronto: University of Toronto Press, 1979), 94–97. Also see Mill's own discussion of this problem in *An Examination of Sir William Hamilton's Philosophy and of the Principal Philosophical Questions Discussed in His Writings* (Boston: William V. Spencer, 1861), 183–84.

90. Mill, *On Liberty*, 220.

91. Michael Kober, "Certainties of a World-Picture: The Epistemological Investigations of *On Certainty*," in *Cambridge Companion to Wittgenstein*, ed. Hans Sluga and David G. Stern (Cambridge: Cambridge University Press, 1996): 412, 419, 419. This formulation challenges Kwame Anthony Appiah's claims regarding Mill's investment in identification: "In identification," Appiah writes (summarizing Mill), "I shape my life by the thought that something is an appropriate aim or an appropriate way of acting for an American, a black man, a philosopher. It seems right to call this 'identification' because the label plays a role in shaping how the agent makes decisions about how to conduct a life." *The Ethics of Identity* (Princeton: Princeton University Press, 2005), 66. Such a model of subject formation bears a close resemblance to precisely the social influence Mill rejected.

92. Kober, "Certainties," 419.

93. Stanley Cavell, *The Claim of Reason: Wittgenstein, Skepticism, Morality, and Tragedy* (1979; New York: Oxford University Press, 1999), 361.

Chapter 2: Harriet Martineau and the Impersonality of Pain

1. Harriet Martineau, *Autobiography* (1877; Peterborough: Broadview, 2006), 39; hereafter abbreviated *A*.

2. Valerie Sanders captures the feeling of the opening of the *Autobiography* when she describes it as "begin[ning] like an impressionistic novel." *Reason over Passion: Harriet Martineau and the Victorian Novel* (Sussex: Harvester, 1986), 138.

3. See Sharon Cameron, *Beautiful Work: A Meditation on Pain* (Durham, NC: Duke University Press, 2000), 41–42, for a strikingly similar description of the experience of meditation.

4. Harriet Martineau, *Life in the Sick-Room* (1844; Peterborough: Broadview, 2003), 116; hereafter abbreviated *L*.

5. Martineau largely defines invalidism in terms of pain, and particularly in terms of chronic pain. She says very little about contagion or death, and seems relatively uninterested in curable disease.

6. See, for example, Dorothy Mermin, *Godiva's Ride: Women of Letters in England, 1830–1880* (Bloomington: Indiana University Press, 1993), 100.

7. Deirdre David, *Intellectual Woman and Victorian Patriarchy: Harriet Martineau, Elizabeth Barrett Browning, George Eliot* (Ithaca, NY: Cornell University Press, 1987), 41. See *A* 149–50 for a vivid account of how unexpectedly quickly the first volume sold out.

8. In addition to politics, Martineau wrote books for children, novels, and works on religion, the laws of man's nature and development, mesmerism, literature, domestic education, the principles of social observation (what we now call sociology), and travel.

9. R. K. Webb, *Harriet Martineau: A Radical Victorian* (New York: Columbia University Press, 1960), 193.

10. Alison Winter, "Harriet Martineau and the Reform of the Invalid in Victorian England," *The Historical Journal* 38, no. 3 (1995): 597. Winter provides an excellent description of the debate over whether Martineau's cure was effected by mesmerism (Martineau's opinion), or was instead due to the movement of a large tumor from her lower to her upper abdomen that fortuitously coincided with the mesmeric cure (the claim of her brother-in-law and physician, Dr. Greenhow). Also see T. H. Greenhow, *Medical Report of the Case of Miss H—M—* (London: Samuel Highley, 1845); and T. H. Greenhow, "Termination of the Case of Miss H. Martineau," *British Medical Journal* (Apr. 14, 1877): 449–50. I discuss Martineau's relation to mesmerism at the end of this chapter.

11. See Winter, "Harriet Martineau," 604; Maria Frawley, Introduction to *Life in the Sick-Room*, by Harriet Martineau, (Peterborough: Broadview, 2003), 11–28.

12. This is a point made repeatedly by her biographers. See, for example, Caroline Roberts, *The Woman and the Hour: Harriet Martineau and Victorian Ideologies* (Toronto: University of Toronto Press, 2002), 117. One important exception to this pattern is Maria Frawley's passing suggestion that "illness provides Martineau with the raw material to explore the intersubjective nature of selfhood and of human experience more generally." "'A Prisoner to the Couch': Harriet Martineau, Invalidism, and Self-Representation," in *The Body and Physical Difference: Discourses of Disability*, ed. David T. Mitchell and Sharon L. Snyder (Ann Arbor: University of Michigan Press, 1997), 176.

13. Trev Lynn Broughton, "Making the Most of Martyrdom: Harriet Martineau, Autobiography and Death," *Literature and History* 2, no. 2 (1993): 26.

14. Anka Ryall, "Medical Body and Lived Experience: The Case of Harriet Martineau," *Mosaic* 33, no. 4 (2000): 38.

15. A. Laura Stef-Praun, "Harriet Martineau's 'Intellectual Nobility': Gender, Genius and Disability," in *Harriet Martineau: Authorship, Society and Empire*, ed. Ella Dzelzainis

and Cora Kaplan (Manchester: Manchester University Press, 2010), 48. Also see Eitan Bar-Yosef on Martineau's claim that hearing impairment aids the traveler. "'With the Practiced Eye of a Deaf Person': Martineau's Travel Writing and the Construction of the Disabled Traveller," in *Harriet Martineau: Authorship, Society, and Empire*, ed. Ella Dzelzianis and Cora Kaplan (Manchester: Manchester University Press, 2010), 170.

16. Roy Porter, "The Patient's View: Doing Medical History from Below," *Theory and Society* 14, no. 2 (1985): 175–98. These efforts are in turn part of a more widespread revaluation of the sickroom and Victorian illness. See, in particular, Maria Frawley, *Invalidism and Identity in Nineteenth-Century Britain* (Chicago: University of Chicago Press, 2004); Miriam Bailin, *The Sickroom in Victorian Fiction: The Art of Being Ill* (Cambridge: Cambridge University Press, 1994); Meegan Kennedy, *Revising the Clinic: Vision and Representation in Victorian Medical Narrative and the Novel* (Columbus: Ohio State University Press, 2010); Martha Stoddard Holmes, *Fictions of Affliction: Physical Disability in Victorian Culture* (Ann Arbor: University of Michigan Press, 2004); Janis McLarren Caldwell, *Literature and Medicine in Nineteenth-Century Britain: From Mary Shelley to George Eliot* (Cambridge: Cambridge University Press, 2004); Athena Vrettos, *Somatic Fictions: Imagining Illness in Victorian Culture* (Stanford, CA: Stanford University Press, 1995).

17. Elaine Hadley, *Living Liberalism: Practical Citizenship in Mid-Victorian Britain* (Chicago: University of Chicago Press, 2010), 104, 9.

18. Harriet Martineau, *Household Education*, (Philadelphia: Lea & Blanchard, 1848), 17; hereafter abbreviated *H*.

19. Joseph Priestley, *Remarks on Dr. Reid's Inquiry into the Principles of the Human Mind on the Principles of Common Sense* (London: J. Johnson, 1775), 2.

20. Webb, *Harriet Martineau*, 77–88.

21. Hartley is now best known for his materialist revision of Locke's theory of mind. Martineau, however, was relatively unfamiliar with this aspect of the philosopher's work since Priestley eliminated most references to his "theory of vibrations" in an effort to make the theory more accessible. See Priestley, *Remarks*, 79.

22. Jad Smith, "Custom, Association, and the Mixed Mode: Locke's Early Theory of Cultural Reproduction," *ELH* 73, no. 4 (Winter 2006): 835. Also see Jenny Davidson's claim that "throughout Locke's writing the idea that children should be considered 'only as white Paper, or Wax, to be moulded and fashioned as one pleases' is balanced by an acknowledgement that individual children possess 'various Tempers, different Inclinations, and particular Defaults.'" *Breeding: A Partial History of the Eighteenth Century* (New York: Columbia University Press, 2009), 40.

23. Smith, "Custom, Association," 835.

24. John Locke, *An Essay Concerning Human Understanding* (1689; Oxford: Oxford University Press, 1975), 55.

25. Richard Allen, "David Hartley," in *The Stanford Encyclopedia of Philosophy*, ed. Edward N. Zalta, summer 2015 ed., http://plato.stanford.edu/archives/sum2015/entries/hartley/. Also see idem, *David Hartley on Human Nature* (Albany: State University of New York Press, 1999).

26. Allen, "David Hartley," 19.

27. Ibid.

28. David Hartley, *Various Conjectures on the Perception, Motion, and Generation of Ideas*, trans. Robert E. A. Palmer (Los Angeles: Williams Andrews Clark Memorial Library, University of California, 1959), 28–29.

29. Contemporary physiologists would largely have agreed with Martineau's basic point that there is an unbridgeable gulf between sensation and the memory or imagination of sensation. As G. H. Lewes wrote, for example, "To feel cold, and to think of cold,

are two markedly different states." *Problems of Life and Mind, First Series*, vol. 1 (London: Trubner & Co., 1874), 149. Also see Alexander Bain, *The Emotions and the Will* (1859; London: Longmans, Green, 1875), 15; and Herbert Spencer, *The Principles of Psychology*, vol. 1, 2nd ed. (London: Williams and Norgate, 1870), 230. It is worth noting that Martineau is also raising the problem that Ludwig Wittgenstein discusses: "Suppose everyone had a box with something in it: we call it a 'beetle.' No one can look into anyone else's box, and everyone says he knows what a beetle is only by looking at *his* beetle.—Here it would be quite possible for everyone to have something different in his box. One might even imagine such a thing constantly changing." *Philosophical Investigations* (1953; Oxford: Blackwell, 200), §293.

30. James Mill, *Analysis of the Phenomena of the Human Mind*, vol. 1 (1829; with notes by John Stuart, Alexander Bain, Andrew Finklater, and George Grote, 1869; London: Longmans, Green, Reader, and Dyer, 1878), xvii.

31. Throughout Martineau's work, one can trace her commitment to the power of education even for those whose basic modes of perception have presumably already been established. *Illustrations of Political Economy* (1832–34; edited by Deborah Ann Logan [Peterborough: Broadview, 2004]), for example, is organized around the assumption that understanding the principles of political economy will affect how people behave.

32. Ibid., 55–136.

33. When she uses it in a positive sense, Martineau usually uses the term "natural" to describe what comes automatically once we have been appropriately trained. So, for example, in "On the Agency of Feelings in the Formation of Habits; and On the Agency of Habits in the Regeneration of Feelings," she claims, "When the selfishness natural to childhood has so far given way as to allow of the exertion of benevolent principle ... various pleasures will arise from the gratitude of the object, the new interests thus opened to us, the consciousness of useful employment; ... and these pleasurable feelings ... will render a repetition of such offices of kindness more an impulse of the inclination ... till we come to do good naturally, and without any express regard to our own peace of mind." *Miscellanies*, vol. 1 (Boston: Hilliard, Gray, & Co., 1836), 210. In this passage, the term "natural" is affixed first to the "selfishness of childhood" and then to the feelings that result from a self-conscious program of cultivation. "Natural" thus means something like, "without thought," rather than without education or training.

34. For claims that Martineau *did* seek martyrdom, see Webb, *Harriet Martineau*, 68; and Broughton, "Making the Most."

35. On Martineau's representation of her relationship with her mother, see Diana Postlethwaite, "Mothering and Mesmerism in the Life of Harriet Martineau," *Signs* 14, no. 3 (1989): 583–609.

36. Roberts has shown how "illness provided Martineau with a means of escape from the conflicts of domestic and professional life," although she also claims that for her, "sickness was less of a virtually sanctioned means of rebellion than it was an atonement for a successful professional career." *Woman and the Hour*, 117, 118.

37. Martineau's letters are punctuated by expressions of guilt. See, for example, her letter of Apr. 26, 1840, to Thomas and Jane Carlyle, "If I live till winter, I hope to have done something wh shall reconcile me to the luxuries of eye & heart in wh I am steeped in this place. If I did not work somewhat, I shd be ashamed to live in such a place as this." Harriet Martineau, *The Collected Letters of Harriet Martineau, Vol. 2: 1837–1845*, ed. Deborah Ann Logan (London: Pickering & Chatto, 2007), 52.

38. Frawley emphasizes, "*Life in the Sick-Room* staked out territory markedly different from books by invalids that ... used the [sickroom] primarily to offer Christian consolation to their fellow afflicted. Concerning herself with the psychology of the invalid, Martineau

envisioned an audience less in need of consolation than of education." *Invalidism and Identity*, 201.

39. Priscilla Maurice, *Sickness, Its Trials and Blessings*, 7th ed. (1850; London: Rivingtons, 1859), 4-5.

40. James Hinton, *The Mystery of Pain: A Book for the Sorrowful* (1866; New York: Mitchell Kennerly, 1914), 39.

41. Ibid., 41.

42. Adam Smith, *The Theory of Moral Sentiments* (1759; Cambridge: Cambridge University Press, 2002), 56-57.

43. Martineau, "On the Agency of Feelings," 214.

44. Ibid., 203.

45. See Holmes's description of Martineau's concern that for the deaf, sympathy "is not only inadequate but also a destructive force ... [because of] its disarming tendency, which in Martineau's eyes leaves deaf people without a constant plan for controlling their lives." *Fictions of Affliction*, 152-53.

46. The idea of "natural magic" goes back at least to Early Modern interest in forms of magic that deal directly with natural forces. The idea of natural magic was revived at the beginning of the nineteenth century by Sir David Brewster in his *Letters on Natural Magic Addressed to Sir Walter Scott* (1832; London: Chattus & Windus, 1883).

47. Charles Dickens, *Dombey and Son* (1844-46. Harmondsworth: Penguin, 1970), 738.

48. It is worth noting that the *Dombey and Son* passage is similarly abstract.

49. Martineau, Letter to Richard Monckton Milnes (Dec. 22, 1843), in *Collected Letters, Vol. 2*, 208.

50. Martineau, Letter to Ralph Waldo Emerson (8 August, 1841), *Collected Letters, Vol. 2*, 89.

51. Ralph Waldo Emerson, *Essays: First Series* (1841; New York: Library of America, 1983), 160.

52. Ibid.

53. As Sharon Cameron goes on to explain, just because we cannot help being attached to self does not mean there is no value to seeking to rid ourselves of that attachment. *Impersonality: Seven Essays* (Chicago: University of Chicago Press, 2007), 106.

54. Stanley Cavell, *The Claim of Reason: Wittgenstein, Skepticism, Morality, and Tragedy* (1979; Oxford: Oxford University Press, 1999), 431.

55. Nowhere is the irrelevance of cognition or understanding made clearer than in Martineau's request that her maid serve as a substitute when the famous Spencer Hall failed to appear for their second appointment: "With the greatest alacrity she complied. Within one minute the twilight and phosphoric lights appeared; and in two or three more, a delicious sensation of ease spread through me,—a cool comfort, before which all pain and distress gave way, oozing out, as it were, at the soles of my feet." *Letters on Mesmerism* (1844; London: Edward Moxon, 1845), 9-10. Martineau eventually found another mesmerist since "the patience and strenuous purpose required in a case of such long and deep-seated disease can only be looked for in an educated person." Ibid., 11. It is nevertheless notable that she gave her maid credit for the turning point in her illness.

56. Henry George Atkinson and Harriet Martineau, *Letters on the Laws of Man's Nature and Development* (Boston: Josiah P. Mendum, 1851), 125. Tamara Ketabgian emphasizes the resemblances between mesmeric fluid and the mysterious forces thought to be at work in factory systems. *The Lives of Machines: The Industrial Imaginary in Victorian Literature and Culture* (Ann Arbor: University of Michigan Press, 2011), 39-44.

57. John Rawls, *A Theory of Justice* (Cambridge, MA: Harvard University Press, 1999), 24.

Chapter 3: Pain and Privacy in Villette

1. A number of other critics have made this point before, so striking and unmistakable is the narrator's hostility toward the reader. See, for example, Gillian Beer's claim that in *Villette*, "the apparent intimacy of first person narration [is] never borne out, the trust breached by opacities in the narrative, so that we are imprisoned within Lucy without full knowledge of her." "'Coming Wonders': Uses of Theatre in the Victorian Novel," in *English Drama: Forms and Development: Essays in Honour of Muriel Clara Bradbrook*, ed. Marie Axton and Raymond Williams (Cambridge: Cambridge University Press, 1977), 181–82. Also see Janice Carlisle, "The Face in the Mirror: *Villette* and the Conventions of Autobiography," *ELH* 46, no. 2 (1979): 275; Garrett Stewart, *Dear Reader: The Conscripted Audience in Nineteenth-Century British Fiction* (Baltimore: Johns Hopkins University Press, 1996), 250.

2. Charlotte Brontë, *Villette* (1853; London: Penguin, 2004), 109; hereafter abbreviated *V*.

3. As Monica L. Feinberg writes, in reading *Villette*, "we cannot avoid but feel excluded —as if the novel itself were too private to let even us in." "The Domestic Interiors of *Villette*," *Novel: A Forum on Fiction* 26, no. 2 (1993): 187.

4. Amanda Anderson, *The Powers of Distance: Cosmopolitanism and the Cultivation of Detachment* (Princeton: Princeton University Press, 2001), 35.

5. Ibid., 59.

6. John Stuart Mill, *On Liberty* (1859; in *Collected Works of John Stuart Mill*, vol. 18, *Essays on Politics and Society*, ed. J. M. Robson [Toronto: University of Toronto Press, 1977]), 220.

7. M. R. C. S., *Confessions of a Hypochondriac; or, Adventures of a Hyp. in Search of a Cure* (London: Saunders and Otley, 1849), 256–57.

8. Ibid., 258. Also see Maria H. Frawley's discussion of this text in *Invalidism and Identity in Nineteenth-Century Britain* (Chicago: University of Chicago Press, 2004), 64–112.

9. The connection between hypochondria and idleness can be traced back at least to George Cheyne's assertion in *The English Malady* (1733) that the supposed nervousness of the English can be attributed to their relative wealth and leisure. Hypochondria, like the more generic "nervousness," was commonly regarded as a problem that arises from excess civilization. For a more extensive discussion of hypochondria, see the introduction.

10. M. R. C. S., *Confessions of a Hypochondriac*, 298–99.

11. Ibid., 309–10. The implicit reference to Hume here suggests the skepticism that bedevils the hypochondriac is less cured than set aside. In responding to the question of how he lives his skepticism, Hume writes: "I dine, I play a game of back-gammon, I converse, and am merry with my friends; and when after three or four hour's amusement, I wou'd return to these speculations, they appear so cold, and strain'd, and ridiculous, that I cannot find in my heart to enter into them any further." *A Treatise of Human Nature* (1739–40; Oxford: Clarendon, 1985), 269. My thanks to an anonymous reader for calling my attention to this resemblance.

12. The term "pathophobia" comes from Esther Fischer-Homberger, "Hypochondriasis of the Eighteenth Century—Neurosis of the Present Century," *Bulletin of the History of Medicine* 46, no. 4 (1972): 397.

13. Although hypochondria has been discussed in relation to *Villette*, it has invariably been understood only as an undesirable pathology. See, for example, Micael M. Clarke's equation of hypochondria and depression. "Charlotte Brontë's *Villette*, Mid-Victorian Anti-Catholicism, and the Turn to Secularism," *ELH* 78, no. 4 (2011): 979. Also see John May-

nard, *Charlotte Brontë and Sexuality* (Cambridge: Cambridge University Press, 1984), 192; Athena Vrettos, *Somatic Fictions: Imagining Illness in Victorian Culture* (Stanford, CA: Stanford University Press, 1995), 66; Sally Shuttleworth, *Charlotte Brontë and Victorian Psychology* (Cambridge: Cambridge University Press, 1996), 231.

14. John Kucich anticipates my argument in his account of "the pleasure Brontë's protagonists take in being at odds with others, in an embattled solitude." For Kucich, however, this pleasure simply constitutes a form of self-intensification, not a religiously and morally mediated practice. *Repression in Victorian Fiction: Charlotte Brontë, George Eliot, and Charles Dickens* (Berkeley: University of California Press, 1987), 58.

15. Mary Jacobus, "The Buried Letter: Feminism and Romanticism in *Villette*," in *Women Writing and Writing about Women*, ed. Mary Jacobus (London: Croom Helm, 1979), 44.

16. The connection between Lucy's solitude (or secrecy) and power has most often been made through the issue of surveillance. See, for example, Joseph Allen Boone's claim that Lucy's "defining inwardness and sense of self ... participates in a ... 'game of secrecy' ... in which the police must also learn to play by *her* rules." "Depolicing *Villette*: Surveillance, Invisibility, and the Female Erotics of 'Heretic Narrative,'" *Novel: A Forum on Fiction* 26, no. 1 (1992), 40–41. Also see Margaret L. Shaw, "Narrative Surveillance and Social Control in *Villette*," *Studies in English Literature, 1500–1900* 34, no. 4 (1994): 817; Kathryn Bond Stockton, *God between Their Lips: Desire between Women in Irigaray, Brontë, and Eliot* (Stanford, CA: Stanford University Press, 1994), 146; Ivan Kreilkamp, *Voice and the Victorian Storyteller* (Cambridge: Cambridge University Press, 2005), 145, 152.

17. Adam Smith, *The Theory of Moral Sentiments* (1759; Cambridge: Cambridge University Press, 2002), 20.

18. Charlotte Brontë, Letter to Elizabeth Gaskell (Jul. 9, 1853), in *Letters of Charlotte Brontë*, vol. 3, *1852–55*, ed. Margaret Smith (Oxford: Clarendon, 2004), 182.

19. Ibid., 182.

20. This overdetermination may be part of what inspired Matthew Arnold to claim that he could see nothing in the novel but "hunger[,] rebellion and rage." Matthew Arnold, Letter to Jane Martha Arnold Forster (Apr. 14, 1853), in *The Letters of Matthew Arnold*, vol. 1, ed. Cecil Y. Lang (Charlottesville: University of Virginia Press, 1996), 262.

21. Peter Allan Dale, "Heretical Narration: Charlotte Brontë's Search for Endlessness," *Religion and Literature* 16, no. 3 (1984): 5. Also see Thomas Vargish's claim that for St. Paul, "suffering is the mark of a special grace: 'For whom the Lord loveth he chasteneth, and scourgeth every son whom he receiveth.'" "Lucy's destiny is to support this assertion," Vargish writes, "to suffer deeply and in a special way." *The Providential Aesthetic in Victorian Fiction* (Charlottesville: University of Virginia Press, 1985), 84.

22. Charlotte Brontë, Letter to Ellen Nussey (Feb. 20?, 1837), in *Letters of Charlotte Brontë*, vol. 1, *1829–1847*, ed. Margaret Smith (Oxford: Clarendon, 1995), 164.

23. Charlotte Brontë, Letter to Amelia Ringrose (Apr. 28?, 1850) in *Letters of Charlotte Brontë*, vol. 2, *1848–1851*, ed. Margaret Smith (Oxford: Clarendon, 2000), 390.

24. Raymond Williams, *The English Novel from Dickens to Lawrence* (1970; London: Hogarth Press, 1984), 73–74.

25. So, for example, when Lucy wakes up after fainting to find herself surrounded by objects she knows from her childhood, she claims to be wholly bewildered. Yet, since we subsequently learn that she had already recognized Dr. John as Graham Bretton, it is difficult to believe she would not imagine his mother might be in town, too.

26. See Avrom Fleishman's claim that the novel can best be understood as a spiritual autobiography in the tradition of Bunyan. *Figures of Autobiography: The Language of Self-Writing in Victorian and Modern England* (Berkeley: University of California Press,

1983), 225. Yet, as Peter Allen Dale notes, "We have in *Villette*, finally, another sort of endlessness than the Christian Eternity, and this is the condition of simply being with an end, without a shape to life." "Heretical Narration," 21.

27. Angus Fletcher, "Allegory without Ideas," *boundary 2* 33, no. 1 (2006), 78.

28. Ibid.

29. Ibid., 79.

30. Ibid., 96, 98.

31. It seems worth noting that shipwreck was sometimes identified as an antidote to hypochondria. See, for example, Spencer Thompson, "Trips after Health, and How to Profit by Them," where he claims, "Surely, if you were the most confirmed of hypochondriacs, they [shipwrecks] will take you out of yourself." *The Sixpenny Magazine* 1 (1861): 444. Harriet Martineau makes a similar point in *Life in the Sick-Room*, pointing to the distraction afforded by shipwreck. (1844; Peterborough: Broadview, 2003), 71.

32. Nor does the remainder of the passage clarify: "To-night, I was not so mutinous, nor so miserable. My Sisera lay quiet in the tent, slumbering; and if his pain ached through his slumbers, something like an angel—the Ideal—knelt near, dropping balm on the soothed temples, holding before the sealed eyes a magic glass, of which the sweet, solemn visions were repeated in dreams, and shedding a reflex from her moonlight wings and robe over the transfixed sleeper, over the tent threshold, over all the landscape lying without. Jael, the stern woman, sat apart, relenting somewhat over her captive; but more prone to dwell on the faithful expectation of Heber coming home. By which words I mean that the cool peace and dewy sweetness of the night filled me with a mood of hope: not hope on any definite point, but a general sense of encouragement and heart-ease" (*V* 121).

33. According to Kucich, Brontë's novels often "protest against certain kinds of deprivation, they compensate for and transform deprivation through an extravagant elaboration of feeling, of inward strength tested and exercised through suffering." This notion of "compensation" seems to me excessively optimistic. *Repression in Victorian Fiction*, 72.

34. Marit Fimland, "On the Margins of the Acceptable: Charlotte Bronte's *Villette*," *Literature and Theology* 10, no. 2 (1996), 152.

35. Stanley Cavell, *The Claim of Reason: Wittgenstein, Skepticism, Morality, and Tragedy* (1979; New York: Oxford University Press, 1999), 425. Cavell's claim constitutes the conclusion of his attempt to parse Wittgenstein's famous thought-experiment regarding a picture (or image, or idea—depending on the translation one consults) of a pot from which steam is escaping. See the introduction for a discussion of this parable.

36. Elaine Freedgood, "The Secret History of Diegesis," lecture at the Radcliffe Institute for Advanced Study (Sept. 2013). My thanks to Elaine Freedgood for allowing me to cite this talk.

37. "*Villette* and *Ruth*," *Putnam's Magazine* 1 (1853): 537.

38. Ibid.

39. See John Stokes on Rachel, in which he quotes George Henry Lewes as claiming that "tragic pathos to be grand should be *impersonal*"—by which Stokes claims Lewes meant sympathy engendered by the absence of self-pity in the tragic protagonist. "'Terrible Beauty': An Actress among the Novelists," *ELH* 51, no. 4 (1984): 790. Mary Wilson Carpenter claims that Vashti's biblical significance is not just that she is disobedient: "The name Vashti speaks to patriarchal denial of a woman's right to speak her own 'language,' even the language of her national or racial identity, and to patriarchal approval of her self-suppression of what might be termed the language of her body." *Imperial Bibles, Domestic Bodies: Women, Sexuality, and Religion in the Victorian Market* (Athens: Ohio University Press, 2003), 79.

40. Rachel Biale, *Women and Jewish Law: The Essential Texts, Their History, and Their Relevance for Today* (New York: Schocken, 1995), 186.

41. According to Susan M. Gilbert and Sandra Gubar, Lucy's illness "is her final, anguished recognition of her own life-in-death." *Madwoman in the Attic: The Woman Writer and the Nineteenth-Century Literary Imagination* (New Haven, CT: Yale University Press, 1979), 414. While I agree, I want to emphasize that it is not clear whether that death is her own or M. Paul's—or whether there is a significant difference between these two events.

42. The passage also serves as a confirmation of Steven Knapp's account of the Romantic concern regarding personifications' "contagious effect on the ostensibly literal agents with which they interacted.... Once the boundaries between literal and figurative agency were erased, it seemed that nothing would prevent the imagination from metaphorizing literal agents as easily as it literalized metaphors." Steven Knapp, *Personification and the Sublime: Milton to Coleridge* (Cambridge, MA: Harvard University Press, 1985), 2.

43. A number of critics have taken at face value the notion that M. Paul's fate is left up to the reader to decide. See, for example, Patricia E. Johnson, "'The Heretic Narrative': The Strategy of the Split Narrative in Charlotte Brontë's *Villette*," *Studies in English Literature, 1500–1900* 30, no. 4 (1990): 629; Terry Eagleton, *Myths of Power: A Marxist Study of the Brontës* (Houndmills: Macmillan, 1975), 73; Luann McCracken Fletcher, "Manufactured Marvels, Heretic Narratives, and the Process of Interpretation in *Villette*," *Studies in English Literature, 1500–1900* 32, no. 4 (1992): 740. This is a notion that Brontë herself supports: as she wrote to George Smith, "With regard to that momentous point—M. Paul's fate—in case any one in future should request to be enlightened thereon—they may be told that it was designed that every reader should settle the catastrophe for himself, according to the quality of his disposition, the tender or the remorseless impulse of his nature. Drowning and Matrimony are the fearful alternatives. The Merciful ... will choose the milder doom—drown him to put him out of pain. The cruel-hearted will on the contrary impale him on the second horn of the dilemma, marrying him without ruth or compunction to that—person—that—that—individual—'Lucy Snowe.'" Letter to George Smith (Mar. 26, 1853), *Letters*, vol. 3, 142. Despite this weight of critical opinion and the textual evidence offered by the letter, the echoes between the two drowning passages, along with the way the reader is invited to imagine a happy counterfactual in each, confirms that we are supposed to imagine that M. Paul does, in fact, drown at the end of the novel.

44. Sigmund Freud, *The Interpretation of Dreams* (1989; in *The Standard Edition of the Complete Psychological Works of Sigmund Freud*, Vol. 5 [London: Hogarth Press, 1994], 509), quoted in Cathy Caruth, *Unclaimed Experience: Trauma, Narrative, and History* (Baltimore: Johns Hopkins University Press, 1996), 93.

45. Caruth, *Unclaimed Experience*, 100.

46. Ibid.

47. Ibid., 106.

48. The bathetic counterexample would be the nun. On the nun, see, in particular, Christina Crosby, "Charlotte Brontë's Haunted Text," *Studies in English Literature, 1500–1900* 24, no. 4 (1984): 701–15.

49. Veena Das, *Life and Words: Violence and the Descent into the Ordinary* (Berkeley: University of California Press, 2007), 39.

Chapter 4: Charles Darwin's Affect Theory

1. Charles Darwin himself sought to soften the implications of his conclusions. See, for example, *The Origin of Species*: "When we reflect on this struggle [for existence], we may console ourselves with the full belief, that the war of nature is not incessant, that no fear is felt, that death is generally prompt, and that the vigorous, the healthy, and the happy survive and multiply." *On the Origin of Species* (1859; Oxford: Oxford University Press, 1996), 62; hereafter abbreviated *O*. Several critics have commented on the contradictions in this passage. See, for example, James R. Moore, "Of Love and Death: Why Darwin 'Gave Up Christianity,'" in *History, Humanity, and Evolution: Essays for John C. Greene*, ed. James R. Moore (Cambridge: Cambridge University Press, 1989), 222; Gillian Beer, *Darwin's Plots: Evolutionary Narrative in Darwin, George Eliot, and Nineteenth-Century Fiction* (Cambridge: Cambridge University Press, 1983), 35.

2. Thomas Robert Malthus, *An Essay on the Principle of Population* (1798; Oxford: Oxford University Press, 2004), 14.

3. Adam Phillips, *Darwin's Worms: On Life Stories and Death Stories* (New York: Basic Books, 1999), 3.

4. Ibid., 7.

5. Benedict de Spinoza, *Ethics* (1677; London: Penguin, 1996), 35. Although it is unlikely that Darwin read Spinoza's work himself, Peter Garratt has pointed out the probable connections between the two thinkers. *Victorian Empiricism: Self, Knowledge, and Reality in Ruskin, Bain, Lewes, Spencer, and George Eliot* (Madison, NJ: Fairleigh Dickinson University Press, 2010), 133. Also see Robert J. Richards, *The Romantic Conception of Life: Science and Philosophy in the Age of Goethe* (Chicago: University of Chicago Press, 2002), 455–58, 481.

6. Spinoza, *Ethics*, 32.

7. Charles Darwin, *Journal of Researches into the Geology and Natural History of the Various Countries Visited by H. M. S. Beagle Under the Command of Captain Fitzroy, R. N., From 1832–1836* (1839; London: Henry Colburn, 1840), 369. Later editions of this text came to be known as *The Voyage of the Beagle*.

8. One version of affect theory has been attentive to antisocial emotions such as disgust, envy, etc.; however, they have rarely engaged the problem of aversive physical experience. See, for example, Sianne Ngai, *Ugly Feelings* (Cambridge, MA: Harvard University Press, 2007); Lauren Berlant, *Cruel Optimism* (Durham, NC: Duke University Press, 2011); Ann Cvetkovich, *Depression: A Public Feeling* (Durham, NC: Duke University Press, 2012). One notable exception is Sara Ahmed, *The Cultural Politics of Emotion* (New York: Routledge, 2004).

9. Bruno Latour, "Why Has Critique Run out of Steam? From Matters of Fact to Matters of Concern," *Critical Inquiry* 30 (2004): 227. Latour advocates "a *stubbornly realist attitude*." The question, he explains, is not "to get *away* from facts but *closer* to them, not fighting empiricism but, on the contrary, renewing empiricism" (231).

10. On the continuities between Darwin and Bell, see Thomas Dixon, *From Passions to Emotions: The Creation of a Secular Psychological Category* (Cambridge: Cambridge University Press, 2003), 165–75.

11. Sir Charles Bell writes: "There exist in [man's] face, not only all those parts, which by their action produce expression in the several classes of quadrupeds, but there is added a peculiar set of muscles to which no other office can be assigned than to serve for expression." *The Anatomy and Philosophy of Expression: As Connected with the Fine Arts*, 5th ed. (London: Henry H. Bohn, 1865), 121. For discussions of the relation between Darwin and Bell, see Janet Browne, "Darwin and the Expression of the Emotions," in *The Darwin-*

ian Heritage, ed. David Kohn (Princeton: Princeton University Press, 1985), 312–13; and Lucy Hartley, *Physiognomy and the Meaning of Expression in Nineteenth-Century Culture* (Cambridge: Cambridge University Press, 2001), 44–79.

12. Hartley, *Physiognomy*, 146.

13. Adrian Desmond and James Moore, introduction to *The Descent of Man, and Selection in Relation to Sex*, by Charles Darwin (1871; London: Penguin, 2004), xxvii. Also see idem, *Darwin's Sacred Cause: How a Hatred of Slavery Shaped Darwin's Views on Human Evolution* (Boston: Houghton Mifflin Harcourt, 2009); Sarah Winter, "Darwin's Saussure: Biosemiotics and Race in *Expression*," *Representations* 107, no. 1 (2009): 129–32; Rosemary Jann, "Evolutionary Physiognomy and Darwin's *Expression of the Emotions*," *Victorian Review* 18, no. 2 (1992): 1–27.

14. Ekman also maintains a close relation to the work of Silvan Tomkins, whose writings on affect have recently been popularized by Eve Kosofsky Sedgwick and Adam Frank. See Eve Kosofsky Sedgwick and Adam Frank, eds., *Shame and Its Sisters: A Silvan Tomkins Reader* (Durham, NC: Duke University Press, 1995). On this history, see Ruth Leys, "The Turn to Affect: A Critique," *Critical Inquiry* 37, no. 3 (2011): 437–39; idem, "How Did Fear Become a Scientific Object and What Kind of Object Is It?" *Representations* 110, no. 1 (2010): 67–70; and Daniel M. Gross, "Defending the Humanities with Charles Darwin's *The Expression of the Emotions in Man and Animals* (1872)," *Critical Inquiry* 37, no. 1 (2010): 38–39.

15. Paul Ekman, introduction to *The Expression of the Emotions in Man and Animals*, by Charles Darwin (Oxford: Oxford University Press, 1998), xxx. (Please note that references to *The Expression* in this chapter are not to this edition.) Although Ekman claims this is a false dichotomy, he is far more committed to expression's function as an index than as a signal. See Leys, "Turn to Affect," for a discussion of the significance of this claim.

16. See Charles S. Peirce's definition of the index in "On a New List of Categories" (1867; in *The Writings of Charles S. Peirce: A Chronological Edition*, vol. 2, *1867–1871*, ed. Peirce Edition Project [Bloomington: Indiana University Press, 1984], 56–58). For a useful discussion of this concept, see Albert Atkin, "Peirce's Theory of Signs," in *The Stanford Encyclopedia of Philosophy*, ed. Edward N. Zalta, summer 2013 ed., http://plato.stanford.edu/archives/sum2013/entries/peirce-semiotics/

17. Paul Ekman, afterword to *The Expression of the Emotions in Man and Animals*, by Charles Darwin (Oxford: Oxford University Press, 1998), 387.

18. Paul Ekman, "How to Spot a Terrorist on the Fly," *The Washington Post* (Oct. 29, 2006), http://www.washingtonpost.com/wp-dyn/content/article/2006/10/27/AR2006102701478.html

19. Gross, "Defending the Humanities," 51.

20. Ibid., 45.

21. John Plotz, "Emotional Intelligence, Darwin-Style: The Work of Feeling in an Era of Objectivity," unpublished essay. My thanks to John Plotz for allowing me to cite this essay.

22. Other critics who have discussed Darwin's rejection of the disaggregation of nature and culture, biology and language, nonhuman and human animals include Janet Browne, *Charles Darwin: A Biography*, vol. 2, *The Power of Place* (Princeton: Princeton University Press, 2002), 340; Robert M. Young, *Darwin's Metaphor: Nature's Place in Victorian Culture* (Cambridge: Cambridge University Press, 1985), 57. Such refusals of the separation of body and mind seem to place Darwin very clearly in the tradition of monism that Dixon and Garratt have shown was reemerging around mid-century. Dixon, *From Passions to Emotions*, and Garratt, *Victorian Empiricism*. As Garratt explains, "double-aspect theory"

implies that "a psychological event such as pain may be accounted for both in mental terms (the qualitative experience of pain) and bodily terms (the occurrence of specific physiological changes) without either description being exhaustively valid or finally preferable." *Victorian Empiricism*, 135. On double-aspect monism, also see Rick Rylance, *Victorian Psychology and British Culture 1850–1880* (Oxford: Oxford University Press, 2000), 251–330.

23. Charles Darwin, *The Expression of the Emotions in Man and Animals* (1872; Chicago: University of Chicago Press, 1965), 28; hereafter abbreviated *E*.

24. My thanks to Sarah Winter for calling my attention to this connection.

25. Darwin explains, "A hungry man, if tempting food is placed before him, may not show his hunger by any outward gesture, but he cannot check the secretion of saliva" (*E* 75–76). Salivating may not be the same thing as feeling hungry, but it has an indexical relation to it. Similarly, "A man when moderately angry, or even when enraged, may command the movements of his body, but he cannot prevent his heart from beating rapidly" (*E* 75). One implication here is that if one's heart does *not* race, one cannot truly be said to be enraged.

26. Brian Massumi, *Parables for the Virtual: Movement, Affect, Sensation* (Durham, NC: Duke University Press, 2002), 29.

27. Ibid., 28.

28. Ibid., 29.

29. Ibid.

30. Ibid., 30.

31. See Susan Pockett, "The Neuroscience of Movement," in *Does Consciousness Cause Behavior?*, ed. Susan Pockett, William P. Banks, and Shaun Gallagher (Cambridge: Massachusetts Institute of Technology Press, 2006), 9–24; Shaun Gallagher, "Where's the Action? Epiphenomenalism and the Problem of Free Will," in *Does Consciousness Cause Behavior?*, edited by Susan Pockett, William P. Banks, and Shaun Gallagher (Cambridge: Massachusetts Institute of Technology Press, 2006), 109–24; Daniel C. Dennett, *Freedom Evolves* (New York: Viking, 2003); M. R. Bennett and P. M. S. Hacker, *Philosophical Foundations of Neuroscience* (Malden, MA: Blackwell, 2003).

32. Leys, "Turn to Affect," 451.

33. Ibid.

34. William E. Connolly, "Brain Waves, Transcendental Fields and Techniques of Thought," *Radical Philosophy* 94 (1999): 20.

35. Ibid.

36. Connolly's choice to rely on a *New York Times* summary rather than on the scientists' own findings represents one example of a much more general ambivalence regarding science in affect studies. This problem is pointed out in Leys, "Turn to Affect," 460.

37. Charles Darwin, *Charles Darwin Notebooks, 1836–1844, Geology, Transmutation of Species, Metaphysical Inquiries*, ed. Paul H. Barrett, Peter J. Gautrey, Sandra Herbert, David Kohn, Sydney Smith (Ithaca, NY: Cornell University Press, 1987), 575. As several critics have pointed out, although the *Notebooks* were written several decades before *The Expression*, certain passages from these notebooks appear nearly verbatim in the much later published work. Janet Browne, *Charles Darwin: A Biography*, vol. 1, *Voyaging* (Princeton: Princeton University Press, 1995), 382–84; idem, *Power of Place*, vol. 2, 201.

38. Darwin, *Notebooks*, 582.

39. Paul White situates Darwin's fascination with tears in the context of a larger cultural shift: while eighteenth-century writings on tears involved the whole body, he argues, new models of emotions centered on nervous physiology. "Darwin Wept: Science and the Sentimental Subject," *Journal of Victorian Culture* 16, no. 2 (2011): 195–213. Also see Sandra Herbert, "Darwin, Malthus, and Selection," *Journal of the History of Biology* 4, no. 1

(1971): 209-17; S. A. Barnett, "The 'Expression of the Emotions,'" in *A Century of Darwin*, ed. S. A. Barnett (London: Heinemann, 1962), 519; Browne, *Power of Place*, vol. 2, 305; Eugenie Brinkema, *The Forms of the Affects* (Durham, NC: Duke University Press, 2014), 11-14; Otniel E. Dror, "On the Blush," in *Histories of Scientific Observation*, ed. Lorraine Daston and Elizabeth Lunbeck (Chicago: University of Chicago Press, 2011), 335-36.

40. Darwin, *Notebooks*, 526.

41. Ibid., 536.

42. It is worth noting that both John Stuart Mill and Harriet Martineau were necessitarians, as well. As I discuss in chapter 1, for Mill, a commitment to necessity says nothing about what it feels like to be a moral agent. Harriet Martineau agreed, "All the world is practically Necessarian [*sic*]. All human action proceeds on the supposition that all the workings of the universe are governed by laws which cannot be broken by human will." *Autobiography* (1877; Peterborough: Broadview, 2006), 106.

43. Spinoza, *Ethics*, 32.

44. Garratt, *Victorian Empiricism*, 137.

45. As Gilles Deleuze explains, this does not mean that attributes constitute an epistemological problem: "Attributes are not ways of seeing pertaining to the intellect, because the Spinozist intellect perceives only what is." *Spinoza: Practical Philosophy* (San Francisco: City Lights, 1988), 51.

46. Gillian Beer suggestively invokes the concept "becoming" in her claim that "Darwin's work is not a search for an originator nor for a true beginning. It is rather the description of a process of becoming, and such process does not move constantly in a single direction." "Darwin's Reading and the Fictions of Development," in *The Darwinian Heritage*, ed. David Kohn (Princeton: Princeton University Press, 1985), 575.

47. According to Elizabeth Grosz, Deleuze and Guattari take from Darwin his "understanding of evolution as the emergence in time of biological innovation and surprise." "Darwin develops an account of a real that is an open and generative force of self-organization and growing complexity," she continues, "a dynamic real that has features of its own which ... are more readily understood in terms of active vectors of change." *The Nick of Time: Politics, Evolution, and the Untimely* (Durham, NC: Duke University Press, 2004), 19. Although this is an accurate account of Deleuze and Guattari's repurposing of Darwin's work, Darwin is in no way as optimistic or as teleological as this account suggests. See, for example, Browne on Darwin's rejection of Lamarckian progressivism. *Voyaging*, vol. 1, 452.

48. Gilles Deleuze, and Felix Guattari, *A Thousand Plateaus: Capitalism and Schizophrenia* (1980; Minneapolis: University of Minnesota Press, 2007), 272.

49. Charles Darwin, *The Various Contrivances by Which Orchids Are Fertilized by Insects* (1862; New York: New York University Press, 1988), 32.

50. Ibid., 101.

51. Deleuze and Guattari, *Thousand Plateaus*, 238.

52. As such, moments like these bear out what Gary Willingham-McLain has identified as Darwin's investment in the mathematical sublime as evidenced in "the infinitely complex web of dynamic relations that produces evolutionary change." "Darwin's 'Eye of Reason': Natural Selection and the Mathematical Sublime," *Victorian Literature and Culture* 25, no. 1 (1997): 68.

53. On Darwin's anthropomorphism, see Beer, *Darwin's Plots*, 44-70; Jane Bennett, *Vibrant Matter: A Political Ecology of Things* (Durham, NC: Duke University Press, 2010), 119-20; John R. Durant, "The Ascent of Nature in Darwin's *Descent of Man*," in *The Darwinian Heritage*, ed. David Kohn (Princeton: Princeton University Press, 1985), 283-306; Jann, "Evolutionary Physiognomy," 17; George Levine, *Darwin Loves You: Natural Selection*

and the Re-Enchantment of the World (Princeton: Princeton University Press, 2006), 150, 169.

54. Darwin, *Journal of Researches*, 260.

55. Ibid., 261.

56. Part of what seems remarkable about moments like these is the leap of imagination such ways of seeing involve. As Darwin writes in his "Recollections," "I am not very skeptical,—a frame of mind which I believe to be injurious to the progress of science." "Recollections of the Development of My Mind and Character (1876-1881)," in *Evolutionary Writings*, ed. James A. Secord (Oxford: Oxford University Press, 2008), 423. This lack of skepticism—otherwise understandable as a wildly imaginative way of perceiving the world—is apparent throughout his work. On Darwin's shifts of attention between the individual and the collective, see, in particular, Cannon Schmitt, *Darwin and the Memory of the Human: Evolution, Savages, and South America* (Cambridge: Cambridge University Press, 2009), 155-62.

57. Darwin, *Notebooks*, 529.

58. Lorraine Daston and Katharine Park, *Wonders and the Order of Nature: 1150-1750* (New York: Zone, 1998), 363. Richards is one of several critics to comment on Darwin's commitment to aesthetic pleasure. See Richards, *Romantic Conception of Life*, 526. Also see Browne, *Voyaging*, vol. 1, 211-33; James Paradis, "Darwin and Landscape," in *Victorian Science and Victorian Values: Literary Perspectives*, ed. James Paradis and Thomas Postlewait (New Brunswick, NJ: Rutgers University Press, 1985), 94-110; James Krasner, "A Chaos of Delight: Perception and Illusion in Darwin's Scientific Writing," *Representations* 31 (1990): 139-40; Levine, *Darwin Loves You*, 209-21; Schmitt, *Darwin and the Memory of the Human*, 10-12.

59. Darwin, *Journal of Researches*, 177n. It thus took great effort to explain to his host that he refrained from spurring his horse not on his host's account, but on the animal's: "He exclaimed, with a look of great surprise, 'Ah Don Carlos que cosa!' It was clear that such an idea had never before entered his head" (ibid.). Such astonishment suggests an utter absence of any compassion or fellow-feeling between rider and horse.

60. Ibid., 177-78.

61. Spinoza, *Ethics*, 105.

62. Ibid., 77.

63. See Darwin, "Recollections," 393.

64. Ibid., 394.

65. Darwin, *Descent*, 121.

66. For a more extended discussion of sympathy, see Rachel Ablow, *The Marriage of Minds: Reading Sympathy in the Victorian Marriage Plot* (Stanford, CA: Stanford University Press, 2007).

67. Darwin clearly manifests an interest in more familiar forms of sympathy, as well. See, for example, the very beginning of *The Expression*, where he argues that "the study of Expression is difficult," for "when we witness any deep emotion, our sympathy is so strongly excited, that close observation is forgotten or rendered almost impossible" (E 12). Sympathy here is powerful and distracting, but it does not seem to have any other consequences of note.

68. Critics who attend to this passage include: Mary Noble, "Darwin among the Novelists: Narrative Strategy and the Expression of the Emotions," *Nineteenth-Century Prose* 38, no. 1 (2011): 113-15; White, "Darwin Wept," 209-11; Randal Keynes, *Darwin, His Daughter, and Human Evolution* (New York: Riverhead, 2002), 299.

69. Leys, "Turn to Affect," 440.

70. Elizabeth A. Wilson, *Psychosomatic: Feminism and the Neurological Body* (Durham, NC: Duke University Press, 2004), 65.

71. Wilson, for example, assumes that Darwin sought to keep nervous action separate from psychology. See ibid., 71. It is difficult to determine the basis for such a claim.

72. Gregory J. Seigworth and Melissa Gregg, "An Inventory of Shimmers," in *The Affect Theory Reader*, ed. Melissa Gregg and Gregory J. Seigworth (Durham, NC: Duke University Press, 2010), 3, 4.

73. Ben Anderson, "Becoming and Being Hopeful: Towards a Theory of Affect," *Environment and Planning D: Society and Space* 24, no. 5 (2006): 733.

74. Teresa Brennan, *The Transmission of Affect* (Ithaca, NY: Cornell University Press, 2004), 65. Brennan bases this claim on scientific accounts of the transmission of pheromones that she admits she may have misunderstood: "The point here is not to claim a property for this or that hormone, or to claim that it inevitably affects us all the same way. I do not have the expertise to make such a claim. The point rather is to use particular instances (even if some of them have been misinterpreted, as a layperson is likely to misinterpret any technical field) to frame hypotheses" (72).

75. Darwin, "Recollections," 394.

76. Levine attempts to appropriate Darwin's wonder for a progressive politics in line with Jane Bennett's notion of "vibrant matter" and William Connolly's "secular enchantment." "As we follow Darwin's tough theodicy," he writes, "we find ourselves in a world worth loving; we become participants and observers in a life larger than any of us, and more meaningful." *Darwin Loves You*, 25. Although I agree that Darwin encourages us to find ourselves in a "world worth loving," that does not mean that he imagines it is therefore "meaningful."

77. Darwin, *Journal of Researches*, 376.

Chapter 5: Wounded Trees, Abandoned Boots

1. Veena Das cites this passage from Wittgenstein in "Language and Body: Transactions in the Construction of Pain." However, she omits Wittgenstein's suggestion that it might be possible to claim that "someone has pains ... in a piece of furniture, or in any empty spot." *Life and Words: Violence and the Descent into the Everyday* (Berkeley: University of California Press, 2007), 39–40. While Das is exclusively interested in the possibility of feeling pain in another *person's* body, in this chapter I argue that Hardy is additionally concerned with what opportunities are made available by the possibility of feeling pain in animals, inanimate objects, counterfactuals, fictions, or empty spaces.

2. On the dreariness of Hardy's plots, see, for example, John Holloway, "Hardy's Major Fiction," in *Hardy: A Collection of Critical Essays*, ed. Albert J. Guerard (Englewood Cliffs, NJ: Prentice Hall, 1963), 52–62.

3. Gillian Beer, *Darwin's Plots: Evolutionary Narrative in Darwin, George Eliot, and Nineteenth-Century Fiction* (Cambridge: Cambridge University Press, 1983), 232.

4. Dorothy Van Ghent is one of the earliest critics to be concerned with the pervasiveness of accident in Hardy's work. "On the earth [as Hardy conceives it], coincidence and accident constitute order, the prime terrestrial order, for they ... are 'the given,' impenetrable by human *ratio*, accountable only as mystery." *The English Novel: Form and Function* (New York: Harper & Row, 1967), 204. Also see J. Hillis Miller, *Thomas Hardy: Distance and Desire* (Cambridge, MA: Harvard University Press, 1970), 209.

5. See Hardy's insistence, reprinted in *The Later Years*, that he is an artist rather than a philosopher: "Like so many critics, Mr. Courtney treats my works of art as if they were a

scientific system of philosophy, although I have repeatedly stated in prefaces and elsewhere that the views in them are *seemings*, provisional impressions only, used for artistic purposes because they represent approximately the impression of the age, and are plausible, till somebody produces better theories of the universe." Florence Emily Hardy, *The Later Years of Thomas Hardy, 1892-1928* (Cambridge: Cambridge University Press, 1930), 175. Just a few of the critics who have insisted that Hardy should be taken at his word when he claims not to have any coherent philosophy are Morton Dauwen Zabel, "Hardy in Defense of His Art: The Aesthetic of Incongruity," *Southern Review* 6 (1940): 145; John Holloway, *The Victorian Sage: Studies in Argument* (New York: Norton, 1953), 6.

6. Mark Asquith, "Philosophy, Metaphysics, and Music in Hardy's Cosmic Vision," in *The Ashgate Research Companion to Thomas Hardy*, ed. Rosemarie Morgan (Farnham: Ashgate, 2010), 181.

7. On Darwin's influence, see Beer, *Darwin's Plots*; Elliott B. Gose, Jr., "Psychic Evolution: Darwinism and Initiation in *Tess of the d'Urbervilles*," *Nineteenth-Century Fiction* 18, no. 3 (1963): 261-72; Holloway, "Hardy's Major Fiction"; Bruce Johnson, "'The Perfection of Species' and Hardy's *Tess*," in *Nature and the Victorian Imagination*, ed. U. C. Knoepflmacher and G. B. Tennyson (Berkeley: University of California Press, 1977), 259-77. On Schopenhauer's influence, see Miller, *Thomas Hardy*, 20-21. (Carl J. Weber points out that although Hardy's copy of *The Four-Fold Root* was cut and marked, since the text was not published in English until *Tess of the d'Urbervilles* was complete, its impact on the earlier novels must have been relatively limited. "Hardy's Copy of Schopenhauer," *Colby Quarterly* 4, no. 12 [1957]: 217-24.) On Frazer's influence, see Gose, "Psychic Evolution." On Spencer's influence, see Kathleen Blake, "Pure Tess: Hardy on Knowing a Woman," *Studies in English Literature, 1500-1900* 22, no. 4 (1982): 689-705. G. Glen Wickens attends to Hardy's connections to Darwin, Huxley, Spencer, Comte, Hume, and Mill. "Literature and Science: Hardy's Response to Mill, Huxley and Darwin," *Mosaic* 14, no. 3 (1981): 63-79. Robert Schweik adds Leslie Stephen, Feuerbach, and Fourier to Spencer, Mill, Comte, and Schopenhauer. "The Influence of Religion, Science, and Philosophy on Hardy's Writings," in *The Cambridge Companion to Thomas Hardy*, ed. Dale Kramer (Cambridge: Cambridge University Press, 1999), 54-72.

8. Hardy, *Later Years*, 217. The passage continues: "This view is quite in keeping with what you call a Pessimistic philosophy (a mere nickname with no sense in it), which I am quite unable to see as 'leading logically to the conclusion that the Power behind the universe is malign'" (ibid.). Although nominally attributed to Florence Emily Hardy, most critics agree that Thomas Hardy was responsible for nearly all the writing of *The Early Life of Thomas Hardy* and *The Later Years of Thomas Hardy*. See Michael Millgate, *Thomas Hardy: A Biography Revisited* (Oxford: Oxford University Press, 2004), 476-79.

9. Hardy, *Later Years*, 97.

10. On the rhetoric of antivivisection, see, in particular, Lucy Bending, *The Representation of Bodily Pain in Late Nineteenth-Century English Culture* (Oxford: Clarendon, 2000), 116-76. Also see Carol Lansbury, "Gynaecology, Pornography, and the Antivivisection Movement," *Victorian Studies* 28, no. 3 (1985): 413-37; Stewart Richards, "Vicarious Suffering, Necessary Pain: Physiological Method in Late Nineteenth-Century Britain," in *Vivisection in Historical Perspective*, ed. Nicholaas A. Rupke (London: Croom Helm, 1987), 125-48; Nicholaas A. Rupke, "Pro-vivisection in England in the Early 1880s: Arguments and Motives," in *Vivisection in Historical Perspective*, ed. Nicholaas A. Rupke (London: Croom Helm, 1987), 188-213; James Turner, *Reckoning with the Beast: Animals, Pain, and Humanity in the Victorian Mind* (Baltimore: Johns Hopkins University Press, 1980), 88-121.

11. Thomas Laqueur, "Bodies, Details, and the Humanitarian Narrative," in *The New Cultural History*, ed. Lynn Hunt (Berkeley: University of California Press, 1989), 181.

12. Ibid., 178.

13. Ludwig Wittgenstein, *The Blue and Brown Books: Preliminary Studies for the "Philosophical Investigations"* (1933–35; New York: Harper Perennial, 1960), 51.

14. Thomas Hardy, *The Woodlanders* (1887; Oxford: Oxford University Press, 2005), 15; hereafter abbreviated *W*.

15. See Steven Knapp and Walter Benn Michaels's account of why "cries" cannot be understood as meaningful unless they are also understood as the product of a subject that intends to communicate something to someone. Either we experience material signs as intentional—and hence, meaningful—or we experience them as accidental, and hence meaningless. "Against Theory," *Critical Inquiry* 8, no. 4 (1982): 728. Such an account helps explain why Hardy's description of the "vocalized sorrows" of the trees makes it seem as if the trees must have consciousness, even though the passage deliberately refuses to offer that as a clear conclusion. Also see Heather Keenleyside's description of how "the eighteenth-century predilection for personification reveals modernity to be marked less by the clear distinction between persons and things than by the persistent instability of these terms." "Personification for the People: On James Thomson's *The Seasons*," *ELH* 76, no. 2 (2009): 448.

16. My thanks to Jules Law for pointing out the ambiguity as to whether these branches are on the same or different trees.

17. William A. Cohen, "Arborealities: The Tactile Ecology of Hardy's *Woodlanders*," *19: Interdisciplinary Studies in the Long Nineteenth Century* 19 (2014), http://www.19.bbk.ac.uk/articles/10.16995/ntn.690/. Also see Ivan Kreilkamp's suggestion that *Far from the Madding Crowd*, in particular, invites a nonanthropocentric reading, and Gillian Beer's insight that Hardy's attempt "to find a scale for the human" results in an "ambiguous anthropomorphism [that] pervades his writing ... which paradoxically ... gives the human a fugitive and secondary role in his system of reference but not in his system of value." Ivan Kreilkamp, "Pitying the Sheep in *Far from the Madding Crowd*," *Novel: A Forum on Fiction* 42, no. 3 (2009): 475; Beer, *Darwin's Plots*, 235. Beer may emphasize the continuing interest in the human in a way that seems to run counter to Kreilkamp's and Cohen's efforts, but all three critics seem to be grappling with the problem of how to determine the exact definition of the human in Hardy.

18. Ann Banfield describes free indirect discourse (or what she calls "represented speech and thought") as a possibility inherent to the "universal grammar" that could only appear as a result "of the transformation of western culture in a literate culture" because of the impossibility of inhabiting its peculiarities as a speaker. *Unspeakable Sentences: Narration and Representation in the Language of Fiction* (London: Routledge, 1983; reprinted in Michael McKeon, ed., *Theory of the Novel: A Historical Approach* [Baltimore: Johns Hopkins University Press, 2000], 527).

19. A long critical tradition sees ambiguities like these as an aesthetic failure on Hardy's part. See, for example, Vernon Lee, "Hardy," in *The Handling of Words, and Other Studies in Literary Psychology* (London: John Lane, 1923), 222–41. David Lodge attempts to defend the novelist against the charge of being a bad writer, but nevertheless admits "a fundamental uncertainty about the author's relation to his readers and to his characters." *Language of Fiction: Essays in Criticism and Verbal Analysis of the English Novel* (London: Routledge & K. Paul, 1966), 168. Also see Penny Boumelha, *Thomas Hardy and Women: Sexual Ideology and Narrative Form* (Sussex: Harvester Press, 1982), 132. Other critics have focused on the relation between the unstable narrator and shifting perspectives in the novel. See, for example, Lucille Herbert, "Hardy's Views in *Tess of the d'Urbervilles*," *ELH* 37, no. 1 (1970): 90; and John Plotz, *Portable Property: Victorian Culture on the Move* (Princeton: Princeton University Press, 2008), 136. While Hardy does often shift

perspective, he also often leaves open the question of whose perspective is ultimately being described.

20. Boumelha, *Thomas Hardy and Women*, 118, 119.

21. Elisha Cohn, for example, argues that while Hardy's early work "evokes a world without human autonomy, agency, or individuality in which animals and humans appear to interpenetrate," his later work, including *Tess*, manifests "an increasing investment in addressing pragmatic moral problems." "'No insignificant creature': Thomas Hardy's Ethical Turn," *Nineteenth-Century Literature* 64, no. 4 (2010): 499. While I agree that ethics for Hardy requires a certain minimal level of differentiation between self and other, the model of sympathy that I see him embracing does not simply involve a straightforward taking of responsibility for the other.

22. Thomas Hardy, *Tess of the d'Urbervilles* (1891; Oxford: Oxford University Press, 2005), 350; hereafter abbreviated *T*.

23. Das, *Life and Words*, 46.

24. Ibid., 47.

25. Ibid. Emphasis in original.

26. Ibid.

27. Ibid., 48.

28. A number of feminist critics have attended to the power of men's words in *Tess* and the relative impotence of women's. See, for example, Margaret R. Higonnet, "Fictions of Feminine Voice," in *Out of Bounds: Male Writers and Gender(ed) Criticism*, ed. Laura Claridge and Elizabeth Langland (Amherst: University of Massachusetts Press, 1990), 201; and Charlotte Thompson, "Language and the Shape of Reality in *Tess of the d'Urbervilles*," *ELH* 50, no. 4 (1983): 732.

29. Laird points out several key changes between the 1st edition 1891 and the 2nd edition of 1892: most importantly, the omission of a medicine bottle from which Alec makes Tess drink before leaving her to determine their location in the woods, and the inclusion of a conversation between two of her fellow field-hands after the baby is born, in which one insists, "A little more than persuading had to do wi' the coming o't [the baby], I reckon. There were they that heard a sobbing one night last year in The Chase" (quoted in J. T. Laird, *The Shaping of Tess of the d'Urbervilles* [Oxford: Clarendon, 1975], 177).

A history of the debate over whether Tess was raped or seduced might begin with David Lodge's 1966 insistence that the following passage proves she was seduced: "She had dreaded him, winced before him, succumbed to adroit advantages he took of her helplessness; then, temporarily blinded by his ardent manners, had been stirred to confused surrender awhile." *Language of Fiction*, 185. Also see Leon Waldoff, "Psychological Determinism in *Tess of the d'Urbervilles*," in *Critical Approaches to the Fiction of Thomas Hardy*, ed. Dale Kramer (London: Macmillan, 1979), 136–37; J. Hillis Miller, *Fiction and Repetition: Seven English Novels* (1970; Cambridge, MA: Harvard University Press, 1982); John Goode, *Thomas Hardy: The Offensive Truth* (Oxford: B. Blackwell, 1988), 124; Elizabeth Bronfen, "Pay As You Go: On the Exchange of Bodies and Signs," in *The Sense of Sex: Feminist Perspectives on Hardy*, ed. Margaret R. Higonnet (Urbana: University of Illinois Press, 1993), 77; Kaja Silverman, "History, Figuration and Female Subjectivity in *Tess of the d'Urbervilles*," *Novel: A Forum on Fiction* 18, no. 1 (1984): 5–28.

30. Elaine Scarry, *Resisting Representation* (New York: Oxford University Press, 2004), 77–78.

31. One might imagine that the narrator himself makes a home for Tess's pain, albeit one she cannot inhabit. "Poor wounded name!" the epigraph to the novel proclaims, quoting from *Measure for Measure*, "My bosom as a bed / Shall lodge thee." The gesture that Angel fails to make, the narrator appears to make in his place, offering a Tess a place of

consolation for her own. Because of its diacritical position, however, such a gesture is necessarily unable to counter Angel's entombment of Tess's pain. Nor is it clear that offering a home to the *name* is exactly the same as offering a home to Tess herself. See Susan David Bernstein's reading of the way Hardy's prefaces, as well as the epigraph, serve to "fashion[] himself as writer into a figure resembling his heroine"; a self-fashioning that seeks to offer a "correlation between pure textual body and pristine female body" in which "both categories maintain their inviolate status as abstractions, as idealized constructions." "Confessing and Editing: The Politics of Purity in Hardy's *Tess*," in *Virginal Sexuality and Textuality in Victorian Literature*, ed. Lloyd Davis (Albany: State University of New York Press, 1993), 160, 178.

32. Das, *Life and Words*, 47.

33. Anne-Lise François argues that in his poems to his dead wife, Hardy rejects the excessive heroism of an ethics of acknowledgement "as a burden for which one is solely responsible": a notion that "presupposes the secular, perhaps paradigmatically Romantic, sense of being alone in the world, the bearer of experiences that without one's broadcast will remain unknown." *Open Secrets: The Literature of Uncounted Experience* (Stanford, CA: Stanford University Press, 2008), 213. Against such heroism, François argues that Hardy embraces a notion of acknowledgment that she identifies with Stanley Cavell, that "limit[s] its status as an 'event' to a slight adjustment in 'attitude,' a change in one's way of seeing others whose expression in a direct, definitive statement may never take place" (214). The notion that Hardy rejects the heroics of acknowledgment has been very important for the argument of this chapter. As I hope the readings make clear, in place of acknowledgment, I argue that Hardy offers something like registration: a way of experiencing the pain of the other that may or may not be conscious and makes no claim regarding its accuracy to the other's experience.

34. Gose, "Psychic Evolution," 266.

35. See, for example, Cohn, "'No insignificant creature,'" 514–15.

36. Hardy returns to similar or related notions of altruism repeatedly in his autobiography. See, for example, the attack on vivisection he reprinted in *The Later Years*: "The discovery of the law of evolution, which revealed that all organic creatures are of one family, shifted the centre of altruism from humanity to the whole conscious world collectively. Therefore the practice of vivisection, which might have been defended while the belief ruled that men and animals are essentially different, has been left by that discovery without any logical argument in its favor. And if the practice, to the extent merely of inflicting slight discomfort now and then, be defended (as I sometimes hold it may) on the grounds of it being good policy for animals as well as men, it is nevertheless in strictness a wrong, and stands precisely in the same category as would stand its practice on men themselves." Hardy, *Later Years*, 138–39.

37. Silverman describes Tess as uniquely in danger of disappearing into her environment and so needing to "be painted, imprinted and patterned in order to be seen"—a problem she sees as unique to female subjects. "History, Figuration," 9. Yet nearly all characters—and working-class characters, in particular—often seem on the verge of dissolving into the landscape in Hardy.

38. Asquith points out how this moment echoes Schopenhauer's account of the way "the act of listening to music ... enables individuals to submerge their will in the wider process and therefore find solace from the misery of life while experiencing a 'picture' of the inner life governed by the will 'but entirely without reality and far removed from their pain.'" "Philosophy, Metaphysics, and Music," 191.

39. Thomas Hardy, *Far from the Madding Crowd* (1874; Oxford: Oxford University Press, 2002), 41; hereafter abbreviated *F*.

40. Kreilkamp argues that Hardy's novel can be read as a rereading of the parable of the rich man who steals the poor man's ewe lamb, kills it, and serves it for dinner. For Hardy, Kreilkamp claims, the proper object of pity in the parable is not just the poor man but also the ewe lamb itself. "The lamb was not just any member of the flock or a possession of the poor man, but rather a member of the intimate family. This is a parable, then, about the power of pastoral care radicalized and literalized so that the animal acquires personhood and should be exempt from an animal's usual transformation into deindividuated meat." "Pitying the Sheep," 480. Kreilkamp offers a wonderfully nuanced account of Hardy's ethics of the nonhuman animal. At the same time, reexamining Gabriel's relationship to his sheep reveals a rather more mobile and ambiguous affective and ethical sensibility than Kreilkamp suggests: Gabriel's relation to his sheep does not just seem to be about care, in other words, but also the mobility of the imagination as an end in itself. Gabriel thus comes to represent the ability to pity even in the absence of an obvious object of that pity—a form of hypothetical or fictional thinking and feeling that enables him not just to attend to others' needs, but to attend to his own sorrows as they pertain to those of others.

Afterword: The Fantasy of the Speaking Body

1. Elaine Scarry, *The Body in Pain: The Making and Unmaking of the World* (Oxford: Oxford University Press, 1985), 28.

2. George Eliot, *Middlemarch* (1871–72; London: Penguin, 1994), 211.

3. For an extended description of nineteenth-century sympathy, see Rachel Ablow, *The Marriage of Minds: Reading Sympathy in the Victorian Marriage Plot* (Stanford, CA: Stanford University Press, 2007).

4. For an extended version of this argument about torture, see Rachel Ablow, "Tortured Sympathies: Victorian Literature and The Ticking Time-Bomb Scenario," *ELH* 80, no. 4 (2013): 1145–71.

5. Page DuBois, *Torture and Truth* (New York: Routledge, 1991), 68.

6. On the history of torture in England, see John H. Langbein, *Torture and the Law of Proof: Europe and England in the Ancien Regime* (1976; Chicago: University of Chicago Press, 2006); James Heath, *Torture and English Law: An Administrative and Legal History from the Plantagenets to the Stuarts* (Westport, CT: Greenwood, 1982); L. A. Parry, *The History of Torture in England* (1934; Montclair, NJ: Patterson Smith, 1975); Talal Asad, *Formations of the Secular: Christianity, Islam, Modernity* (Stanford, CA: Stanford University Press, 2003).

7. Lisa Silverman, *Tortured Subjects: Pain, Truth, and the Body in Early Modern France* (Chicago: University of Chicago Press, 2001), 9.

8. Ibid., 22.

9. Ibid., 167. In making this argument, Silverman is disputing the longstanding belief that torture was finally abolished in Europe in the eighteenth century as a consequence of the work of Beccaria and Voltaire in sentimentalizing the issue. She is also attempting to complicate Langbein's revisionist claim in *Torture and the Law* that changes in the law of proof obviated the need for torture. Although she recognizes the partial legitimacy of the other two accounts, Silverman argues that the abolition of torture was also due to a shift in common understandings of the relationship between the body, pain, and truth.

10. Cesare Beccaria, *On Crimes and Punishments* (1764; Englewood Cliffs, NJ: Prentice Hall, 1963), 32.

11. Eliot, *Middlemarch*, 792.

12. Ibid., 795.

13. George Eliot, "The Lifted Veil," in *The Lifted Veil and Brother Jacob* (1859; Oxford: Oxford University Press, 2009), 19–20.

14. Ibid., 41.

15. Ibid., 42.

16. On the use of MRIs and other imaging technologies in the courtroom, see Silvia Camporesi, Barbara Bottalico, and Giovanni Zamboni, "Can We Finally 'See' Pain? Brain Imagining Techniques and Implications for the Law," *Journal of Consciousness Studies* 18, no. 9–10 (2011), 257–76. On medical professionals' attempts to distinguish "real" pain from false, see Renee Montaigne, "Doctors Grapple with When to Prescribe Opioids for Pain" (Mar. 31, 2016), http://www.npr.org/2016/03/31/472501001/doctors-grapple-with-when-to-prescribe-opioids-for-pain

17. Veena Das, *Life and Words: Violence and the Descent into the Ordinary* (Berkeley: University of California Press, 2007), 40.

WORKS CITED

Ablow, Rachel. *The Marriage of Minds: Reading Sympathy in the Victorian Marriage Plot*. Stanford, CA: Stanford University Press, 2007.
———. "Tortured Sympathies: Victorian Literature and the Ticking Time-Bomb Scenario." *ELH* 80, no. 4 (2013): 1145–71.
Abrams, M. H. *The Mirror and the Lamp: Romantic Theory and the Critical Tradition*. New York: Oxford University Press, 1953.
Ahmed, Sara. *The Cultural Politics of Emotion*. New York: Routledge, 2004.
Allen, Richard. "David Hartley." In *The Stanford Encyclopedia of Philosophy*, edited by Edward N. Zalta. Summer 2015 ed. http://plato.stanford.edu/archives/sum2015/entries/hartley/
———. *David Hartley on Human Nature*. Albany: State University of New York Press, 1999.
Anderson, Amanda. *The Powers of Distance: Cosmopolitanism and the Cultivation of Detachment*. Princeton: Princeton University Press, 2001.
Anderson, Ben. "Becoming and Being Hopeful: Towards a Theory of Affect." *Environment and Planning D: Society and Space* 24, no. 5 (2006): 733–52.
Andral, M. "Lectures on Medical Pathology." *The Lancet* (Jan. 26, 1833): 550–56.
Appiah, Kwame Anthony. *The Ethics of Identity*. Princeton: Princeton University Press, 2005.
Armstrong, Dr. "From Lectures on the Principles and Practice of Physic." *The Lancet* (Jul. 23, 1825): 65–72.
Armstrong, Nancy. *Desire and Domestic Fiction: A Political History of the Novel*. New York: Oxford University Press, 1987.
Arnold, Matthew. *The Letters of Matthew Arnold*. Vol. 1. Edited by Cecil Y. Lang. Charlottesville: University of Virginia Press, 1996.
Asad, Talal. *Formations of the Secular: Christianity, Islam, Modernity*. Stanford, CA: Stanford University Press, 2003.
Asquith, Mark. "Philosophy, Metaphysics and Music in Hardy's Cosmic Vision." In *The Ashgate Research Companion to Thomas Hardy*, edited by Rosemarie Morgan, 181–98. Farnham: Ashgate, 2010.
Atkin, Albert, "Peirce's Theory of Signs." In *The Stanford Encyclopedia of Philosophy*, edited by Edward N. Zalta. Summer 2013 ed. http://plato.stanford.edu/archives/sum2013/entries/peirce-semiotics/
Atkinson, Henry George, and Harriet Martineau. *Letters on the Laws of Man's Nature and Development*. Boston: Josiah P. Mendum, 1851.
Bailin, Miriam. *The Sickroom in Victorian Fiction: The Art of Being Ill*. Cambridge: Cambridge University Press, 1994.
Bain, Alexander. *The Emotions and the Will*. 1859. London: Longmans, Green, 1875.
———. *John Stuart Mill: A Criticism; with Personal Recollections*. 1882. London: Longmans, Green, 1882.
———. *The Senses and the Intellect*. 1855. London: Longmans, Green, 1868.
Banfield, Ann. *Unspeakable Sentences: Narration and Representation in the Language of Fiction*. London: Routledge, 1983.

Barnett, S. A. "The 'Expression of the Emotions.'" In *A Century of Darwin*, edited by S. A. Barnett, 206–30. London: Heinemann, 1962.

Bar-Yosef, Eitan. "'With the Practiced Eye of a Deaf Person': Martineau's Travel Writing and the Construction of the Disabled Traveller." In *Harriet Martineau: Authorship, Society, and Empire*, edited by Ella Dzelzainis and Cora Kaplan, 165–79. Manchester: Manchester University Press, 2010.

Beccaria, Cesaire. *On Crimes and Punishments*. 1764. Englewood Cliffs, NJ: Prentice Hall, 1963.

Beer, Gillian. "'Coming Wonders': Uses of Theatre in the Victorian Novel." In *English Drama: Forms and Development: Essays in Honour of Muriel Clara Bradbrook*, edited by Marie Axton and Raymond Williams, 164–85. Cambridge: Cambridge University Press, 1977.

———. *Darwin's Plots: Evolutionary Narrative in Darwin, George Eliot, and Nineteenth-Century Fiction*. Cambridge: Cambridge University Press, 1983.

———. "Darwin's Reading and the Fictions of Development." In *The Darwinian Heritage*, edited by David Kohn, 543–88. Princeton: Princeton University Press, 1985.

Bell, Sir Charles. *The Anatomy and Philosophy of Expression: As Connected with the Fine Arts*, 5th ed. London: Henry H. Bohn, 1865.

Bending, Lucy. *The Representation of Bodily Pain in Late Nineteenth-Century English Culture*. Oxford: Clarendon Press, 2000.

Bennett, Jane. *Vibrant Matter: A Political Ecology of Things*. Durham, NC: Duke University Press, 2010.

Bennett, M. R., and P. M. S. Hacker. *Philosophical Foundations of Neuroscience*. Malden, MA: Blackwell, 2003.

Bentham, Jeremy. *Bentham: Selected Writings of John Dinwiddy*. Edited by William Twining. Stanford, CA: Stanford University Press, 2004.

———. *An Introduction to the Principles of Morals and Legislation*. 1781. Amherst, NY: Prometheus Books, 1988.

———. "Table of the Springs of Action." 1817. In *The Works of Jeremy Bentham*. Vol. 1. Edited by John Bowring. Edinburgh: William Tait, 1843.

Berlant, Lauren. *Cruel Optimism*. Durham, NC: Duke University Press, 2011.

Berlin, Isaiah. *Four Essays on Liberty*. London: Oxford University Press, 1969.

Bernstein, Susan David. "Confessing and Editing: The Politics of Purity in Hardy's *Tess*." In *Virginal Sexuality and Textuality in Victorian Literature*, edited by Lloyd Davis, 159–78. Albany: State University of New York Press, 1993.

Biale, Rachel. *Women and Jewish Law: The Essential Texts, Their History, and Their Relevance for Today*. New York: Schocken, 1995.

Blake, Kathleen. "Pure Tess: Hardy on Knowing a Woman." *Studies in English Literature, 1500–1900* 22, no. 4 (1982): 689–705.

Boone, Joseph Allen. "Depolicing *Villette*: Surveillance, Invisibility, and the Female Erotics of 'Heretic Narrative.'" *Novel: A Forum on Fiction* 26, no. 1 (1992): 20–42.

Boumelha, Penny. *Thomas Hardy and Women: Sexual Ideology and Narrative Form*. Sussex: Harvester Press, 1982.

Bourke, Joanna. *The Story of Pain: From Prayer to Painkillers*. New York: Oxford University Press, 2014.

Brennan, Teresa. *The Transmission of Affect*. Ithaca, NY: Cornell University Press, 2004.

Brewster, Sir David. *Letters on Natural Magic Addressed to Sir Walter Scott*. 1832. London: Chattus & Windus, 1883.

Brinkema, Eugenie. *The Forms of the Affects*. Durham, NC: Duke University Press, 2014.

Bronfen, Elizabeth. "Pay As You Go: On the Exchange of Bodies and Signs." In *The Sense of Sex: Feminist Perspectives on Hardy*, edited by Margaret R. Higonnet. Urbana: University of Illinois Press, 1993.
Brontë, Charlotte. *Letters of Charlotte Brontë*. Edited by Margaret Smith. 3 vols. Oxford: Clarendon, 1995-2004.
———. *Villette*. 1853. London: Penguin, 2004.
Broughton, Trev Lynn. "Making the Most of Martyrdom: Harriet Martineau, Autobiography and Death." *Literature and History* 2, no. 2 (1993): 24-45.
Browne, Janet. *Charles Darwin: A Biography*. Vol. 1, *Voyaging*; Vol. 2, *The Power of Place*. Princeton: Princeton University Press, 1995-2002.
———. "Darwin and the Expression of the Emotions." In *The Darwinian Heritage*, edited by David Kohn, 307-26. Princeton: Princeton University Press, 1985.
Buckley, Jerome H. "John Stuart Mill's 'True' Autobiography." *Studies in the Literary Imagination* 23, no. 2 (1990): 223-31.
Burston, W. H. *James Mill on Philosophy and Education*. London: Athlone, 1973.
Buxton, A. St. Clair. "Letter to the Editor: Pain and Its Interpretation." *The Lancet* (Sept. 24, 1887): 635.
Bynum, W. F. *Science and the Practice of Medicine in the Nineteenth Century*. Cambridge: Cambridge University Press, 1994.
Caldwell, Janis McLarren. *Literature and Medicine in Nineteenth-Century Britain: From Mary Shelley to George Eliot*. Cambridge: Cambridge University Press, 2004.
Cameron, Sharon. *Beautiful Work: A Meditation on Pain*. Durham, NC: Duke University Press, 2000.
———. *Impersonality: Seven Essays*. Chicago: University of Chicago Press, 2007.
Camporesi, Silvia, Barbara Bottalico, and Giovanni Zamboni. "Can We Finally 'See' Pain? Brain Imagining Techniques and Implications for the Law." *Journal of Consciousness Studies* 18, no. 9-10 (2011): 257-76.
Carlisle, Janice. "The Face in the Mirror: *Villette* and the Conventions of Autobiography." *ELH* 46, no. 2 (1979): 262-89.
———. *John Stuart Mill and the Writing of Character*. Athens: University of Georgia Press, 1991.
Carlyle, Thomas. *Sartor Resartus*. 1833-34. Oxford: Oxford University Press, 1987.
Carpenter, Mary Wilson. *Imperial Bibles, Domestic Bodies: Women, Sexuality, and Religion in the Victorian Market*. Athens: Ohio University Press, 2003.
Caruth, Cathy. *Unclaimed Experience: Trauma, Narrative, and History*. Baltimore: Johns Hopkins University Press, 1996.
Cassell, Eric J. "The Nature of Suffering and the Goals of Medicine." *New England Journal of Medicine* 306, no. 11 (1982): 639-45.
Cavell, Stanley. *The Claim of Reason: Wittgenstein, Skepticism, Morality, and Tragedy*. 1979. New York: Oxford University Press, 1999.
———. *Must We Mean What We Say? A Book of Essays*. New York: Charles Scribner's and Sons, 1969.
Chambers, Thomas King. "Lecture on Hypochondriasis." *British Medical Journal* (Jul. 5, 1873): 6-8.
Checkland, S. G. *The Rise of Industrial Society in England, 1815-1885*. New York: St. Martin's Press, 1964.
Clark, Michael J. "'Morbid Introspection,' Unsoundness of Mind, and British Psychological Medicine, c. 1830-c.1900." In *The Anatomy of Madness: Essays in the History of Psychiatry*. Vol. 3, *The Asylum and Its Psychiatry*, edited by W. F. Bynum, Roy Porter, and Michael Shepherd, 71-101. London: Routledge, 1988.

Clarke, Micael M. "Charlotte Brontë's *Villette*, Mid-Victorian Anti-Catholicism, and the Turn to Secularism." *ELH* 78, no. 4 (2011): 967–89.

Clutterbuck, Dr. "Lectures on the Diseases of the Nervous System." *The Lancet* (Aug. 14, 1827): 550–54.

Cohen, William A. "Arborealities: The Tactile Ecology of Hardy's *Woodlanders*." *19: Interdisciplinary Studies in the Long Nineteenth Century* 19 (2014). http://www.19.bbk.ac.uk/articles/10.16995/ntn.690/

Cohn, Elisha. "'No insignificant creature': Thomas Hardy's Ethical Turn." *Nineteenth-Century Literature* 64, no. 4 (2010): 494–520.

Collins, W. J. "Letter to the Editor: Pain and Its Interpretation." *The Lancet* (Aug. 20, 1887): 391–92.

Connolly, William E. "Brain Waves, Transcendental Fields and Techniques of Thought." *Radical Philosophy* 94 (1999): 19–28.

Conolly, John. "The Croonian Lectures, Lecture III: Description of General Paralysis." *The Lancet* (Oct. 27, 1849): 443–46.

Crawford, Cassandra S. *Phantom Limb: Amputation, Embodiment, and Prosthetic Technology*. New York: New York University Press, 2014.

Crosby, Christina. "Charlotte Brontë's Haunted Text." *Studies in English Literature, 1500–1900* 24, no. 4 (1984): 701–15.

Cvetkovich, Ann. *Depression: A Public Feeling*. Durham, NC: Duke University Press, 2012.

Dale, Peter Allan. "Heretical Narration: Charlotte Brontë's Search for Endlessness." *Religion and Literature* 16, no. 3 (1984): 1–24.

Dames, Nicholas. *Amnesiac Selves: Nostalgia, Forgetting, and British Fiction, 1810–1870*. New York: Oxford University Press, 2001.

Darwin, Charles. *Charles Darwin Notebooks, 1836–1844. Geology, Transmutation of Species, Metaphysical Inquiries*. Edited by Paul H. Barrett, Peter J. Gautrey, Sandra Herbert, David Kohn, and Sydney Smith. Ithaca, NY: Cornell University Press, 1987.

———. *The Descent of Man and Selection in Relation to Sex*. 1871. London: Penguin, 2004.

———. *The Expression of the Emotions in Man and Animals*. 1872. Chicago: University of Chicago Press, 1965.

———. *Journal of Researches into the Geology and Natural History of the Various Countries Visited by H. M. S. Beagle Under the Command of Captain Fitzroy, R. N., From 1832–1836*. 1839. London: Henry Colburn, 1840.

———. *On the Origin of Species*. 1859. Oxford: Oxford University Press, 1996.

———. "Recollections of the Development of My Mind and Character (1876–1881)." In *Evolutionary Writings*, edited by James A. Secord, 355–425. Oxford: Oxford University Press, 2008.

———. *The Various Contrivances by Which Orchids Are Fertilized by Insects*. 1862. New York: New York University Press, 1988.

Das, Veena. *Life and Words: Violence and the Descent into the Ordinary*. Berkeley: University of California Press, 2007.

Daston, Lorraine. "The Theory of Will versus the Science of Mind." In *The Problematic Science: Psychology in Nineteenth-Century Thought*, edited by William R. Woodward and Mitchell G. Ash, 88–115. New York: Praeger, 1982.

Daston, Lorraine, and Katharine Park. *Wonders and the Order of Nature: 1150–1750*. New York: Zone, 1998.

David, Deirdre. *Intellectual Woman and Victorian Patriarchy: Harriet Martineau, Elizabeth Barrett Browning, George Eliot*. Ithaca, NY: Cornell University Press, 1987.

Davidson, Jenny. *Breeding: A Partial History of the Eighteenth Century*. New York: Columbia University Press, 2009.

Davies, Jeremy. *Bodily Pain in Romantic Literature*. New York: Routledge, 2014.
Deleuze, Gilles. *Spinoza: Practical Philosophy*. San Francisco: City Lights, 1988.
Deleuze, Gilles, and Felix Guattari. *A Thousand Plateaus: Capitalism and Schizophrenia*. 1980. Minneapolis: University of Minnesota Press, 2007.
Dennett, Daniel C. *Freedom Evolves*. New York: Viking, 2003.
Desmond, Adrian, and James Moore. *Darwin's Sacred Cause: How a Hatred of Slavery Shaped Darwin's Views on Human Evolution*. Boston: Houghton Mifflin Harcourt, 2009.
———. Introduction to *The Descent of Man, and Selection in Relation to Sex*, by Charles Darwin, xi–lviii. London: Penguin, 2004.
Dickens, Charles. *Dombey and Son*. 1844–46. Harmondsworth: Penguin, 1970.
———. *Hard Times*. 1854. London: Penguin, 2003.
Digby, Anne. *Making a Medical Living: Doctors and Patients in the English Market for Medicine, 1720–1911*. Cambridge: Cambridge University Press, 1994.
Dixon, Thomas. *From Passions to Emotions: The Creation of a Secular Psychological Category*. Cambridge: Cambridge University Press, 2003.
Donner, Wendy. *The Liberal Self: John Stuart Mill's Moral and Political Philosophy*. Ithaca, NY: Cornell University Press, 1991.
Dormandy, Thomas. *The Worst of Evils: The Fight against Pain*. New Haven, CT: Yale University Press, 2006.
Dror, Otniel E. "On the Blush." In *Histories of Scientific Observation*, edited by Lorraine Daston and Elizabeth Lunbeck, 326–48. Chicago: University of Chicago Press, 2011.
DuBois, Page. *Torture and Truth*. New York: Routledge, 1991.
Durant, John R. "The Ascent of Nature in Darwin's *Descent of Man*." In *The Darwinian Heritage*, edited by David Kohn, 283–306. Princeton: Princeton University Press, 1985.
Durham, John. "The Influence of John Stuart Mill's Mental Crisis on His Thoughts." *American Imago* 20, no. 4 (1963): 369–84.
Eagleton, Terry. *Myths of Power: A Marxist Study of the Brontës*. Houndmills: Macmillan, 1975.
Ekman, Paul. "How to Spot a Terrorist on the Fly." *The Washington Post* (Oct. 29, 2006). http://www.washingtonpost.com/wp-dyn/content/article/2006/10/27/AR2006102701478.html
———. Introduction and afterword to *The Expression of the Emotions in Man and Animals*, by Charles Darwin, xxi–xxxvi, 363–93. Oxford: Oxford University Press, 1998.
Eliot, George. "The Lifted Veil." In *The Lifted Veil and Brother Jacob*. 1859. Oxford: Oxford University Press, 2009.
———. *Middlemarch*. 1871–72. London: Penguin, 1994.
Elliotson, John. "St. Thomas's Hospital: Clinical Lecture." *The Lancet* (Nov. 3, 1832): 161–67.
Emerson, Ralph Waldo. *Essays: First Series*. 1841. New York: Library of America, 1983.
Esquirol, Etienne. *Mental Maladies: Treatise on Insanity*. 1838. Philadelphia: Lea and Blanchard, 1845.
Feinberg, Monica L. "The Domestic Interiors of *Villette*." *Novel: A Forum on Fiction* 26, no. 2 (1993): 170–91.
Ferguson, Frances. "Belief and Emotions (from Stanley Fish to Jeremy Bentham and John Stuart Mill)." In *Politics and the Passions, 1500–1850*, edited by Victorian Kahn, Neil Saccamano, and Daniela Coli, 231–50. Princeton: Princeton University Press, 2006.
Fimland, Marit. "On the Margins of the Acceptable: Charlotte Brontë's *Villette*." *Literature and Theology* 10, no. 2 (1996): 148–59.

Fischer-Homberger, Esther. "Hypochondriasis of the Eighteenth Century—Neurosis of the Present Century." *Bulletin of the History of Medicine* 46, no. 4 (1972): 391–401.
Fissell, Mary. "The Disappearance of the Patient's Narrative and the Invention of Hospital Medicine." In *British Medicine in an Age of Reform*, edited by Roger French and Andrew Wear, 92–109. London: Routledge, 1991.
Flathman, Richard E. *Toward a Liberalism* .... Ithaca, NY: Cornell University Press, 1989.
Fleishman, Avrom. *Figures of Autobiography: The Language of Self-Writing in Victorian and Modern England*. Berkeley: University of California Press, 1983.
Fletcher, Angus. "Allegory without Ideas." *boundary 2* 33, no. 1 (2006): 77–98.
Fletcher, Luann McCracken. "Manufactured Marvels, Heretic Narratives, and the Process of Interpretation in *Villette*." *Studies in English Literature, 1500–1900* 32, no. 4 (1992): 723–46.
Fogelin, Robert J. "Wittgenstein's Critique of Philosophy." In *Cambridge Companion to Wittgenstein*, edited by Hans Sluga and David G. Stern, 34–45. Cambridge: Cambridge University Press, 1996.
"Foreign Department: Hypochondria Politica in Germany." *The Lancet* (Jun. 17, 1848): 669.
Foucault, Michel. *The Birth of the Clinic: An Archaeology of Medical Perception*. 1973. New York: Vintage, 1994.
François, Anne-Lise. *Open Secrets: The Literature of Uncounted Experience*. Stanford, CA: Stanford University Press, 2008.
Frawley, Maria. Introduction to *Life in the Sick-Room*, by Harriet Martineau, 11–28. Peterborough: Broadview, 2003.
———. *Invalidism and Identity in Nineteenth-Century Britain*. Chicago: University of Chicago Press, 2004.
———. " 'A Prisoner to the Couch': Harriet Martineau, Invalidism, and Self-Representation." In *The Body and Physical Difference: Discourses of Disability*, edited by David T. Mitchell and Sharon L. Snyder, 174–88. Ann Arbor: University of Michigan Press, 1997.
Freedgood, Elaine. "The Secret History of Diegesis." Lecture at the Radcliffe Institute for Advanced Study. Sept. 2013.
"The Function of Physical Pain: Anaesthetics." *Westminster Review* 40, no. 1 (1871): 198–205.
Furst, Lilian R. *Between Doctors and Patients: The Changing Balance of Power*. Charlottesville: University Press of Virginia, 1998.
Gallagher, Catherine. *The Body Economic: Life, Death, and Sensation in Political Economy and the Victorian Novel*. Princeton: Princeton University Press, 2006.
Gallagher, Shaun. "Where's the Action? Epiphenomenalism and the Problem of Free Will." In *Does Consciousness Cause Behavior?*, edited by Susan Pockett, William P. Banks, and Shaun Gallagher, 109–24. Cambridge: Massachusetts Institute of Technology Press, 2006.
Gardiner, H. N., Ruth Clark Metcalf, and John G. Beebe-Center. *Feeling and Emotion: A History of Theories*. Westport, CT: Greenwood Press, 1970.
Garforth, F. W. *John Stuart Mill's Theory of Education*. New York: Barnes & Noble, 1979.
Garratt, Peter. *Victorian Empiricism: Self, Knowledge, and Reality in Ruskin, Bain, Lewes, Spencer, and George Eliot*. Madison, NJ: Fairleigh Dickinson University Press, 2010.
Gilbert, Sandra M., and Susan Gubar. *The Madwoman in the Attic: The Woman Writer and the Nineteenth-Century Literary Imagination*. New Haven, CT: Yale University Press, 1979.
Gillies, H. Cameron. "The Interpretation of Disease, Part III: The Life-Saving Value of Pain and Disease." *The Lancet* (Aug. 13, 1887): 305–7.

Goode, John. *Thomas Hardy: The Offensive Truth*. Oxford: B. Blackwell, 1988.
Gose, Elliott B., Jr. "Psychic Evolution: Darwinism and Initiation in *Tess of the d'Urbervilles*." *Nineteenth-Century Fiction* 18, no. 3 (1963): 261-72.
Greenhow, T. M. *Medical Report of the Case of Miss H—M—*. London: Samuel Highley, 1845.
———. "Termination of the Case of Miss H. Martineau." *British Medical Journal* (Apr. 14, 1877): 449-50.
Grinnell, George C. *The Age of Hypochondria: Interpreting Romantic Health and Illness*. New York: Palgrave Macmillan, 2010.
Gross, Daniel M. "Defending the Humanities with Charles Darwin's *The Expression of the Emotions in Man and Animals* (1872)." *Critical Inquiry* 37, no. 1 (2010): 34-59.
Grosz, Elizabeth. *The Nick of Time: Politics, Evolution, and the Untimely*. Durham, NC: Duke University Press, 2004.
Gull, William Withey, and Francis Edmund Anstie. "On Hypochondria or Hypochondriasis." In *A System of Medicine*, edited by J. Russell Reynolds, 623-30. London: Macmillan, 1876.
Hadley, Elaine. *Living Liberalism: Practical Citizenship in Mid-Victorian Britain*. Chicago: University of Chicago Press, 2010.
Halévy, Elie. *The Growth of Philosophic Radicalism*. New York: Macmillan, 1928.
Haley, Bruce. *The Healthy Body and Victorian Culture*. Cambridge, MA: Harvard University Press, 1978.
Hardy, Florence Emily. *The Early Life of Thomas Hardy, 1840-1891*. Cambridge: Cambridge University Press, 1928.
———. *The Later Years of Thomas Hardy, 1892-1928*. Cambridge: Cambridge University Press, 1930.
Hardy, Thomas. *Far from the Madding Crowd*. 1874. Oxford: Oxford University Press, 2002.
———. *Tess of the d'Urbervilles*. 1891. Oxford: Oxford University Press, 2005.
———. *The Woodlanders*. 1887. Oxford: Oxford University Press, 2005.
Harpham, Geoffrey Galt. "Elaine Scarry and the Dream of Pain." *Salmagundi* 130/131 (2001): 202-34.
Harrison, John P. "On the Physiology, Pathology and Therapeutics of Pain." *Western Lancet and Hospital Reporter* 9 (1849): 349-54.
Hartley, David. *Various Conjectures on the Perception, Motion, and Generation of Ideas*. Translated by Robert E. A. Palmer. Los Angeles: William Andrews Clark Memorial Library, University of California, 1959.
Hartley, Lucy. *Physiognomy and the Meaning of Expression in Nineteenth-Century Culture*. Cambridge: Cambridge University Press, 2001.
Hartman, Geoffrey H. *Wordsworth's Poetry, 1787-1814*. New Haven, CT: Yale University Press, 1964.
Heath, James. *Torture and English Law: An Administrative and Legal History from the Plantagenets to the Stuarts*. Westport, CT: Greenwood, 1982.
Herbert, Lucille. "Hardy's Views in *Tess of the d'Ubervilles*." *ELH* 37, no. 1 (1970): 77-94.
Herbert, Sandra. "Darwin, Malthus, and Selection." *Journal of the History of Biology* 4, no. 1 (1971): 209-17.
Hertz, Neil. *The End of the Line: Essays on Psychoanalysis and the Sublime*. New York: Columbia University Press, 1985.
Higonnet, Margaret R. "Fictions of Feminine Voice." In *Out of Bounds: Male Writers and Gender(ed) Criticism*, edited by Laura Claridge and Elizabeth Langland, 197-218. Amherst: University of Massachusetts Press, 1990.

Hilton, Boyd. *The Age of Atonement: The Influence of Evangelicalism on Social and Economic Thought, 1785–1865*. Oxford: Oxford University Press, 1992.

Hinton, James. *The Mystery of Pain: A Book for the Sorrowful*. 1866. New York: Mitchell Kennerly, 1914.

"Hints to the Public and the Legislature, on the Nature and Effect of Evangelical Preaching." *Quarterly Review* 8 (Nov. 1810): 480–514.

Hobbes, Thomas. *Leviathan*. 1651. Cambridge: Cambridge University Press, 1991.

Hodgkiss, A. D. "Chronic Pain in Nineteenth-Century British Medical Writings." *History of Psychiatry* 2, no. 5 (1991): 27–40.

Holloway, John. "Hardy's Major Fiction." In *Hardy: A Collection of Critical Essays*, edited by Albert J. Guerard, 52–62. Englewood Cliffs, NJ: Prentice Hall, 1963.

———. *The Victorian Sage: Studies in Argument*. New York: Norton, 1953.

Holmes, Martha Stoddard. *Fictions of Affliction: Physical Disability in Victorian Culture*. Ann Arbor: University of Michigan Press, 2004.

Hume, David. *A Treatise of Human Nature*. 1739–40. London: Penguin, 1985.

Jacobus, Mary. "The Buried Letter: Feminism and Romanticism in *Villette*." In *Women Writing and Writing about Women*, edited by Mary Jacobus, 42–60. London: Croom Helm, 1979.

Jann, Rosemary. "Evolutionary Physiognomy and Darwin's *Expression of the Emotions*." *Victorian Review* 18, no. 2 (1992): 1–27.

Jewson, N. D. "The Disappearance of the Sick Man from Medical Cosmology, 1770–1870." *Sociology* 10, no. 2 (1976): 225–44.

Johnson, Bruce. "'The Perfection of Species' and Hardy's *Tess*." In *Nature and the Victorian Imagination*, edited by U. C. Knoepflmacher and G. B. Tennyson, 259–77. Berkeley: University of California Press, 1977.

Johnson, Patricia E. "'This Heretic Narrative': The Strategy of the Split Narrative in Charlotte Brontë's *Villette*." *Studies in English Literature, 1500–1900* 30, no. 4 (1990): 617–31.

Keenleyside, Heather. "Personification for the People: On James Thomson's *The Seasons*." *ELH* 76, no. 2 (2009): 447–72.

Kennedy, Meegan. *Revising the Clinic: Vision and Representation in Victorian Medical Narrative and the Novel*. Columbus: Ohio State University Press, 2010.

Ketabgian, Tamara. *The Lives of Machines: The Industrial Imaginary in Victorian Literature and Culture*. Ann Arbor: University of Michigan Press, 2011.

Keynes, Randal. *Darwin, His Daughter, and Human Evolution*. New York: Riverhead, 2002.

Kleinman, Arthur. *The Illness Narratives: Suffering, Healing, and the Human Condition*. New York: Basic Books, 1988.

Kleinman, Arthur, Veena Das, and Margaret M. Lock, eds. *Social Suffering*. Berkeley: University of California Press, 1997.

Knapp, Steven. *Personification and the Sublime: Milton to Coleridge*. Cambridge, MA: Harvard University Press, 1985.

Knapp, Steven, and Walter Benn Michaels. "Against Theory." *Critical Inquiry* 8, no. 4 (1982): 723–42.

Kober, Michael. "Certainties of a World-Picture: The Epistemological Investigations of *On Certainty*." In *Cambridge Companion to Wittgenstein*, edited by Hans Sluga and David G. Stern, 411–41. Cambridge: Cambridge University Press, 1996.

Krasner, James. "A Chaos of Delight: Perception and Illusion in Darwin's Scientific Writing." *Representations* 31 (1990): 118–41.

Kreilkamp, Ivan. "Pitying the Sheep in *Far from the Madding Crowd*." *Novel: A Forum on Fiction* 42, no. 3 (2009): 474–81.

———. *Voice and the Victorian Storyteller*. Cambridge: Cambridge University Press, 2005.
Kucich, John. *Repression in Victorian Fiction: Charlotte Brontë, George Eliot, and Charles Dickens*. Berkeley: University of California Press, 1987.
Laird, J. T. *The Shaping of Tess of the d'Urbervilles*. Oxford: Clarendon, 1975.
Langbein, John H. *Torture and the Law of Proof: Europe and England in the Ancien Regime*. 1976. Chicago: University of Chicago Press, 2006.
Lansbury, Coral. "Gynaecology, Pornography, and the Antivivisection Movement." *Victorian Studies* 28, no. 3 (1985): 413–37.
Laqueur, Thomas. "Bodies, Details, and the Humanitarian Narrative." In *The New Cultural History*, edited by Lynn Hunt, 176–204. Berkeley: University of California Press, 1989.
Latour, Bruno. "Why Has Critique Run Out of Steam? From Matters of Fact to Matters of Concern." *Critical Inquiry* 30 (2004): 225–48.
Lee, Vernon. *The Handling of Words, and Other Studies in Literary Psychology*. London: John Lane, 1923.
Levi, A. W. "The 'Mental Crisis' of John Stuart Mill." *Psychoanalytic Review* 32 (1945): 86–101.
Levine, George. *Darwin Loves You: Natural Selection and the Re-Enchantment of the World*. Princeton: Princeton University Press, 2006.
Lewes, George Henry. *Problems of Life and Mind, First Series*. Vol. 1. London: Trubner & Co., 1874.
Leys, Ruth. "How Did Fear Become a Scientific Object and What Kind of Object Is It?" *Representations* 110 (2010): 66–104.
———. "The Turn to Affect: A Critique." *Critical Inquiry* 37, no. 3 (2011): 434–72.
Locke, John. *An Essay Concerning Human Understanding*. 1689. Oxford: Oxford University Press, 1975.
Loesberg, Jonathan. *Fictions of Consciousness: Mill, Newman, and the Reading of Victorian Prose*. New Brunswick, NJ: Rutgers University Press, 1986.
Lodge, David. *Language of Fiction: Essays in Criticism and Verbal Analysis of the English Novel*. London: Routledge & K. Paul, 1966.
Logan, Peter Melville. *Nerves and Narratives: A Cultural History of Hysteria in Nineteenth-Century British Prose*. Berkeley: University of California Press, 1997.
Magnuson, Paul. *Coleridge and Wordsworth: A Lyrical Dialogue*. Princeton: Princeton University Press, 1988.
Malthus, Thomas Robert. *An Essay on the Principle of Population*. 1798. Oxford: Oxford University Press, 2004.
Manser, Anthony. "Pain and Private Language." In *Studies in the Philosophy of Wittgenstein*, edited by Peter Winch, 166–83. London: Routledge & K. Paul, 1969.
Marmontel, Jean François. *Memoirs of Marmontel, Written by Himself*. 1804. London: H. S. Nichols, 1895.
Martin, Revd. George. *Our Afflicted Prince: A Sermon the Substance of Which Was Preached in the Lewisham High Road Congregational Church on Sunday Morning, December 17, 1871*. London: Elliot Stock, 1871.
Martineau, Harriet. *Autobiography*. 1877. Peterborough: Broadview, 2006.
———. *The Collected Letters of Harriet Martineau, Vol. 2: 1837–1845*. Edited by Deborah Ann Logan. London: Pickering & Chatto, 2007.
———. *Household Education*. Philadelphia: Lea & Blanchard, 1848.
———. *Illustrations of Political Economy*. Edited by Deborah Ann Logan. Peterborough: Broadview, 2004.
———. *Letters on Mesmerism*. 1844. London: Edward Moxon, 1845.
———. *Life in the Sick-Room*. 1844. Peterborough: Broadview, 2003.

———. "On the Agency of Feelings in the Formation of Habits; And on the Agency of Habits in the Regeneration of Feelings." In *Miscellanies*. Vol. 1, 201–15. Boston: Hilliard, Gray, & Co., 1836.

Massumi, Brian. *Parables for the Virtual: Movement, Affect, Sensation*. Durham, NC: Duke University Press, 2002.

Maurice, Priscilla. *Sickness, Its Trials and Blessings*. 7th ed. 1850. London: Rivingtons, 1859.

Maynard, John. *Charlotte Brontë and Sexuality*. Cambridge: Cambridge University Press, 1984.

McKeon, Michael, ed. *Theory of the Novel: A Historical Approach*. Baltimore: Johns Hopkins University Press, 2000.

"Medical Annotations." *The Lancet* (Jun. 13, 1863): 664–66.

Melzack, Ronald. "Gate Control Theory: On the Evolution of Pain Concepts." *Journal of Pain* 5, no. 2 (1996): 128–38.

Melzack, Ronald, and Patrick D. Wall. *The Challenge of Pain*. London: Penguin, 1996.

———. "Pain Mechanisms: A New Theory." *American Association for the Advancement of Science* 150, no. 3699 (1965): 971–79.

Mermin, Dorothy. *Godiva's Ride: Women of Letters in England, 1830–1880*. Bloomington: Indiana University Press, 1993.

Mill, James. *Analysis of the Phenomena of the Human Mind*. 2 vols. 1829. With notes by John Stuart, Alexander Bain, Andrew Finklater, and George Grote, 1869. London: Longmans, Green, Reader, and Dyer, 1878.

———. *The Article "Education" Reprinted from the Supplement to the* Encyclopaedia Britannica. London: J. Innes, 1825.

Mill, John Stuart. *The Collected Works of John Stuart Mill*. 33 vols. Edited by J. M. Robson. Toronto: University of Toronto Press, 1963–91.

———. *An Examination of Sir William Hamilton's Philosophy and of the Principal Philosophical Questions Discussed in His Writings*. Boston: William V. Spencer, 1861.

Miller, Andrew H. *The Burdens of Perfection: On Ethics and Reading in Nineteenth-Century British Literature*. Ithaca, NY: Cornell University Press, 2008.

Miller, J. Hillis. *Fiction and Repetition: Seven English Novels*. 1970. Cambridge, MA: Harvard University Press, 1982.

———. *Thomas Hardy: Distance and Desire*. Cambridge, MA: Harvard University Press, 1970.

Millgate, Michael. *Thomas Hardy: A Biography Revisited*. Oxford: Oxford University Press, 2004.

Montaigne, Renee. "Doctors Grapple with When to Prescribe Opioids for Pain" (Mar. 31, 2016) http://www.npr.org/2016/03/31/472501001/doctors-grapple-with-when-to-prescribe-opioids-for-pain

Moore, James R. "Of Love and Death: Why Darwin 'Gave Up Christianity.'" In *History, Humanity, and Evolution: Essays for John C. Greene*, edited by James R. Moore, 195–252. Cambridge: Cambridge University Press, 1989.

Morris, David B. *The Culture of Pain*. Berkeley: University of California Press, 1991.

Moscoso, Javier. *Pain: A Cultural History*. Basingstoke: Palgrave Macmillan, 2012.

Mouffe, Chantal. *The Democratic Paradox*. London: Verso, 2000.

Mulhall, Stephen. *Wittgenstein's Private Language: Grammar, Nonsense, and Imagination in Philosophical Investigations, §243–315*. Oxford: Oxford University Press, 2007.

Nagel, Thomas. *The View from Nowhere*. New York: Oxford University Press, 1986.

Ngai, Sienne. *Ugly Feelings*. Cambridge, MA: Harvard University Press, 2007.

Noble, Mary. "Darwin among the Novelists: Narrative Strategy and the Expression of the Emotions." *Nineteenth-Century Prose* 38, no. 1 (2011): 99–126.

Otis, Laura. *Networking: Communicating with Bodies and Machines in the Nineteenth Century.* Ann Arbor: University of Michigan Press, 2001.
———. *Organic Memory: History and the Body in the Late Nineteenth and Early Twentieth Centuries.* Lincoln: University of Nebraska Press, 1994.
"Pain." *Taxonomy: International Association for the Study of Pain.* http://www.iasp-pain.org/Taxonomy#Pain
Paradis, James. "Darwin and Landscape." In *Victorian Science and Victorian Values: Literary Perspectives,* edited by James Paradis and Thomas Postlewait, 94–110. New Brunswick, NJ: Rutgers University Press, 1985.
Parry, L. A., *The History of Torture in England.* 1934. Montclair, NJ: Patterson Smith, 1975.
Peirce, Charles S. "On a New List of Categories." 1867. Reprinted in *The Writings of Charles S. Peirce: A Chronological Edition, Vol. 2: 1867–1871,* edited by Peirce Edition Project, 49–59. Bloomington: Indiana University Press, 1984.
Perkin, Harold. *The Origins of Modern English Society, 1780–1880.* London: Routledge & K. Paul, 1969.
Pernick, Martin S. *A Calculus of Suffering: Pain, Professionalism, and Anesthesia in Nineteenth-Century America.* New York: Columbia University Press, 1985.
Phillips, Adam. *Darwin's Worms: On Life Stories and Death Stories.* New York: Basic Books, 1999.
Pitkin, Hanna Fenichel. *Wittgenstein and Justice: On the Significance of Ludwig Wittgenstein for Social and Political Thought.* Berkeley: University of California Press, 1993.
Plotz, John. "Emotional Intelligence, Darwin-Style: The Work of Feeling in an Era of Objectivity." Unpublished essay.
———. "Mediated Involvement: John Stuart Mill's Antisocial Sociability." In *The Feeling of Reading: Affective Experience and Victorian Literature,* edited by Rachel Ablow, 69–92. Ann Arbor: Michigan University Press, 2010.
———. *Portable Property: Victorian Culture on the Move.* Princeton: Princeton University Press, 2008.
Pockett, Susan. "The Neuroscience of Movement." In *Does Consciousness Cause Behavior?,* edited by Susan Pockett, William P. Banks, and Shaun Gallagher, 9–24. Cambridge: Massachusetts Institute of Technology Press, 2006.
Porter, Roy. *Mind Forg'd Manacles: A History of Madness in England from the Restoration to the Regency.* Cambridge, MA: Harvard University Press, 1987.
———. "Pain and Suffering." In *Companion Encyclopedia of the History of Medicine.* Vol. 2, edited by W. F. Bynum and Roy Porter, 1574–91. London: Routledge, 1997.
———. "The Patient's View: Doing Medical History from Below." *Theory and Society* 14, no. 2 (1985): 175–98.
Postlethwaite, Diana. "Mothering and Mesmerism in the Life of Harriet Martineau." *Signs* 14, no. 3 (1989): 583–609.
Priestley, Joseph. *Remarks on Dr. Reid's Inquiry into the Principles of the Human Mind on the Principles of Common Sense.* London: J. Johnson, 1775.
Ranking, W. H. "Observations on Spermatorrhoea; or the Involuntary Discharge of the Seminal Fluid." *The Lancet* (Oct. 14, 1843): 46–53.
Rawls, John. *A Theory of Justice.* Revised edition. Cambridge, MA: Harvard University Press, 1999.
Reed, Edward S. *From Soul to Mind: The Emergence of Psychology, from Erasmus Darwin to William James.* New Haven, CT: Yale University Press, 1997.
Rejali, Darius. *Torture and Democracy.* Princeton: Princeton University Press, 2007.
Rey, Roselyne. *The History of Pain.* Cambridge, MA: Harvard University Press, 1995.
Reynolds, J. Russell. "Fashions in Medicine." *British Medical Journal* (Sept. 2, 1871): 256–57.

Richards, Robert J. *The Romantic Conception of Life: Science and Philosophy in the Age of Goethe.* Chicago: University of Chicago Press, 2002.

Richards, Stewart. "Vicarious Suffering, Necessary Pain: Physiological Method in Late Nineteenth-Century Britain." In *Vivisection in Historical Perspective,* edited by Nicolaas A. Rupke, 125–48. London: Croom Helm, 1987.

Richardson, Alan. *British Romanticism and the Science of the Mind.* Cambridge: Cambridge University Press, 2001.

Roberts, Caroline. *The Woman and the Hour: Harriet Martineau and Victorian Ideologies.* Toronto: University of Toronto Press, 2002.

Robinson, Christopher C. "Why Wittgenstein is Not Conservative." *Theory and Event* 9, no. 3 (2006). https://muse.jhu.edu/journals/theory_and_event/v009/9.3robinson.html

——. *Wittgenstein and Political Theory: The View from Somewhere.* Edinburgh: Edinburgh University Press, 2009.

Robson, John M. "J. S. Mill's Theory of Poetry." In *Mill: A Collection of Critical Essays,* edited by J. S. Schneewind, 251–79. Notre Dame: University of Notre Dame Press, 1969.

Rothfield, Lawrence. *Vital Signs: Medical Realism in Nineteenth-Century Fiction.* Princeton: Princeton University Press, 1992.

Rowell, G. A. *An Essay on the Beneficent Distribution of the Sense of Pain.* Oxford: Published and sold by the author, 1857.

Rupke, Nicolaas A. "Pro-vivisection in England in the Early 1880s: Arguments and Motives." In *Vivisection in Historical Perspective,* edited by Nicolaas A. Rupke, 188–213. London: Croom Helm, 1987.

Ryall, Anka. "Medical Body and Lived Experience: The Case of Harriet Martineau," *Mosaic* 33, no. 4 (2000): 35–43.

Ryan, Alan. Introduction to *The Collected Works of John Stuart Mill.* Vol. 9, *An Examination of William Hamilton's Philosophy and of the Principal Philosophical Questions Discussed in his Writings,* edited by John M. Robson, vii–cii. Toronto: University of Toronto Press, 1979.

——. *The Philosophy of John Stuart Mill.* 2nd ed. Houndmills: Macmillan, 1987.

Rylance, Rick. *Victorian Psychology and British Culture 1850–1880.* Oxford: Oxford University Press, 2000.

S., M. R. C. *Confessions of a Hypochondriac; or, Adventures of a Hyp. in Search of a Cure.* London: Saunders and Otley, 1849.

Sanders, Valerie. *Reason over Passion: Harriet Martineau and the Victorian Novel.* Sussex: Harvester, 1986.

Sankey, W. H. O. "Illustrations of the Different Forms of Insanity." *British Medical Journal* (Feb. 13, 1864): 175–76.

Scarry, Elaine. *The Body in Pain: The Making and Unmaking of the World.* Oxford: Oxford University Press, 1985.

——. *Resisting Representation.* New York: Oxford University Press, 2004.

Schmitt, Cannon. *Darwin and the Memory of the Human: Evolution, Savages, and South America.* Cambridge: Cambridge University Press, 2009.

Schweik, Robert. "The Influence of Religion, Science, and Philosophy on Hardy's Writings." In *The Cambridge Companion to Thomas Hardy,* edited by Dale Kramer, 54–72. Cambridge: Cambridge University Press, 1999.

Sedgwick, Eve Kosofsky, and Adam Frank, eds. *Shame and Its Sisters: A Silvan Tomkins Reader.* Durham, NC: Duke University Press, 1995.

Seigworth, Gregory J., and Melissa Gregg. "An Inventory of Shimmers." *The Affect Theory Reader,* edited by Melissa Gregg and Gregory J. Seigworth, 1–28. Durham, NC: Duke University Press, 2010.

Sharpless, F. Parvin. *The Literary Criticism of John Stuart Mill*. The Hague: Mouton, 1967.
Shaw, Margaret L. "Narrative Surveillance and Social Control in *Villette*." *Studies in English Literature, 1500–1900* 34, no. 4 (1994): 813–33.
Shuttleworth, Sally. *Charlotte Brontë and Victorian Psychology*. Cambridge: Cambridge University Press, 1996.
Silverman, Kaja. "History, Figuration and Female Subjectivity in *Tess of the d'Urbervilles*." *Novel: A Forum on Fiction* 18, no. 1 (1984): 5–28.
Silverman, Lisa. *Tortured Subjects: Pain, Truth, and the Body in Early Modern France*. Chicago: University of Chicago Press, 2001.
Singer, Peter. "Review Essay: Unspeakable Acts: The Body in Pain (Scarry) and Torture (Peters)." *The New York Review of Books* (Feb. 27, 1986). http://www.nybooks.com/articles/1986/02/27/unspeakable-acts/
Small, Helen. *Love's Madness: Medicine, the Novel, and Female Insanity, 1800–1865*. Oxford: Clarendon Press, 1996.
Smith, Adam. *The Theory of Moral Sentiments*. 1759. Cambridge: Cambridge University Press, 2002.
Smith, Jad. "Custom, Association, and the Mixed Mode: Locke's Early Theory of Cultural Reproduction." *ELH* 73, no. 4 (2006): 831–53.
Spencer, Herbert. *The Principles of Psychology*. Vol. 1. 2nd ed. London: Williams and Norgate, 1870.
Spinoza, Benedict de, *Ethics*. 1677. London: Penguin, 1996.
Stef-Praun, A. Laura. "Harriet Martineau's 'Intellectual Nobility': Gender, Genius and Disability." In *Harriet Martineau: Authorship, Society and Empire*, edited by Ella Dzelzainis and Cora Kaplan, 38–51. Manchester: Manchester University Press, 2010.
Stewart, Garrett. *Dear Reader: The Conscripted Audience in Nineteenth-Century British Fiction*. Baltimore: Johns Hopkins University Press, 1996.
Stockton, Kathryn Bond. *God between Their Lips: Desire between Women in Irigaray, Brontë, and Eliot*. Stanford, CA: Stanford University Press, 1994.
Stokes, John. "Rachel's 'Terrible Beauty': An Actress among the Novelists." *ELH* 51, no. 4 (1984): 771–93.
Taylor, Jenny Bourke, and Sally Shuttleworth, eds. *Embodied Selves: An Anthology of Psychological Texts, 1830–1890*. Oxford: Clarendon, 1998.
Terada, Rei. "Seeing is Reading." In *The Legacies of Paul de Man*, edited by Marc Redfield, 162–77. New York: Fordham University Press, 2007.
Thomas, William. "John Stuart Mill and the Uses of Autobiography." *History* 56, no. 188 (1971): 341–59.
Thompson, Charlotte. "Language and the Shape of Reality in *Tess of the d'Urbervilles*." *ELH* 50, no. 4 (1983): 729–62.
Thompson, Spencer. "Trips after Health, and How to Profit by Them." *The Sixpenny Magazine* 1 (1861): 443–53.
Thornton, John. *A Companion for the Sick Chamber: or, The Uses of Affliction Briefly Stated and Illustrated, with Examples and Prayers*. London: Frederick Westley and A. H. David, 1835.
Tougaw, Jason Daniel. *Strange Cases: The Medical Case History and the British Novel*. New York: Routledge, 2006.
Turner, James. *Reckoning with the Beast: Animals, Pain, and Humanity in the Victorian Mind*. Baltimore: Johns Hopkins University Press, 1980.
Van Ghent, Dorothy. *The English Novel: Form and Function*. New York: Harper & Row, 1967.
Vargish, Thomas. *The Providential Aesthetic in Victorian Fiction*. Charlottesville: University of Virginia Press, 1985.

"*Villette* and *Ruth.*" *Putnam's Magazine* 1 (1853): 535–39.
Vrettos, Athena. *Somatic Fictions: Imagining Illness in Victorian Culture.* Stanford, CA: Stanford University Press, 1995.
Waldoff, Leon. "Psychological Determinism in *Tess of the d'Urbervilles.*" In *Critical Approaches to the Fiction of Thomas Hardy,* edited by Dale Kramer, 135–54. London: Macmillan, 1979.
Webb, R. K. *Harriet Martineau: A Radical Victorian.* New York: Columbia University Press, 1960.
Weber, Carl J. "Hardy's Copy of Schopenhauer." *Colby Quarterly* 4, no. 12 (1957): 217–24.
"What Is Pain?" *The Lancet* (Aug. 13, 1887): 333–34.
White, Paul. "Darwin Wept: Science and the Sentimental Subject." *Journal of Victorian Culture* 16, no. 2 (2011): 195–213.
Wickens, G. Glen. "Literature and Science: Hardy's Response to Mill, Huxley and Darwin." *Mosaic* 14, no. 3 (1981): 63–79.
Williams, E. R. "Letter to the Editor: Pain and Its Interpretation." *The Lancet* (Sept. 17, 1887): 593–94.
Williams, Raymond. *The English Novel from Dickens to Lawrence.* 1970. London: Hogarth Press, 1984.
Willingham-McLain, Gary. "Darwin's 'Eye of Reason': Natural Selection and the Mathematical Sublime." *Victorian Literature and Culture* 25, no. 1 (1997): 67–85.
Wilson, Elizabeth A. *Psychosomatic: Feminism and the Neurological Body.* Durham, NC: Duke University Press, 2004.
Winter, Alison. "Harriet Martineau and the Reform of the Invalid in Victorian England." *Historical Journal* 38, no. 3 (1995): 597–616.
———. *Mesmerized: Powers of Mind in Victorian Britain.* Chicago: Chicago University Press, 1998.
Winter, Sarah. "Darwin's Saussure: Biosemiotics and Race in *Expression.*" *Representations* 107, no. 1 (2009): 128–61.
Wittgenstein, Ludwig. *The Blue and Brown Books: Preliminary Studies for the "Philosophical Investigations."* 1933–35. New York: Harper Perennial, 1960.
———. *Philosophical Investigations.* 1953. Oxford: Blackwell, 2001.
Wood, Jane. *Passion and Pathology in Victorian Fiction.* Oxford: Oxford University Press, 2001.
Wozniak, Robert H. *Mind and Body: René Descartes to William James.* Bethesda, MD: National Library of Medicine, 1992.
Young, Robert M. *Darwin's Metaphor: Nature's Place in Victorian Culture.* Cambridge: Cambridge University Press, 1985.
Yousef, Nancy. *Isolated Cases: The Anxieties of Autonomy in Enlightenment Philosophy and Romantic Literature.* Ithaca, NY: Cornell University Press, 2004.
Zabel, Morton Dauwen. "Hardy in Defense of His Art: The Aesthetic of Incongruity." *Southern Review* 6 (1940): 125–49.

INDEX

Ablow, Rachel, 164n66
Abrams, M. H., 46
acknowledgment, 4, 6, 7, 22, 122, 140, 147n8, 169n33. *See also* Cavell, Stanley; Das, Veena; Wittgenstein, Ludwig
affect, 4, 9, 23, 65, 93–113 passim, 116, 117, 120–21, 132, 160n8, 161n14, 162n36, 165n74, 170n40
allegory, 72–74, 80–86, 88, 91, 139. *See also* personification
Allen, Richard, 55
analgesics, 2
Anderson, Amanda, 73
Anderson, Ben, 112
anesthetics, 2–3, 11–12, 75, 144n50
Andral, M., 20
Anstie, Francis Edmund, 20
antivivisection, 116, 166n10, 169n36. *See also* vivisection
Appiah, Kwame Anthony, 151n91
Armstrong, Dr., 20
Armstrong, Nancy, 157n17
Arnold, Matthew, 157n22
Asquith, Mark, 115, 169n38
associationism, 11, 22, 25, 28–36, 38, 42, 51, 54–57, 148n31, 149n51. *See also* education
Atkinson, Henry George, 70

Bain, Alexander, 10–11, 26, 28
Banfield, Ann, 167n18
Beccaria, Cesaire, 136
becoming, 104–7 passim, 110, 112, 113, 163n46. *See also* Deleuze, Gilles; Guattari, Félix
Beer, Gillian, 114–15, 156n1, 163n46, 167n17
Bell, Sir Charles, 96, 160nn10 and 11
Bending, Lucy, 10, 14
Bennett, Jane, 165n76
Bennett, M. R., 100
Bentham, Jeremy, 21, 24, 25, 27–28, 30–32, 43, 54, 57, 70, 147n6, 149n44

Berlin, Isaiah, 150n56
Bernstein, Susan David, 168–69n31
Boone, Joseph Allen, 157n18
Boumelha, Penny, 121
Bourke, Joanna, 12, 21
Brennan, Teresa, 112, 165n74
Brewster, Sir David, 155n46
Brontë, Charlotte, 8, 9, 22, 72–92, 117, 137, 140
Broughton, Trev Lynn, 52
Browning, Elizabeth Barrett, 69
Buckley, Jerome H., 35
Bunyan, John, 18, 158n28
Buxton, A. St. Claire, 14
Byron, Lord George Gordon, 41–43

Cameron, Sharon, 9, 68, 152n3, 155n53
Carlisle, Janice, 26–27, 42–43
Carlyle, Jane, 154n37
Carlyle, Thomas, 35–36, 154n37
Carpenter, Mary Wilson, 158–59n42
Caruth, Cathy, 90–91
Cassell, Eric J., 141–42n15
Cavell, Stanley, 4, 6–8, 47, 68, 85, 91, 143n28, 158n38, 169n33
Chambers, Thomas King, 17, 18
Cheyne, George, 156n9
chloroform, 2, 11, 75
chronic pain, 6, 142n18, 146n95, 152n5
Clark, Michael J., 18–19
Cohen, William A., 118, 167n17
Cohn, Elisha, 168n21
Collins, W. J., 15
Confessions of a Hypochondriac; or, Adventures of a Hyp. in Search of a Cure, 74–75, 146n84
Connolly, William E., 97, 100–101, 162n36, 165n76
Conolly, John, 18

Dale, Peter Allen, 80, 158n28
Damasio, Antonio, 97
Darwin, Charles, 3, 8–10, 17, 22–23, 93–113, 115, 117, 140, 161–62n22,

Darwin, Charles (*continued*)
162n25, 162–63n39, 163nn47, 52, and 53, 164n58, 165nn71 and 76; and Bell, Sir Charles, 96, 160n10, 160–61n11; *Descent of Man*, 108; *Expression of the Emotions in Man and Animals*, 10, 96–103, 108–13, 162n25; *Journal of Researches*, 94, 106, 107, 113, 164n59; *M and N Notebooks*, 101–3, 106, 112, 162n37; *On the Origin of Species*, 105, 160n1; "Recollections of the Development of My Mind and Character," 107, 113, 164n56; and Spinoza, Benedict de, 94–95, 104, 112–13, 160n5; *Various Contrivances by which Orchids are Fertilised by Insects*, 105; *Voyage of the Beagle* (see *Journal of Researches*)

Darwin, Erasmus, 106
Das, Veena, 4, 7–8, 17, 21, 92, 116, 123–24, 126, 140, 147n8, 165n1
Daston, Lorraine, 10–11, 106
Davidson, Jenny, 153n22
Davies, Jeremy, 147n6
Deleuze, Gilles, 104–5, 163nn45 and 47. *See also* becoming
Dennett, Daniel C., 100
Desmond, Adrian, 96
determinism, 36, 41, 102–3, 115. *See also* necessitarianism
Dickens, Charles, 1, 9, 27–28, 30, 65, 81, 134, 137
Digby, Anne, 16
Dixon, Thomas, 160n10, 161–62n22
Donner, Wendy, 26
Dormandy, Thomas, 11
dual aspect theory. *See* monism
du Bois, Page, 136
Durham, John, 27

education, 25–34, 37, 44, 50, 53–58, 103, 149n37, 154nn31 and 33, 154–55n38
Ekman, Paul, 96–97, 161nn14 and 15
Eliot, George, 81, 135, 137–40
Emerson, Ralph Waldo, 67–68
Escher, M. C., 41
Esquirol, Etienne, 146n92
ether, 2, 11, 75
evolution, theory of, 12, 14–15, 97, 105, 106, 110, 112, 144n65, 163nn47 and 52, 169n36

Facial Action Coding System (FACS), 97
Feinberg, Monica L., 156n3
Ferguson, Frances, 27
Fimland, Marit, 85
Fischer-Homberger, Esther, 17, 156n13
Fissell, Mary, 16
Fleishman, Avrom, 158n28
Fletcher, Angus, 81–82
form of life, 26. *See also* Wittgenstein, Ludwig
Foster, J. Edgar, 2
Foucault, Michel, 16–17, 52, 145n77
François, Anne-Lise, 169n33
Frank, Adam, 161n14
Frawley, Maria H., 145–46n84, 152n12, 154–55n38
Freedgood, Elaine, 85
free will, 102–3, 35–37. *See also* determinism; necessitarianism
Freud, Sigmund, 90

Gallagher, Catherine, 3, 149n44
Gallagher, Shaun, 100
Garratt, Peter, 104, 160n5, 161–62n22
Gaskell, Elizabeth, 79, 137
Gate Control Theory of Pain, 142n20
Gilbert, Susan M., 159n44
Gillies, H. Cameron, 14–16, 144n65
Greenhow, T. H., 152n10
Gregg, Melissa, 112
Gross, Daniel, 97
Grosz, Elizabeth, 163n47
Guattari, Félix, 104–5, 163n47. *See also* becoming
Gubar, Susan, 159n44
Gull, William Withey, 20

Hacker, P. M. S., 100
Hadley, Elaine, 53, 149n44
Halévy, Elie, 32, 149n42
Hall, Spencer, 155n55
Hamlet, 110–12
Hardy, Florence, 166n8
Hardy, Thomas, 8, 9, 23, 114–34, 140, 165nn2 and 4, 165–66n5, 166nn7 and 8, 167–68n19, 169n33, 169n38; *Far from the Madding Crowd*, 123, 129–31, 134, 167n17, 170n40; *Jude the Obscure*, 118; *The Later Years of Thomas Hardy*, 115, 165–66n5, 166n8, 169n36; *Tess of*

INDEX [189]

the d'Urbervilles, 121–34, 168nn21, 28, and 29, 168–69n31, 169n37; *The Woodlanders*, 117–21, 123, 129, 134
Harrison, John P., 11
Hartley, David, 22, 42, 51, 52, 54–55, 57, 148n31, 153n21
Hartley, Lucy, 96
Hartman, Geoffrey, 45
Hertz, Neil, 40
Hinton, James, 12, 60–61
Hobbes, Thomas, 3–4
Hodgkiss, A. D., 146n95
Holmes, Martha Stoddard, 155n45
humanitarian narrative, 116–17, 121–23, 137
Hume, David, 156n12
hypnosis, 75. *See also* mesmerism
hypochondria, 17–20, 74–80 passim, 91, 145–46n84, 146nn85, 92, 94, and 95, 156n9, 156–57n14, 158n33

illness, 16–20 passim, 22, 48–71 passim, 91, 145n77, 152n12, 153n16, 154n36; vs. disease, 145n73
impersonality, 1, 3, 9, 22, 25, 48–71 passim, 73, 112, 128, 158n42
International Association for the Study of Pain, 142n20
invalidism, 22, 47, 48–71 passim, 145n81, 152n5, 154–55n38

Jackson, Stonewall, 18
Jacobus, Mary, 77

Keenleyside, Heather, 167n15
Ketabgian, Tamara, 155n56
Kleinman, Arthur, 145n73, 147n8
Knapp, Steven, 159n45, 167n15
Kober, Michael, 47
Kreilkamp, Ivan, 167n17, 170n40
Kucich, John, 157n15, 158n35

Lacan, Jacques, 90
Laird, J. T., 125, 168n29
Langbein, John H., 170n9
language game, 3, 6, 7, 22, 25, 26, 34, 45, 47, 73. *See also* Wittgenstein, Ludwig
Laqueur, Thomas, 116, 122
Latour, Bruno, 95, 160n9
Le Doux, Joseph, 97

Levi, A. W., 26, 37
Levine, George, 165n76
Lewes, G. H., 153–54n29, 158n42
Leys, Ruth, 100, 112, 161n15, 162n36
liberalism, 4, 7–8, 21–23, 25, 50, 52–53, 68, 73–74, 92, 135
Libet, Benjamin, 99–100
Lister, Joseph, 14
Lock, Margaret, 147n8
Locke, John, 30, 54–55, 148n34, 153nn21 and 22
Lodge, David, 167–68n19, 168n29
Loesberg, Jonathan, 35–37, 148n14

Maeterlinck, Maurice, 115
Magnuson, Paul, 151n81
Malthus, Thomas, 2–4, 22–23, 32, 51, 57, 93, 141nn7 and 8, 149n42
Manto, Sa'adat Hasan, 123–24, 126
Marmontel, Jean François, 26, 37–41, 150n63
Martin, Rev. George, 13
Martineau, Harriet, 8, 9, 17, 22, 48–71, 73–74, 92, 117, 140, 152nn1, 5, 7, and 8, 153–54n29, 154nn31, 35, 36, and 37, 164n42; *Autobiography*, 48–50, 51, 53, 55, 58–60, 69, 71, 152n7; *The Crofton Boys*, 51; and deafness, 49, 51, 67, 152–53n15, 155n45; *Deerbrook*, 51; *Household Education*, 53, 57, 58; *How to Observe*, 51; *Illustrations of Political Economy*, 51, 52, 57, 154n31; "Letter to the Deaf," 51, 67; *Letters on Mesmerism*, 51, 155n55; *Letters on the Laws of Man's Nature and Development*, 70–71; *Life in the Sick-Room*, 50-2, 54, 55–57, 62–68 passim; and martyrdom, 58–59, 152n12, 154n34; and mesmerism, 152n10, 155nn55 and 56; "On the Agency of Feelings in the Formation of Habits," 61–62, 154n33
Massumi, Brian, 97, 99–101
Maurice, Priscilla, 12–13, 60–61
Melzack, Ronald, 142n20
mesmerism, 17, 51, 70–71, 152n10, 155n55 and 56
Michaels, Walter Benn, 167n15
Mill, James, 21, 24–33 passim, 37–40, 42, 51, 54, 57, 148n31, 149nn37 and 51; *Analysis of the Phenomena of the*

Mill, James (*continued*)
   Human Mind, 28, 29, 33–38 passim, 43, 57; "Education," 31, 149n37
Mill, John Stuart, 8, 9, 21–22, 24–47, 50, 52, 53, 54, 57, 58, 73–74, 92, 117, 140, 148n31, 151nn89 and 91, 163n42; *Autobiography*, 8, 21–24, 25, 26, 33–47 passim, 148n14, 150n63; *An Examination of William Hamilton's Philosophy and of The Principal Philosophical Questions Discussed in his Writings*, 151n89; "Inaugural Address Delivered to the University of St. Andrews," 149n37; *On Liberty*, 45–47, 74, 150n56; on Philosophical Necessity, 35–36; "Sedgwick's Discourse," 28; *A System of Logic*, 36, 149n51, 150nn56 and 77; "Thoughts on Poetry and Its Varieties," 45–46, 150n67
Miller, Andrew H., 143n28
Milnes, Richard Monckton, 67
monism, 95, 108–9, 161–62n22
Moore, James, 96
Morris, David B., 21
Moscoso, Javier, 21

natural magic, 64–65, 67, 155n46
natural selection, 3, 96, 102, 113. *See also* Darwin, Charles
necessitarianism, 35–36, 102–3, 150n56, 163n42. *See also* determinism
nerve force, 98–102, 108–10. *See also* Darwin, Charles
nerves, 2, 10–11, 14, 18, 19–20, 76, 112, 149n51, 156n9, 162n39, 165n71. *See also* nerve force
neurology, 100, 143–44n40
Nightingale, Florence, 69
Noyes, Alfred, 115
Nussey, Ellen, 80

pain: and affect, 93–113 passim (*see also* affect); and certitude, 1, 5–6; definition of, 10–11, 21; desirability of, 11–16 passim; educability of, 24–71 passim (*see also* education); epistemological model of, 4–8, 23, 135–40; eradicability of, 2; and evolution (*see* evolution); Gate Control Theory of, 142n20;
history of, 1–3, 9–23, 74–75; impersonality of (*see* impersonality); ineradicability of, 2–3; International Society for the Study of, 142n20; medical understandings of, 2–3, 4, 6, 10–12, 14–20, 171n16; physical vs. psychological, 5, 10–11, 21; privacy of, 72–92 passim (*see also* privacy); religious understandings of, 1–4, 12–15; social model of, 3, 4, 6–8, 24–47 passim; vs. suffering, 141–42n11 (*see also* suffering). *See also* analgesics; anesthetics; Cavell, Stanley; Das, Veena; hypochondria; illness; invalidism; nerve force; Scarry, Elaine; sympathy; Wittgenstein, Ludwig
pain behavior, 4, 7, 26. *See also* Wittgenstein, Ludwig
Park, Katharine, 106
pathophobia, 17, 76, 156n13
Peirce, Charles Sanders, 96
Perkin, Harold, 32
Pernick, Martin, 11
personification, 72, 81, 86–89, 91, 118, 159n45, 167n15. *See also* allegory
pessimism, 115–17, 141n7, 166n8. *See also* Hardy, Thomas
phantom limb, 6
Phillips, Adam, 93–94
Plotz, John, 40, 97
Pockett, Susan, 100
population, *See* Malthus, Thomas
Porter, Roy, 52
Priestley, Joseph, 54, 153n21
privacy, 8, 22, 26, 29, 33, 34, 45, 47, 72–92 passim, 140
private language, 8, 92, 142n25

race, 96, 102, 144n50
Ranking, W. H., 19
Rawls, John, 27, 71, 148n21
Rejali, Darius, 6
Reynolds, J. Russell, 16
Ricardo, David, 51
Richardson, Samuel, 126
Ringrose, Amelia, 80
Roberts, Caroline, 154n36
Robinson, Christopher C., 45
Robson, John M., 26

Rowell, G. A., 12
Ryall, Anka, 52
Ryan, Alan, 36, 43, 151n89

Sanders, Valerie, 152n2
Scarry, Elaine, 4–8, 10, 30, 125–26, 135, 142nn18, 20, and 21
Schmitt, Cannon, 164n56
Schopenhauer, Arthur, 115, 169n38
Sedgwick, Eve Kosofsky, 161n14
Seigworth, Gregory J., 112
Sharpless, F. Parvin, 43
Silverman, Kaja, 169n37
Silverman, Lisa, 136, 170n9
Singer, Peter, 6
skepticism, 6–7, 17, 20, 26, 42, 52, 57, 66, 68, 73–75, 79, 85, 92, 95, 117, 128, 140, 143n28, 151n89, 156n12. *See also* Cavell, Stanley; Das, Veena; François, Anne-Lise; Miller, Andrew H.; Wittgenstein, Ludwig
Smith, Adam, 61, 74, 78, 85, 91, 127
Smith, Jad, 54
Spencer, Herbert, 99, 115
Spinoza, Benedict de, 9, 94–95, 104–5, 107–8, 112–13, 160n5, 163n45
Stef-Praun, Laura, 52
Stokes, John, 158–59n42
sublime, 28, 40–41, 163n52
suffering: vs. pain, 141–42n11; social, 147n8. *See also* pain
sympathy, 13, 22, 24, 27, 30, 32–33, 38–40, 45, 58–64, 68–71, 73–74, 78–79, 81, 85, 91, 108–9, 116, 117, 127, 128, 135, 138, 155n45, 158n42, 164nn66 and 67,
168n21; religious approaches to, 60–61

Thompson, Spencer, 158n33
Thornton, John, 13
torture, 6, 136–140 passim, 170nn4 and 9
tragedy, 117

utilitarianism, 1, 10, 21, 22, 25–34 passim, 50, 57, 71, 140, 149n42

vaccination, 2
Van Ghent, Dorothy, 165n4
Vargish, Thomas, 157n23
vivisection, 137. *See also* antivivisection
Von Hartmann, Edward, 115
Vrettos, Athena, 145n77

Wall, Patrick, 142n20
Webb, R. K., 54
White, Paul, 162–63n39
Williams, E. R., 15
Williams, Raymond, 81
Willingham-McLain, Gary, 163n52
Wilson, Elizabeth A., 97, 112, 165n71
Winter, Allison, 51, 152n10
Wittgenstein, Ludwig, 1, 3, 4, 6–8, 22, 25, 26, 45–47, 92, 117, 142n25, 143n28, 154n29, 158n38, 165n1. *See also* form of life; language game; private language; skepticism
Wordsworth, William, 24, 26, 40–47, 151n81

Yousef, Nancy, 26, 148n14, 150n67

A NOTE ON THE TYPE

{≡≡≡W≡≡≡}

THIS BOOK has been composed in Miller, a Scotch Roman typeface designed by Matthew Carter and first released by Font Bureau in 1997. It resembles Monticello, the typeface developed for The Papers of Thomas Jefferson in the 1940s by C. H. Griffith and P. J. Conkwright and reinterpreted in digital form by Carter in 2003.

Pleasant Jefferson ("P. J.") Conkwright (1905–1986) was Typographer at Princeton University Press from 1939 to 1970. He was an acclaimed book designer and AIGA Medalist.

The ornament used throughout this book was designed by Pierre Simon Fournier (1712–1768) and was a favorite of Conkwright's, used in his design of the *Princeton University Library Chronicle*.

GPSR Authorized Representative: Easy Access System Europe - Mustamäe tee
50, 10621 Tallinn, Estonia, gpsr.requests@easproject.com

www.ingramcontent.com/pod-product-compliance
Lightning Source LLC
Chambersburg PA
CBHW030624230426
43661CB00053B/2129